1976

This book may be kept

FOURTEEN DAYS

THE CONSTITUTIONAL DECISIONS OF
JOHN MARSHALL

Volume I

THE CONSTITUTIONAL DECISIONS

of

JOHN MARSHALL

Edited by Joseph P. Cotton, Jr.

New Preface by Alpheus Thomas Mason
Doherty Professor of Government and Law
University of Virginia

Volume I

DA CAPO PRESS • NEW YORK • 1969

A Da Capo Press Reprint Edition

First Da Capo Printing — July 1969
Second Da Capo Printing — January 1971

This Da Capo Press edition of
The Constitutional Decisions of John Marshall
is an unabridged republication of the first
edition published in New York in 1905.

Portions of Professor Mason's Preface appeared
originally in his *The Supreme Court*, published
by the University of Michigan Press.

Library of Congress Catalog Card Number 67-25445

THE CONSTITUTIONAL DECISIONS OF
JOHN MARSHALL

Volume I

PREFACE

John Marshall was the fourth Chief Justice of the United States. His three distinguished predecessors were John Jay of New York, John Rutledge of South Carolina, and Oliver Ellsworth of Connecticut. Ten Chief Justices have followed, including Taney, Chase, Charles Evans Hughes, and Harlan Fiske Stone, yet Marshall's preeminence as "the great Chief Justice" remains unchallenged.

The emergence of Earl Warren as the first Chief Justice in our history who might be considered to match Marshall in creative power gives special relevance to this new edition of *The Constitutional Decisions of John Marshall,* edited by Joseph P. Cotton, Jr. A leading federal judge thinks that "Chief Justice Warren will go down in history second only to Chief Justice Marshall. I am not referring to Warren's intellect, legal acumen, style, or personal ascendancy, but to his insight as to the central purposes and potentialities of the society in which he functioned, and to his capacity to make judicial power a chief instrument for their realization." John Marshall possessed all the qualities withheld from Warren, along with those credited to him.

That day in January, 1801, when John Marshall stood before President Adams with John Jay's letter declining a second appointment as Chief Justice was a crucial moment in American history. To some the Judiciary then seemed "almost the only security left us." After slight hesitation, the President, not knowing what to do, announced: "I believe I must nominate you." Pleased and surprised, the future Chief Justice bowed in silence. "I had never before heard myself named for the office," Marshall recalled several years later, "and had not even thought of it." Quite fortuitously, it seemed, President Adams had nominated a judge "equal to a Hale, a Holt or a Mansfield."

But the selection of Marshall at this particular juncture as the Court's titular head was not a "wild freak," as New Jersey Senator Jonathan Dayton asserted. "In the future administration of our country," President Adams had remarked, December 19, 1800, offering the post to former Chief Justice Jay, "the firmest security we can have against the effects of visionary schemes of fluctuating theories, will be in a solid judiciary. . . ." It had even been suggested that Adams might appoint himself Chief Justice and resign as President. In discrediting this bizarre idea, he explained: "The office of Chief Justice is too important for any man to hold of sixty-five years of age, who has wholly neglected the study of law for six and twenty years. I have already, by the nomination of a gentleman in the full vigor of middle age, in the full habits of business, and whose reading in the science is fresh in his head, to this office, put it wholly out of my power, and, indeed, it never was in my hopes or wishes."

"I hope nothing will prevent his [Marshall's] acceptance of that office," Charles Cotesworth Pinckney wrote Theodore Sedgwick from Savannah on February 10, 1801; "at a time when attempts are making to construe away the energy of our constitution, to unnerve our Government, and to overthrow that system by which we have risen to our present prosperity, it is all important that our supreme Judiciary should be filled by men of elevated talents, sound federal principles and unshaken firmness."

Others were less certain of Marshall's qualifications. "General Marshall is a leader," George Cabot declared. "But you see in him the faults of a Virginian. . . . He thinks too much of that state, and he expects the world will be governed according to the Rules of Logic." Cabot believed that the new Chief Justice had "much to learn on the subject of practicable theories of free government." Others suspected that Marshall might be soft on Republicanism. Charles Cotesworth Pinckney reassured one alarmist: "You may rely on his federalism, and be certain that he will not unite with Jefferson and the Jacobins."

Certain objections were more narrowly focused. In nominating Marshall, the President had by-passed Associate Justice Paterson, disappointing the hopes and expectations of the veteran Justice's friends, both in and out of Congress. The day before Marshall was confirmed, Senator Jonathan Dayton of New Jersey wrote Justice Paterson "with grief, astonishment and almost indignation":

> The delay which has taken place was upon my motion for postponement, and was intended to afford an opportunity for ascertaining whether the President could be induced under any circumstances whatever to nominate you. . . . It must be gratifying to you to learn that all voices, with the exception of one only, were united in favor of the conferring of this appointment on you. The President alone was inflexible, and declared he would never nominate you.

The new Chief Justice, forty-four years old, took office February 4, 1801, the Court sitting for the first time in the federal city of Washington. Few saw this, or anything else, as signaling a new day for the Supreme Court or for its titular head. President Jefferson and Democratic-Republicans now dominated the political branches of the government. The Federalists' only chance of exercising a continuing influence in national affairs lay in the Judiciary. The Adams administration demonstrated firm determination to dig in, Chief Justice Marshall, in the celebrated case of *Marbury* v. *Madison,* seizing the first opportunity to establish the Court as supreme arbiter over both Congress and the Executive. A hint of the reason for his overpowering sense of urgency may be found in the autobiographical essay Chief Justice Marshall wrote at the request of Justice Story.

Prior to 1798, Marshall's primary interests were professional, not political. In 1789, he decined the office of U.S. District Attorney at Richmond. In 1795, he turned down the offices of Attorney General and Secretary of War. In 1796, he rejected the opportunity to become Minister to France. In 1798, he refused President Adams' offer to succeed James Wilson as Associate Justice of the Supreme Court. By the late 1790's, Federalist dominance was drawing to a close. Then, at the strong urging of General Washington, Marshall reluctantly consented to run for Congress. Elected in 1798, he found himself in the cross fire of bitter party conflict. Federalism was on the defensive. He had hardly taken his seat in Congress when President Adams nominated him Secretary of State. Marshall recalled the considerations moving him to remain in politics rather than return to the bar: "I never felt more doubt than on the question of accepting or declining this office. My decided preference was still for the bar. But on becoming a candidate for Congress I was given up as a lawyer, and considered generally as a political man."

What turned the scales toward acceptance of political office was the inability of his political enemies to withhold their fire. The press, Marshall wrote, "teemed with so much falsehood, with such continued and irritating abuse of me that I could not bring myself to yield to it. I could not conquer a stubbornness of temper which determines a man to make head against and struggle with injustice. . . . I determined to accept the office."

Marshall's nationalism, imbibed during the revolutionary struggle, was deeply ingrained. Harassments of "the critical period" confirmed him in "the habit of considering America as my country, and Congress as my government." Experience in the Virginia state legislature "proved that everything was afloat, and that we had no safe anchorage ground." All this gave "high value in my estimation to that article in the constitution [Art. I, Sec. 10] which imposes restrictions on states. I was consequently a determined advocate for its adoption, and became a candidate for the convention to which it was to be submitted."

In 1803, the year *Marbury* v. *Madison* was decided, Marshall must again have felt that "stubbornness of temper which determines a man to make head against and struggle with injustice." Both Congress and the

President were then brought to heel. The victory Marshall scored over a Chief Executive of the highest political acumen was to stand unmatched until our own time. It was not until 1937, when President Franklin D. Roosevelt was joined in a furious political contest with Chief Justice Charles Evans Hughes, that the palm of victory again went so completely to the Court's titular head.

Marshall's juristic response to the Democratic-Republican challenge would be hard to match. The Chief Justice grounded his nationalism in "established principles"—those Jefferson himself had immortalized in the Declaration of Independence. The decision reached in *Marbury* seemed to be the only one consistent with reason, common sense, and the Constitution. With a single stroke the Chief Justice encompassed the higher law background of our constitutional heritage and delineated its implications for the functioning of the American system of free government. Eschewing precedents, authorities, and documentation, he took the high road of principle. Disavowing novelty, Marshall described the issue of judicial review as "interesting but not intricate." In grounding his opinion in "established principles," he wrote in the tradition of the Declaration of Independence. Marshall no more than Jefferson aimed at originality. Both voiced the conviction, as Marshall put it, that "the people have an original right to establish, for their future government, such principles as, in their opinion, shall most induce to their own happiness." "The whole American fabric has been erected" on this proposition. Having reinforced specific provisions of the Constitution with high principle,

Marshall invoked, without ever mentioning it by name, the clincher—separation of powers. "It is emphatically the province and duty of the judicial department to say what the law is."

Marshall's gifts as a debater are well known. Less appreciated are the literary skills he invariably demonstrated. The Chief Justice fused the ingredients Judge B. N. Cardozo singled out as prerequisites for persuasiveness—overtones of sincerity and fire, the mnemonic power of alliteration and antithesis, the terseness and tang of the proverb and the maxim. "Neglect the help of these allies," Cardozo warns, "and it [the opinion] may never win its way." Such qualities make an opinion "magisterial" and "imperative." It "eschews ornament. It is meager in illustration and analogy. If it argues, it does so with the downward rush and overwhelming conviction of the syllogism, seldom with tentative gropings toward the inductive apprehension of a truth imperfectly discerned."

"We hear," Cardozo wrote of Marshall's commanding prose, "the voice of the law speaking by its consecrated ministers with the calmness and assurance that are born of a sense of mastery and power. Thus Marshall seemed to judge, and a hush falls upon us even now as we listen to his words. Those organ tones of his were meant to fill cathedrals or the most exalted of tribunals."

William Wirt divined the quality that flavors all the Chief Justice's great opinions. "Marshall's maxim," said Wirt, "seems always to have been, 'aim exclusively *at Strength.*'" In his *Age of Fable,* Bulfinch tells the story of Antheus "whose strength was invincible as long as he remained in contact with his Mother Earth." Chief Justice Marshall's Mother Earth was the Constitution, construed in light of firsthand knowledge of the views and hardened experience which inspired it. His purpose, like that of the author of the Declaration of Independence, was modest—"to place before mankind the common sense of the subject," and to do so "in terms so plain and firm as to command their assent." A catalyst rather than an innovator, Marshall marked the path America was impelled to take.

At the end of Marshall's long judicial career, the Philadelphia Bar paid him homage. Using the occasion to comment on his judicial stewardship, the Chief Justice boasted that his Court had "never sought to enlarge judicial power beyond its proper bounds, nor feared to carry it to the fullest extent duty requires." Marshall thought he understood the narrow line that separates judicial *review* and judicial *supremacy*. He had met the demanding requirements of both *self-restraint* and *duty*. Provisions of the Constitution must neither "be restricted into insignificance, nor extended to objects not comprehended in them nor contemplated by its framers." Judicial review was both a power-releasing and power-breaking function. For Marshall, as for Judge Cardozo, its chief worth lay not "in the few cases in which the legislature has gone beyond the lines that mark the limits of discretion," but "in making vocal and audible the ideals that might otherwise be silenced, in giving them continuity of life and of expression, in guiding and directing choice within the limits where choice ranges." Marshall deserves to be remembered as much, if not more, for *McCulloch* v. *Maryland,* in which the Court affirmed the power of Congress to incorporate a bank, nontaxable by the state, thus laying the foundations of national power, as for *Marbury* v. *Madison,* in which, for the first time, the Court set aside an act of Congress. Marshall did not repeat the prerogative he claimed for the judiciary. That remained for his successor, Chief Justice Taney, in the ill-fated *Dred Scott* case.

For Marshall the question whether a law, national or state, is void was a matter of "much delicacy," seldom "to be decided in the affirmative, in a doubtful case." But when impelled by "duty" to render such a judgment, the Court would, he said, "be unworthy of its station," if it were "unmindful of the solemn obligations which that station imposes." Judicial duty required him to take, on appeal, state court decisions in cases arising under the Constitution or laws of the United States, otherwise America would suffer the chaos of "hydra in government"—each state would "possess a *veto* on the will of the whole. . . . We have no more right to decline the exercise of jurisdiction which is given," he declared, "than to usurp that which is not given. The one or the other would be treason to the Constitution." Judicial duty commanded the Chief Justice to save the charter of Dartmouth College from New Hampshire's attempt to destroy it. Precluding state action was not only the constitutional injunction against impairing the obligation of contracts in Article I, Section 10—"a Bill of Rights for the people of each State," he called it—but also the sanctity which enshrouds property and contract rights; and Marshall was as adept in fashioning political theory ("penumbra" in modern terminology) in defense of property as in support of nationalist goals: "It may well be doubted whether the nature of society and of government does not prescribe some limits to the legislative power; and, if any be prescribed, where are they to be found, if property of an individual, fairly and honestly acquired, may be seized without compensation?"

Chief Justice Marshall insisted that judicial duty is heightened when political checks are ineffective or unavailable. When a state, as in *McCulloch* v. *Maryland,* taxes an instrumentality of the national government, "it acts upon institutions created, not by their own constituents, but by people over whom they claim no control." Since the people of the United States were not represented in the Maryland legislature which enacted the offending law, the usual political restraints for correcting abuse of power were not operative; hence an enlarged judicial responsibility.

The burden of Chief Justice Marshall's constitutional jurisprudence throughout is that the Supreme Court's primary task is positive and creative. He deplored any construction which attempts "to explain away the Constitution," leaving "it a magnificent structure . . . to look at, but totally unfit for use." The Judiciary, like other agencies of government, should facilitate achievement of the great objectives mentioned in the Constitution's Preamble.

In the exercise of this task Chief Justice Marshall demonstrated the quality Woodrow Wilson identified with great statesmanship—"Large vision of things to come." On the one hundredth anniversary of the day on which Marshall took his seat as Chief Justice, Holmes wrote: "Time has been on Marshall's side; . . . the theory for which Hamilton argued, and he decided, and Webster spoke, and Grant fought, and Lincoln died, is now our cornerstone."

Princeton University
January 1967

Alpheus Thomas Mason

John Marshall

om the portrait by Chester Harding in the Athenæum, Boston

THE CONSTITUTIONAL DECISIONS

OF

JOHN MARSHALL

EDITED, WITH AN INTRODUCTORY ESSAY

BY

JOSEPH P. COTTON, JR.

OF THE NEW YORK BAR

IN TWO VOLUMES

VOL. I.

G. P. PUTNAM'S SONS

NEW YORK   LONDON
27 WEST TWENTY-THIRD STREET   24 BEDFORD STREET, STRAND

The Knickerbocker Press

1905

The Knickerbocker Press, New York

PREFATORY NOTE.

It is not possible to bring to the study of Marshall's life and work any great new light. Of his intimate personal life comparatively little, save the bare outlines, is known. His work is universally acknowledged to have been more important than that of any other man in formulating and expounding the doctrines of the American system of constitutional law. It is the intention of these volumes to present all of his decisions (in the Supreme Court and on circuit) on that branch of the law (they are nowhere else completely collected), to show how far they have affected or been changed by subsequent cases, to describe the political conditions existing at the time they were given, and to indicate, as far as may be practicable, their effect on constitutional history. So common has been the habit of American lawyers of accepting Marshall's opinions as the final expression of the law, and so firmly have his theories become imbedded in our governmental system, that the praise of his work has been often indiscriminating, and with little understanding, and the task of analyzing his decisions becomes more difficult. The editor has attempted in these volumes, by notes to each case, to give its setting in the history of Marshall's time and

iii

its place in the system of constitutional law ; and, in an introductory monograph, to bring together and formulate the results of that analysis. This work has been, in a large measure, the proving and carrying on of the opinions of the late Professor James Bradley Thayer, of the Harvard Law School, who, more than any other man of recent years, has contributed to the better understanding of Marshall's genius.

CONTENTS

INTRODUCTION.

It is a national habit and tradition to regard Marshall as the greatest American lawyer, and, save Washington, Hamilton, and Lincoln, no American stands higher as a constructive statesman in the work of the evolution of the Union. It is the peculiarity of his work of statesmanship that,—practically without exception,—all of it found expression in the course of judicial opinions as Chief Justice, given in litigated cases, as, from time to time, from 1801 to his death in 1835, constitutional questions came before the Supreme Court of the United States. These opinions were, in form, the opinions of the whole Court, and in that Court there were at least two other men of great ability ; the first, Story, a man of remarkable legal learning, his ablest follower, the second, William Johnson, a figure too little understood and valued, who served almost as long as Marshall and, alone in that Court, exercised an independent judgment on constitutional questions, free from Marshall's domination, with a curious foresight and comprehension of the actual workings of the system which Marshall created. It is to be remembered, too, that those cases were argued before Marshall by the ablest group of counsel that have ever practiced before an

American court, men great not only as lawyers, but as leaders and statesmen : Adams, Pinckney, Wirt, Martin, Ogden, Binney, Hopkinson, Taney, Benton, Webster, Clay, and a dozen more. But Marshall's was the dominating mind, completely overshadowing and pervading the Court during his whole term of service. He created the American system of constitutional law, the theory was his, the form and vigor of the opinions were his, and this body of decision is fairly his achievement and his service.

It is not proposed here to give even an outline of Marshall's life,[1] but one aspect of it calls for particu-**Marshall's** lar emphasis. Marshall was born in 1755, **Life** of good Virginia stock, and seems to have received as good an education as was possible outside the colleges. In his youth, he lived the hardy life of the Virginia frontier ; in 1775, he was drilling a company of soldiers. He served through the Revolution,

---

[1] There is no entirely satisfactory biography of Marshall. The material is scanty, his letters were few, and his personal life of so simple and intimate a nature that almost the only important sources of information are the essays published shortly after his death by Story and Binney (which are variously republished). In the observance of John Marshall Day on February 4, 1901, by the Bar Associations of the various states, many addresses were delivered concerning him in various parts of the country. None contained important new information, save an address of the late Justice Horace Gray at Richmond, Va., before the Bar Association of that state, in which is preserved an autobiography of Marshall, lately discovered, of touching brevity and simplicity. These various addresses on John Marshall Day were collected and edited by the Hon. John F. Dillon and published by Callaghan & Co. (3 vols., Chicago, 1903). One other source of information in regard to his life is the monograph on " John Marshall " by the late Professor Thayer of the Harvard Law School (Houghton, Mifflin & Co., Cambridge, 1901), in which many hitherto unpublished data are collected. This book is frequently referred to in these volumes. It is certainly the most important recent contribution to the subject.

first as lieutenant, then as captain, frequently in the fighting, often serving as judge advocate, and thus coming into personal relations with Washington and Hamilton. In 1780, he was admitted to the Virginia bar, and rose rapidly to the head of it ; he served often in the Virginia legislature, in the Federal Convention in Virginia in 1788, and in 1798 he was sent to Congress for Virginia. In 1795, he declined the office of Attorney General of the United States, and in 1796, that of Minister to France. In 1797, with Pinckney and Gerry, he was special envoy to France, and to him is attributed the authorship of the American side of the famous X. Y. Z. Correspondence. In 1798, he refused an appointment by Adams as associate justice of the Supreme Court, but later became his secretary of war. In all his public life, he had been closely associated with Washington and the leaders of the Federalist party ; and, perhaps more important, his early military and political service and his association with the great Federalists had bred in him a devotion to the Union and a belief in it that underlay his whole theory of constitutional government. He himself said :

"I am disposed to ascribe my devotion to the Union, and to a government competent to its preservation, at least as much to casual circumstances as to judgment. I had grown up at a time . . . when the maxim 'United we stand, divided we fall,' was the maxim of every orthodox American, and I had imbibed those sentiments so thoroughly that they constituted a part of my being. I carried them with me into the army, where I found myself associated with brave men from different States who were risking life and everything valuable in a common cause, . . . and where I was confirmed in the habit of considering America as my country and Congress my government."

As Professor Thayer has said: "It was this con-firmed 'habit of considering America as my country' communicated by him to his countrymen, which en-abled them to carry through the great struggle of forty years ago, and to save for us all, North and South, the inestimable treasure of the Union." [1] That is the key-note of all his work—a profound and stable conviction, abiding with him through his dark-est hours till his death in his eightieth year, that the salvation of the Republic lay in the full and complete powers of the Federal government; and in the light of that conviction he expounded the constitution.

It was a crucial time in the affairs of the nation when, in 1801, just at the end of his term, Adams appointed Marshall Chief Justice of the Supreme Court. During Washington's second term and Adams' administration, the power and influ-ence of the men who had accomplished the Revolution and the establishment of the constitution were coming to an end, and the principles of Washing-ton and Hamilton, the belief in the necessity of a strong Federal government, had ceased to represent the majority of the people of the country. The popular unrest, the growth of the new communities

The last days of the Federalist Party

---

[1] *John Marshall*, p. 23.

along the Ohio and the Mississippi, and the spread
of democratic principles had undermined Federalism.
The change manifested in the triumphant election
of Jefferson in 1800 was more than political; the
whole habit of the people, the system of government
and of social conditions had shifted. The history of
that change has been many times written at large;
it was the triumph of the new-made American democracy, the manifestation in America of the radical-
ism of the French Revolution, the success of the
party of strict construction that had put forth the
Virginia and Kentucky Resolutions of 1798 and 1799
and believed the constitution a compact to which the
states were the integral parties having the power to
determine and remedy its violations, even by nullification. At such a time Marshall became Chief
Justice. From every other department of government Federalism was ousted and from that day
began the rapid disintegration of the Federalist
party.

Up to that time, the Supreme Court had played
but little part in the governmental system. Its
Marbury jurisdiction was limited, its judges had been
v. men of little calibre, or had despaired of
Madison creating an efficient court; but the whole
character of the tribunal was changed by a single
step which Marshall took almost on the threshold
of his service. At the end of Adams' term, with
their last moments of power, the Federalists had
passed an amendment to the Judiciary Act creating
a new system of inferior Federal courts, relieving

the Supreme Court judges from service on circuit, and providing, *inter alia*, that the next vacancy in the Supreme Court should not be filled. New judges were created for the District of Columbia in so great a hurry that their appointments were confirmed on the last day of Adams' term, and their commissions were signed on the very night of his retirement, but never delivered. It was but natural that the first act of the Jeffersonians was to repeal the amendment to the Judiciary Act and to deny commissions to the "midnight judges." In 1801, one of these judges, Marbury, applied for a mandamus to require the issue of his commission, and in 1803 Marshall delivered his opinion on that application. (See note *Marbury* v. *Madison, infra*, Vol. I., p. 1.) That opinion is the beginning of the American system of constitutional law. In it Marshall announced the right of the Supreme Court to review the constitutionality of acts of the national legislature and the executive, the co-ordinate branches of the government. Such a power had been spoken of in certain opinions, and indeed occasionally acted on in unimportant cases in the state courts,[1] but never in the Federal courts. Common as this conception of the powers of our courts now is, it is hard to comprehend the amazing quality of it then. No court in England had such a power; there was no express warrant for it in the words of the constitution; the existence of it was denied by every other branch of the government and by the dominant

---

[1] *Stuart* v. *Laird*, 1 Cranch 299. *Hayburn's Case*, 2 Dallas 409.

majority of the country. Moreover, no such power had been clearly anticipated by the framers of the constitution, nor was it a necessary implication from the scheme of government they had established.[1]

If that doctrine were to be law, the Supreme Court was indeed a final power in a democracy beyond the reach of public opinion.

It is not surprising that *Marbury* v. *Madison* infuriated Jefferson to the last degree, nor was his temper improved by the fact that the doc- The Impeachment trine so announced was stated and explained Trials with gratuitous strength and vigor where it might, perhaps, have been passed over.[2] The case was made the signal for an immediate counter attack, the importance of which has usually been curiously overlooked. On February 3, 1803, Jefferson recommended the impeachment of John Pickering, District Judge of New Hampshire, for drunkenness and incompetency. On February 24, Marshall gave his opinion on Marbury's case, and immediately afterwards Pickering was impeached by the House. At the next session of Congress, Jefferson aimed a final blow at the independence of the Federal judiciary by

---

[1] This aspect of Marshall's doctrine, *i.e.*, that it was in no sense a necessary implication from the constitution, has, in the course of time, as Marshall's theory has become accepted been generally overlooked. The best consideration of it, and of the position of the case in our system of constitutional law, is found in the work of the late Professor Thayer. (See Thayer's *Cases on Constitutional Law*, vol. i., p. 146, an article in *Harvard Law Review*, vii. p. 129, *et seq.*, and in *John Marshall*, p. 61, *et seq.*)

[2] The portion of the opinion bearing on the right of the Court to pass on the constitutionality of acts of the executive branch of the government, which is the main theme of the opinion, is not the point on which the case turned.

the process of impeachment, a method of controlling the judges which was still open. If that were unsuccessful, then it was apparent that, as Martin Van Buren pungently remarked long after,[1] the Federalist party had been "conducted to the judicial department of the government, as to an ark of future safety which the constitution placed beyond the reach of public opinion."

The most hated of all the Federalist judges was Samuel Chase, of Maryland, and he had earned that hatred. He had been most prominent and most violent in the enforcement of the obnoxious Alien and Sedition laws, and had ever preached Federalist politics from the bench; after the impeachment of Pickering, he had made a charge to the grand jury in Baltimore full of intemperate, vituperative attack on Jefferson and the government. At the beginning of the session in 1804, he was impeached. The action of the Senate on that case, though then merely a chapter in a political controversy, is second in importance only to *Marbury* v. *Madison.* At the time of Pickering's trial he was hopelessly insane, no counsel appeared for him, and he was summarily removed. Far different from that drumhead court martial was the trial of Chase.[2] There were then nine Federalists in the Senate and twenty-five Republicans; the vote of twenty-three was necessary to convict. Vice-President Aaron Burr was its presiding

---

[1] *Political Parties in the United States*, p. 278.

[2] The best account of the trial of Chase is in Henry Adams' *History of the United States*, vol. ii., chap. x., p. 218.

officer. The manager of an ill-planned prosecution was John Randolph, of Virginia, assisted by six second-rate men. For Chase appeared the best lawyers of the Federalist party, first, Luther Martin, then Robert Goodloe Harper, Charles Lee, P. B. Key, and Joseph Hopkinson. No act of Chase which was made the basis of impeachment came within any definition of a crime; and the theory of the defence was that, under the constitution, no judge could be impeached save for an act which the law had made criminal. The greatest number of votes for removal on any charge was nineteen, and the impeachment failed ingloriously. But the principle there established, that the Senate sits in impeachment trials as a criminal court, meant that the Federal judiciary was permanently free from control of the dominant party, and that, as Mr. Adams says, impeachment was a " scarecrow." [1]

Marshall again infuriated Jefferson in the case of *Ex parte Bollman and Swartwout* (see note to that

---

[1] The importance of that trial of Chase seems too little noted. Recalling the impeachment of Hastings, a dozen years before, Mr. Adams says (*History of the United States*, vol. ii., p. 218):

" . . . but in the infinite possibilities of American democracy, the questions to be decided in the Senate Chamber had a weight for future ages beyond any that were settled in the House of Lords. Whether Judge Chase should be removed from the bench was a trifling matter; whether Chief Justice Marshall and the Supreme Court should hold their power and principles against this combination of State rignts conservatives and Pennsylvania democrats was a subject for grave reflection."

Immediately after the failure of the impeachment trial, Randolph proposed an amendment to the constitution that " the judges of the Supreme Court of the United States shall be removed by the President on the joint address of both Houses of Congress."

case, *infra*, Vol. I., p. 68), and by his conduct while presiding at the trial of Aaron Burr for treason (see note in regard to that trial, *infra*, Vol. I., p. 100), in refusing to yield to the popular demand for a conviction, and particularly in issuing a subpœna to Jefferson to appear before him; but neither of those cases decided any fundamental question, and, save *Marbury* v. *Madison*, Marshall delivered no constitutional opinion of note during Jefferson's administrations.

It is not correct to suppose that Marshall's opinions had triumphed, or that his doctrines of constitutional law were accepted, in that time. Marbury had never applied for his writ of mandamus and had never obtained his office, and the co-ordinate branches of government had never accepted the power of the Supreme Court to pass on their acts; one great thing had been accomplished, all efforts of Jefferson and the Republicans to control the judiciary had failed, but the real power of the Supreme Court had not been exercised, and Marshall had not set out his scheme of constitutional government.

In the years before the War of 1812, the fundamental Republican doctrine of strict construction of the constitution had been departed from by the Republicans themselves in the actual conduct of the national affairs; extensive foreign relations were en-
The New   tered into, Louisiana had been purchased, a
National   commercial embargo used, and the powers
Spirit   of the executive had in fact greatly increased. The Jeffersonians who, out of office, had

cried out against the liberal powers of the Federal government, when in office had found them convenient; the violations of governmental theory so obnoxious to the minority seemed less important when that minority became a majority with the problem of running the nation on its hands, so that the doctrines of strict construction became a legacy of the disgruntled New England Federalists. In 1810, Marshall delivered the opinion in the case of *Fletcher* v. *Peck* (see note to that case, *infra*, Vol. I., p. 228). That controversy was in its nature political, and Marshall's decision, as a practical matter, did not settle it at all; the Supreme Court announced its law and Georgia disregarded the announcement. In 1812, Marshall delivered the opinion in *New Jersey* v. *Wilson* (*infra*, Vol. I., p. 255), another case limiting the right of a state to impair its contracts, but the case seems to have attracted little notice, and been little understood.   No other important constitutional case was decided by the Court until the close of the War of 1812.

When the war ended in 1816, it was evident that the theories of the country as to constitutional government had been radically changed since the first administration of Jefferson.   As Mr. Henry Adams tersely said :

"Between 1801 and 1815 great changes in the American people struck the most superficial observer.   The rights of men occupied public thoughts less, and the price of cotton more,—" [1]

------

[1] *History of the United States*, vol. ix., p. 104.

In the last year of the war, the national government was practically bankrupt and New England talked of separation, commerce and manufacture were paralyzed, and there was no currency. The question of what was constitutional gave way to the question of what was possible. "In politics as in theology, the practical system which resulted from sixteen years of experience seemed to rest on the agreement not to press principles to a conclusion."[1] It was obviously necessary to return to Washington's theories of "a strong government" which Hamilton had toasted. In the years immediately following the war then there appeared a new national spirit.[2] This spirit, which the nation's lesson in the facts of government had taught it since 1800, was immediately manifested in the legislation of 1816 in the increasing of the activity of

---

[1] *History of the United States*, vol. ix., p. 191.

[2] These tendencies are elaborately and significantly treated in *The Middle Period* by Professor John W. Burgess (Scribners', 1900). See also an essay by Nicholas Murray Butler published in 1887 in John Hopkins University Studies, Fifth Series VII. The growth of the national spirit is curiously shown in a letter of Gallatin (Adams' *Writings of Gallatin* (Putnams'), vol. ii., p. 300) written May 7, 1816, where he says:

"The war has been productive of evil and good, but I think the good predominates. Independent of the loss of lives and of the losses in property by individuals, the war has laid the foundation of permanent taxes and military establishments which the Republicans had deemed unfavorable to the happiness and free institutions of the country. But under our former system we were becoming too selfish, too much attached exclusively to the acquisition of wealth, above all, too much confined in our political feelings to local and State objects. The war has renewed and reinstated the national feelings which the Revolution has given and which were daily lessened. The people have now more general objects of attachment with which their pride and political feelings are connected. They are more Americans ; they feel and act more as a nation, and I hope the permanency of the Union is thereby better secured."

the Federal government.   Madison's first message after the war recommended reorganization of the army and navy, the creation of a national currency, national improvements of highways, and a national university.   In 1816, Congress passed a bill creating a new national bank, and only one member of either House questioned the constitutionality of the bill which five years before and for twenty years after was bitterly denounced as a usurpation of the rights of the states.   In 1816, too, Congress passed the first Tariff Act, perhaps hardly to be regarded as a protective measure for American manufactures, but so championed even then by Calhoun, and surely the beginning of the protective tariff.   The same Congress provided a thorough reorganization of the army on a permanent peace footing, and the retirement of over eighteen hundred superannuated officers.   Additions were made to the navy and a bill was passed to provide a permanent fund for national improvements. [1]

Too often this aspect of the constitutional development of the country is passed over in any study of Marshall.   The doctrines of *McCulloch* v. *Maryland* in 1819, three years after, that the federal government must have all powers convenient and suitable to carry on the nation, were the very doctrines under which the government had been operated in the years following the war.   Too much emphasis can hardly be put upon the conclusion that in 1816 the nation was starting afresh in the governmental experiment

[1] This bill was, however, vetoed by Madison on the ground that it was unconstitutional as not pertaining to national objects.

on the very basis from which it had departed in the last decade of the eighteenth century, and that Marshall's theories were the justification of the actual practice of the American government at that time.

It was not until after the war and after the new national spirit that Marshall began his great series of McCulloch opinions construing the national powers and *v.* Maryland the limitations on the states, and the doctrines of the Supreme Court began to be felt as a cogent governmental power. First in importance, though not in time, was the great case of *McCulloch* v. *Maryland* in 1819. (See note to that case, *infra*, Vol. I., p. 302). The Bank of the United States, established immediately after the war, was, it seems, not operated on sound or conservative lines. By 1818, the depression of commerce and manufacture caused, probably, by the embargo and the war combined, with imprudent banking and insufficient currency, had brought the country to "hard times," particularly in the west. From 1814 on there had been numbers of banks chartered by the states which issued worthless and irredeemable paper.[1] Every evil of wild-cat banking and fraudulent over-issue was present. In Pennsylvania and the western states there came a condition akin to universal bankruptcy, and popular indignation made the Bank of the United States the scapegoat for conditions really brought about mainly by popular folly. The course of the Bank in forcing

---

[1] The banking conditions are fully set out in McMaster's *History of the United States*, vol. iv., ch. xxxvi. and in W. G. Sumner's *Life of Jackson*, American Statesmen Series (Houghton & Mifflin, 1888).

the state banks to early resumption of specie payment undoubtedly had the result of withdrawing currency from circulation in the debtor communities of the west and did force a general liquidation in those communities. In the general bankruptcy that followed a strong effort was made to repeal its charter. Failing that, the states commenced a systematic campaign to tax out of existence this Bank which seemed the immediate source of all trouble, and which was now freely denounced as unconstitutional. The resistance to the Maryland tax came before the Supreme Court in *McCulloch* v. *Maryland* and Marshall there laid down, in the broadest terms the extent of the national power to do all things necessary and convenient for the ends of government and the doctrine that their exercise under the constitution was paramount and free from all restraint by the states. The conflict that followed that decision and the persistent disregard for the authority of the Supreme Court are the subject of the notes to that case (*infra*, Vol. I., p. 302) and to *Osborn* v. *Bank* (*infra*, Vol. II., p. 84) and *Weston* v. *Charleston* (*infra*, Vol. II., p. 261). The Supreme Court's decision did not settle that controversy, and it was not until 1826 that normal conditions of banking were restored. Shortly after that Jackson saw fit to begin his operations against the Bank, again declaring that it was unconstitutional. Yet in nearly every discussion of *McCulloch* v. *Maryland* that historical setting is lost sight of. Marshall's doctrine of implied powers was the exposition of the national powers which, immediately after the war, had been vital to

the existence of the government; he was upholding
the Bank which was created by a Congress in which
only one man questioned its constitutionality, and
which the majority of the solvent communities of
the country still believed in and supported.

In the "hard times" of 1818 it was but natural
that the constitutional restrictions on the state
The Lesson powers bore harshly on the debtor states,
of State and that they were constantly violated,
Honesty secretly and openly. Kentucky, as Professor W. G. Sumner says,[1] "was the scene of the
strongest and longest conflict between the constitutional guaranties of vested rights and the legislative
measures for relieving persons from contract obligations." In this "application of political forces to the
relations of debtor and creditor" Marshall and the
Supreme Court, by precept and by example, played a
most important part. By 1819, all the banks of Kentucky and Ohio had suspended specie payments, the
population of both states was falling off, and the
majority of the people who remained were actually
bankrupt. Illinois and Tennessee were in, or soon
came to, a like condition. Tennessee passed a relief
law making property sold under execution redeem-
able within two years. The Supreme Court of Tennessee declared the law unconstitutional. Kentucky
laid a tax of $60,000 on each branch bank of the
United States (this was entirely similar to the Ohio
law declared unconstitutional in *Osborn* v. *Bank*

---

[1] *Life of Jackson*, p. 118, American Statesmen Series, (Houghton &
Mifflin, 1888.)

(*infra*, Vol. II., p. 84). In 1819, Kentucky passed a law suspending sales on execution under legal process for sixty days. A law similar to the Tennessee relief law was passed in 1820.[1] The State Bank of Kentucky had reached substantially the position of issuing unlimited unredeemable paper. In 1822, an attempt was made to remove Judge Clark, of the Kentucky Supreme Court, who declared a replevin act of Kentucky unconstitutional, and that attempt barely failed. In 1823, the Governor denounced the action of the courts. In 1823, the Court again declared the relief system unconstitutional; in 1824, the legislature affirmed it, and the issue in the next campaign was to remove the judges. Again the attempt narrowly failed, but the legislature created a new Court of Appeals—that, too, was declared unconstitutional, and Kentucky had two rival court systems. It was not until 1827 that a compromise was effected and the old courts restored. Affairs were only a little better in Ohio and Missouri, though the eastern states, save Pennsylvania, where business and banking had been on a fairly stable basis, had no such conditions to contend with.

In that stormy period the Supreme Court stood firmly by the constitutional guaranties of vested rights, and denounced and defeated the dishonest policy of the debtor states, without a moment's weakening or hesitation. The value of that service can hardly be overestimated. In 1819, in *Sturges* v. *Crowninshield* (*infra*, Vol. I., p. 281), Marshall had

---

[1] 23 Niles Register, 153.

denied the right of the states to pass bankrupt laws, a harsh doctrine that the Supreme Court later refused to follow, and in the same year he decided that the Bank, which the west believed the root of all evil, was constitutional.   In *Osborn* v. *Bank,* in 1824, not only were the attempts to strangle the branch banks of the United States overthrown, but the Supreme Court declared in substance, that it had final jurisdiction of every suit of every kind to which the Bank was a party.   In *Bank of the United States* v. *Halstead,* 1825, 10 Wheaton, 51, the Supreme Court decided that it had jurisdiction of all suits to which the Bank was a party, and that a Kentucky relief law which forbade sales of lands on execution for less than three fourths of the appraised value was to be construed as not applying to executions out of Federal courts.   In *Wayman* v. *Southard,* 10 Wheaton, 1, decided in the same year, the Supreme Court held that the replevin law of Kentucky giving a period of redemption on executions did not apply to executions out of the Federal courts.   Both cases were in substance declarations of unconstitutionality of the relief laws.   In *Bank of the United States* v. *Planters Bank* (see note to that case, *infra,* Vol. II., p. 143) it was decided substantially that a state was suable and in so far lost the attributes of sovereignty if it became a party to a banking enterprise,—certainly the safeguard of the Eleventh Amendment did not stand in Marshall's way.   In *Green* v. *Biddle,* 1823, 8 Wheaton, 1, the Supreme Court decided that the Kentucky laws of 1812, which reduced the amounts recoverable in land controversies were void as in violation of the contract of separation of Virginia and Kentucky. In 1816 had come *Martin* v. *Hunter's Lessee*, 1 Wheaton, 304, and in 1821 *Cohens* v. *Virginia* (*infra*, Vol. I., p. 400), declaring the final power of the Supreme Court to review the decisions of the state courts on federal questions.

In 1830, in *Craig* v. *Missouri* (*infra*, Vol. II., p. 275), the Supreme Court gave Missouri the touch of the whip, declaring its relief law providing a state currency unconstitutional. Later decisions of the Supreme Court — perhaps unwisely — have construed away some of the harshness which Marshall's view of the constitution laid upon the powers of the states, but the part that the Supreme Court, and the courts of Kentucky and Tennessee, then played in teaching the lesson of state honesty, is too little understood.

The period from the close of the war to the first administration of Jackson,—important as were the economic changes in the nation, and deplorable as was the financial situation in the west,—was a slack time in politics and political theories. After the Missouri Compromise, slavery was not a direct issue, prosperity was slowly returning to the country, and the tariff was benefiting the seaboard and manufacturing communities of the north. Except for the southern agitation on the tariff in the latter part of that time and the beginning of slavery troubles, the country was disturbed by no great political issue, and the powers of the national government were oppressive to no great part of the people. In that period,

Marshall created the American system of constitutional government.

It is necessary to review several other lines of cases to show more thoroughly how far-reaching his achieve-
The Power of the Federal Courts
ment had been, and how great a range his cases had covered. First, as to the power of the Federal courts. The original Judiciary Act of 1789 was drawn soon after the adoption of the constitution with a view of giving to the Federal courts the fullest jurisdiction granted them under the constitution. That great national act, and the clauses in the constitution on which it rested, were substantially first construed by Marshall and his Court,—and surely he construed them in a large way for the purpose of establishing a court of ample jurisdiction and complete power—such a court as the world had never seen.

By *Marbury* v. *Madison* (*infra*, Vol. I., p. 1) he had declared the power of the Court to check violations of the constitution by the co-ordinate branches of the Federal government and by 1830, the exercise of that power was generally, though not completely, acquiesced in. In the long line of cases beginning with *Fletcher* v. *Peck*, the *Dartmouth College* case and the Kentucky and Tennessee cases he had established the Court as the guardian of constitutional guaranties of vested rights of individuals against the encroachments of the states. And more, a practical step of hardly less significance, he had established the Supreme Court as the final judge of constitutional questions over all the state courts.

The constitution in terms gave the Supreme Court no jurisdiction or power of review over the decisions of the state courts on subjects of which the Federal courts had jurisdiction, yet it was vital to the supremacy of Marshall's doctrines. The chain of reasoning by which he found such a power implied in the constitution was announced by Judge Story in *Martin* v. *Hunter's Lessee,* 1 Wheaton, 304, and by Marshall in the noble opinion in *Cohens* v. *Virginia (infra,* Vol. I., p. 400) the most satisfying perhaps of all his decisions.[1]

The ground of that appellate jurisdiction Marshall found in the declaration that the constitution and the laws of the United States were to be the supreme law, in the clauses of the constitution defining the appellate jurisdiction of the Supreme Court in "all other cases," and in the general purpose of the constitution to establish a harmonious and complete judicial system. The astounding quality of that reasoning, convincing as it is, lies in the fact that the Eleventh Amendment forbade any citizen of one state commencing any suit against another state. Yet *Cohens* v. *Virginia* declared the right of a citizen to appeal from a state court to the Supreme Court on a federal question, though that had the indirect result of summoning a state before the bar of the Supreme Court. No one of Marshall's cases save *Marbury* v. *Madison,* and *McCulloch* v. *Maryland* excited more violent and bitter opposition than this.

[1] The jurisdiction asserted in these two cases had been previously exercised unchallenged in other cases.

It is not surprising that, in constructing his scheme
of constitutional law, in which the most important
part was the strengthening of the powers
Marshall's
Limitations of the national government, Marshall con-
on State strued, perhaps too literally and harshly,
Powers the limitations in the powers of the states.
It is in that branch of the law only that Marshall's
decisions have been departed from.[1]

In *New Jersey* v. *Wilson* (see note to that case,
infra, Vol. I., p. 255), Marshall had decided that a
state contract for tax exemption was inviolate.   That
doctrine, thus barely stated, is still law, but, as a matter of experience, to guard against improvident grants
of exemptions in the early stages of the country's
development, the Supreme Court has of necessity
established the strictest rules for construing tax exemptions.   The conditions which Marshall there construed as a contract of exemption would now be
construed as no contract at all.   The courts have become astute to escape the doctrine—of questionable
soundness in the beginning—because it came to work
a substantial inequality.   *Sturges* v. *Crowninshield*
(see note, *infra*, Vol. I., p. 281) was expressly overruled in Marshall's time, and though the scheme of
government propounded by it may be the wiser one,
Marshall's opinion seems clearly wrong.[2]   The Dartmouth College case (see note, *infra*, Vol. I., p. 346),
like *New Jersey* v. *Wilson*, established the inviolability

---

[1] This is noted by Professor Thayer almost alone of Marshall's commentators.

[2] A mass of expert opinion to the contrary notwithstanding.

of corporate charters as contracts; the value of that principle as giving stability to corporate enterprise in the beginning of the nation can hardly be over-emphasized; it is the main element of strength in the American corporate system, but almost immediately improvident legislation made it the instrument of oppression by rapacious corporations. Still it sets the point of view of the courts in dealing with these questions; it is no longer the rule of conduct and the exceptions have half eaten away the rule, but the rule established fair treatment of the corporate charters as a judicial principle,[1] the exceptions were such as became necessary to make possible fair treatment to the public and to protect them from their legislatures. So also the doctrine of *Craig* v. *Missouri* (see note to that case) proved in practice an unnecessarily stringent restriction on the state power to relieve local currency troubles, and the sweeping statements of *McCulloch* v. *Maryland* (see note to that case, *infra*, Vol. I., p. 302) as to the powers of the states to tax the instruments of the national government have been substantially departed from in later cases. Yet it will not do to note those reversals as errors. By and large, the country has taken kindly to the exercise of the constitutional power of review

---

[1] As Professor S. E. Baldwin significantly remarked:

"So did the little phrase 'impair the obligation of contracts'—like the genius of some Arabian tale—at the touch of the magic wand of Chief Justice Marshall, rise and spread into the form of that invincible champion of chartered franchises, by which the whole theory of American corporations was to be revolutionized once and again." (P. 12, *Modern Political Institutions*, Little, Brown & Co., Boston, 1898.)

by the courts, and each succeeding state constitution partakes more largely of the nature of a code of fundamental law and less of the nature of a scheme of government, and each tends to place stricter limits on the improvidence and the unfairness of the legislative branches and greater power of oversight in the courts. To that result, which many of the wisest deem unfortunate, Marshall's method of interpreting the limitations on state powers has led the way. Wise or unwise, it has become a habit of government, a new function of the courts, a practical growth of their powers to an accomplished revolution, natural enough, though in no wise consciously planned by Marshall and his court.

One other great line of cases remains to be dealt with, those construing that clause of the constitution The Com- reading, "Congress shall have power to merce regulate commerce with foreign nations, and Clause among the several states, and with the Indian Tribes," which has produced more difficulties of interpretation than any other clause in that instrument, and is still a source of perplexity to the Supreme Court. Marshall's first opinion construing that clause, five years after the War of 1812 and ten after the Embargo, was *The Brig Wilson (Ivory Huntress, claimant,)* v. *The United States*, a decision delivered in the Circuit Court, in 1820, reported in 1 *Brockenbrough*, 234 (*infra*, Vol. II., p. 401). It is a cases eldom cited, but of real importance. The constitution left entirely to the states the question of the importation of negroes before 1808, but, in 1803,

Congress passed a law providing, in effect, for the seizure of ships in which persons of color were imported into states which (by their local law) forbade such traffic. Marshall's opinion holds this Federal law constitutional as an exercise of the commerce power, giving to commerce a sufficiently broad interpretation to include all navigation. It is notable that in this instance Congress was using its commerce power as a means of regulating a certain form of traffic which the constitution had expressly left to local regulations by the states. That decision, the first of all, forecasted the enormous powers which the national government now wields by virtue of that clause. If the commerce clause gave to Congress, by indirection, the power to regulate a traffic, which power the constitution, in terms, forbade it, it is not remarkable that Congress has exercised this power by the Interstate Commerce Commission to regulate the conduct of common carriers within the states, and to provide the machinery to be used on all railroads dealing with interstate commerce (see *Johnson* v. *Southern Pacific Co.*, 196 U. S., 1), or to regulate monopolies and railroad competition (*The Northern Securities case*, 193 U. S. 197), nor will it be surprising if the national government shall in the future claim the right of supervision of the affairs of all corporations as a condition of the right to allow them to engage in interstate commerce— though the objects of that exercise of power have no direct relation to commerce. Such a conception of the scope of the commerce power goes no

farther than this early and well-nigh forgotten case
of Marshall.

Marshall's best-known contribution to this difficult
subject of the commerce power is the oft-quoted case
of *Gibbons* v. *Ogden* (see note, *infra*, Vol. II., p. 36),
which came before the Supreme Court in 1824. In
that case, Marshall defined commerce as including not
only all navigation but all "commercial intercourse,"
and first laid down the doctrine that the national
power over commerce is "exclusive" and "indivisi-
ble," and is inconsistent with the existence of a concurrent power in the states. Marshall's opinion in
that case turns finally on the conflict of the New
York grant of a steamboat monopoly with the national
coasting regulations, but the reasoning of that portion
of the opinion is hardly satisfactory, and the case has
been almost universally accepted as standing for the
larger doctrine.[1]

It has been pointed out that the only actual decision in *Gibbons* v. *Ogden* was that commerce at least

[1] The concurring opinion of Mr. Justice Johnson, in *Gibbons* v. *Ogden*—one
of the most acute opinions of that most able judge—is really more satisfactory
than Marshall's. Briefly that opinion reviews the history of the insufficient government of the Confederation because of the lack of power over commerce, which
was the prime cause of the adoption of the constitution, and concludes that
the national power is of necessity the sum of the powers residing in the states
under the Confederation, and as such necessarily exclusive of any residuum of
power in the states,—though not inconsistent with the existence of power in
the states to make any laws for the carrying out of local purposes in so far as
they may affect the objects or means of commerce, provided such laws do not
conflict with the exercise of the national power. That doctrine—perhaps more
exactly stated by Webster in his argument of the case—is the real basis of the
decision thirty years later in *Cooley* v. *Board of Port Wardens*, which is nom-
inally the law of the Supreme Court, where it is laid down that the power of
Congress is exclusive only as to objects of national concern.

included navigation, and was under federal control, that in so far Marshall's statement that the power of Congress was exclusive represented the accepted doctrine and was no new thing, and that the decision was not supposed at the time to be in conflict with the power then constantly exercised by the states of granting monopolies of land and ferry travel to common carriers.[1] In *Brown* v. *Maryland* he decided that a state law, taxing imports from foreign countries before they had been sold or incorporated into the general property of the state, was unconstitutional, both as a tax on imports and, by inference, as an attempt by a state to regulate commerce. The decision is now explained by the Supreme Court as applying only to foreign commerce,[2] but the case has been accepted as proclaiming a larger doctrine. Accepted literally, that doctrine, which would seem to go so far as to say that the states had no power to pass any law which should have even an indirect effect on commerce, soon showed itself unworkable. Even in Marshall's time there grew up, with the building of highways and the extension of commerce, an entirely new set of questions as to the validity of state laws which, though they were necessary for the regulation of the health or welfare of the states, or to supplement the national commercial system, yet did deal with commerce. The general doctrine was later adopted by the Supreme Court that

---

[1] Chief Justice Marshall on Federal Regulations of Interstate Carriers, by E. Parmalee Prentice.—*Columbia Law Review*, vol. iv., p. 77.

[2] *American Steel and Wire Co.* v. *Speed*, 192 U. S., 500.

the national power over commerce was exclusive, though not affirmatively exercised, over objects of national concern, and, when exercised, as to the whole domain of commerce. But the effect of *Gibbons* v. *Ogden* is notable as establishing the helplessness of the states to pass laws dealing directly with commerce and the subjects of commerce.[1]

In *Willson* v. *Blackbird Creek, etc.* (see note, *infra*, Vol. II., p. 228), this phase of the commerce question was briefly and rather unsatisfactorily dealt with. The case was seemingly lightly and hurriedly considered. Marshall decided that a Delaware law authorizing the damming of a tide-water creek was not an interference with the federal power over commerce until it came in conflict with the positive provisions of some federal statute. The case is not consistent with the language of *Gibbons* v. *Ogden*, though entirely consistent with the law it later developed.

It is fair to say, then, that Marshall's decisions on the commerce clause were less illuminating than on any other topic of constitutional law, that while setting out clearly the scope of the federal power,—and that may, in the future, prove the most important phase of the subject, as it undoubtedly was in his time,—Marshall failed to understand clearly the scope of the power of the states to pass laws which might affect commerce, a fact that becomes the less notable when one considers that at no later period has the Supreme Court

---

[1] The extent of the acceptance of this doctrine by the Supreme Court is curiously shown in a recent decision. *Central of Georgia Ry. Co.* v. *Murphy*, 196 U. S., 194.

been able to reach a satisfactory, or a stable, opinion on that subject. But certainly he declared very clearly and strongly the breadth of the national power over commerce, and laid the way for the assumption of the pervading powers which the federal government now exercises.

Such was Marshall's work, so magnificent his achievement. It is not easy to measure that greatness with Lilliputian words, or to point to brick and stone as his creation. A nation has delighted to honor him and no voice has dissented from that praise. The final comment seems that he saw most clearly the evils of the Confederation and their causes in the jealousy of the states and the lack of a strong government, that he read the constitution and all its phrases as subordinate to the central idea of the creation of a mighty federal government, complete with every national power, and that, with the imagination of greatness, he created an opportunity and made the Supreme Court of the United States the interpreter of the constitution for every department of the nation. More, with a marvellous prophetic instinct of the course of national greatness in the years to follow, he implanted that conception of complete federal powers so firmly in the judicial system, in the whole frame of government, and in the minds of all who came after him, that it has made simpler and more natural every step in the development of the United States toward national greatness—from the first denial of the doctrine of nullification, to the final denial of that doctrine by arms, to the accession of power over the action of the states by the Fourteenth Amendment and the large construction which the courts have placed upon it, to the strengthening of the power of the federal executive in the hands of Lincoln and the recent presidents, and to the complex and pervasive system of national regulation of commerce which the United States now has.

To the accomplishment of that task Marshall brought the master-mind of American constitutional government, hardly the perfection of legal reasoning and learning, but so sound a common-sense for the practical working of legal theory, so just an instinct for the national welfare, and so austere and unswerving a judicial fairness and openness of mind that no judge since may be compared with him. And he voiced his opinions with absolute clearness of speech and reasoning, with the tremendous earnestness and vigor of sincere conviction, and in language and style so fitting, so dignified, and yet so luminous that they stand as monuments of judicial reasoning and English prose. It was his fortune and virtue to have led a life of great achievement with so much piety and simplicity and beauty that he won alike the admiration and love of all who knew him. In his character there abode, from day to day, and from year to year, from his stainless youth to his splendid death, a passionate and exalted love of country that, even in her darkest hours, he builded strongly for the future of a mighty nation.

THE CONSTITUTIONAL DECISIONS

OF

JOHN MARSHALL.

Marbury *v.* Madison.

NOTE.

THIS was Marshall's first opinion involving constitutional questions—it is perhaps the best known and most lauded of all his cases. In it he first authoritatively declared the American doctrine of constitutional law—that the federal constitution is the supreme law of the land, and that the judiciary will declare all other laws of the state or national governments which conflict with it unconstitutional and void. The meaning, the scope, the importance of that doctrine and the position of this case in our law are commented on in the introduction to these volumes, but the story of political troubles that gave rise to the case is not without interest or point in a study of Marshall's career. For the case was the outcome of a bitter and famous political quarrel in the closing days of the power of the Federalists.

In December 1800 it became certain that the Federalists had been overwhelmingly defeated at the polls, that both branches of Congress would be Republican, and that Jefferson would be the next President. And in that brief period until March 4, 1801, the Federalists evidently set out to pass certain frankly partisan laws which should—after the manner of modern politics, though with loftier motives—provide offices for many Federalists and saddle the country with a Federalist judiciary. The judiciary at that time was perhaps the most unpopular branch of the federal government. The decision of the Supreme Court in *Chisholm* v. *Georgia*, which brought the sovereign State of Georgia before that Court. the life tenure of the judges, the assumption by the courts, both State and United States, to pass on the constitutionality of laws, and the arrogance of the federal judges were alike odious. More than that, there was in the country at large a real hostility to the courts as such. The general poverty, the lack of manufactures, the want of a sound financial system, the republican sentiments of freedom and equality of men, and the jealousy of the national government that had seated Jefferson made the whole machinery of the courts hateful to the dominant element in politics.

Thus in the last days of the Adams administration a bill was passed by the Federalists changing the national judicial system, enlarging it, bringing it to every man's door: the Supreme Court judges were no longer to go on circuit, six circuit and twenty-two district courts were established and new judges created. Such legislation was regarded by the Jeffersonians as pure Federalist defiance. In addition an act of February 27, 1801, created certain justiceships for the District of Columbia and to one of these was appointed William Marbury. This appointment was confirmed by the Senate on March third, and on that night his commission was signed by Adams and sealed by Marshall, then his secretary of state, and newly appointed chief justice. When Jefferson took office he forbade the commissions to be issued.

In the latter part of the December term, 1801, the Supreme Court on the petition of Marbury granted a rule commanding Madison, then Jefferson's secretary of state, to show cause why a writ of mandamus should not be issued directing the delivery of the commission. The hearing was set down for the August term of the Court but before that term began the Republican Congress amended the Judiciary Act, sent the Supreme Court judges on circuit, and abolished the August term. In February 1803, in response to a message from Jefferson a committee of the House recommended the impeachment of Pickering, circuit judge. A week later Marbury's motion came before the Supreme Court—over a year after the order to show cause had been granted. Madison did not appear in opposition to the motion or in any way notice it.

The decision of the case turned on the point that the Supreme Court had no power to issue such a writ—inasmuch as the

Constitution gave to the Court no original jurisdiction in such a case, and the Judiciary Act in so far as it attempted to increase the jurisdiction conflicted with the Constitution and was void. The actual decision then was against Marbury, and more, this first opinion limited and restrained the Supreme Court from exercising the power Congress had granted to it. But—and here lay the sting —Marshall's opinion preceded the decision on this point by an elaborate exposition of the system of individual rights under the Constitution and declared the power of the Court to pass on the validity of Acts of Congress and decide whether they were in conflict with the provisions of the Constitution. It cannot be denied that such an opinion was highly calculated to inflame the Jeffersonians, who contended that Congress, not the Supreme Court of Federalists, had the right to decide the constitutionality of its laws. The decision enraged Jefferson and the Republicans and was the signal for the impeachment of Pickering and a violent attack on the judiciary culminating in the unsuccessful attempt to impeach Justice Chase.

Yet Marshall's opinion contains nowhere a hint of this partisan quarrel that underlay the case—only in the opening words he said: " The peculiar delicacy of this case, the novelty of some of its circumstances, and the real difficulty attending the points which occur in it, require a complete exposition of the principles on which the opinion to be given by the court is founded." And again on page *169 : " The intimate political relation subsisting between the President of the United States and the heads of departments necessarily renders any legal investigation of the acts of one of those high officers peculiarly irksome, as well as delicate; and excites some hesitation with respect to the propriety of entering into such investigation. Impressions are often received without much reflection or examination, and it is not wonderful, that in such a case as this the assertion by an individual, of his legal claims in a court of justice, to which claims it is the duty of that court to attend, should at first view be considered by some as an attempt to intrude into the cabinet, and to intermeddle with the prerogatives of the executive." Such is the temper of the opinion of the man who had been a leader of the

Federalists, who had seen his party broken and dissolved—and this to his bitterest political enemy, Jefferson.

If the opinion be overlauded, and it seems it is, if it lays down too barely and didactically, with too small a basis of argument and history the American doctrine of constitutional law, it is alike remarkable for its courage and its temperance.

William Marbury

v.

James Madison, Secretary of State of the United States.

[1 Cranch, 137.]

February, 1803.

Mr. Charles Lee for the motion.

OPINION OF THE COURT.

At the last term on the affidavits then read and filed with the clerk, a rule was granted in this case, requiring the secretary of state to show
* 154 cause why a mandamus *should not issue, directing him to deliver to William Marbury his commission as a justice of the peace for the county of Washington, in the District of Columbia.

No cause has been shown, and the present motion is for a mandamus. The peculiar delicacy of this case, the novelty of some of its circumstances, and the real difficulty attending the points which occur in it, require a complete exposition of the principles on which the opinion to be given by the court is founded.

These principles have been, on the side of the applicant, very ably argued at the bar. In rendering the opinion of the court, there will be some departure in form, though not in substance, from the points stated in that argument.

In the order in which the court has viewed this subject, the following questions have been considered and decided.

1st. Has the applicant a right to the commission he demands?

2d. If he has a right, and that right has been violated, do the laws of his country afford him a remedy?

3d.   If they do afford him a remedy, is it a mandamus issuing from this court?

The first object of inquiry is,

1st. Has the applicant a right to the commission he demands?

His right originates in an act of congress passed in February, 1801, concerning the District of Columbia.

After dividing the district into two counties, the 11th section of this law enacts, " that there shall be appointed in and for each of the said counties, such number of discreet persons to be justices of the peace as the president of the United States shall, from time to time, think expedient, to continue in office for five years.

* *155*   * It appears, from the affidavits, that in compliance with this law, a commission for William Marbury, as a justice of the peace for the county of Washington, was signed by John Adams, then President of the United States; after which the seal of the United States was affixed to it; but

the commission has never reached the person for whom it was made out.

In order to determine whether he is entitled to this commission, it becomes necessary to inquire whether he has been appointed to the office. For if he has been appointed, the law continues him in office for five years, and he is entitled to the possession of those evidences of office, which, being completed, became his property.

The 2d section of the 2d article of the constitution declares, that "the president shall nominate, and, by and with the advice and consent of the senate, shall appoint, ambassadors, other public ministers and con-suls, and all other officers of the United States, whose appointments are not otherwise provided for."

The 3d section declares, that "he shall commission all the officers of the United States."

An act of congress directs the secretary of state to keep the seal of the United States, "to make out and record, and affix the said seal to all civil commissions to officers of the United States, to be appointed by the president, by and with the consent of the senate, or by the president alone ; provided, that the said seal shall not be affixed to any commission before the same shall have been signed by the President of the United States."

These are the clauses of the constitution and laws of the United States, which affect this part of the case. They seem to contemplate three distinct operations :

1st. The nomination. This is the sole act of the president, and is completely voluntary.

2d. The appointment. This is also the act of the president, and is also a voluntary act, though it can only be performed by and with the advice and consent of the senate.

* *156*   * 3d. The commission. To grant a commission to a person appointed, might, perhaps, be deemed a duty enjoined by the constitution. " He shall," says the instrument, "commission all the officers of the United States."

The acts of appointing to office, and commissioning the person appointed, can scarcely be considered as one and the same; since the power to perform them is given in two separate and distinct sections of the constitution. The distinction between the appointment and the commission will be rendered more apparent by averting to that provision in the second section of the second article of the constitution, which authorizes congress "to vest, by law, the appointment of such inferior officers, as they think proper, in the president alone, in the courts of law, or in the heads of departments;" thus contemplating cases where the law may direct the president to commission an officer appointed by the courts, or by the heads of departments. In such a case, to issue a commission would be apparently a duty distinct from the appointment, the performance of which, perhaps, could not legally be refused.

Although that clause of the constitution which requires the president to commission all the officers of the United States, may never have been applied to officers appointed otherwise than by himself, yet it would be difficult to deny the legislative power to apply it to such cases. Of consequence, the constitutional distinction between the appointment to an office and the commission of an officer who has been appointed, remains the same as if in practice the president had commissioned officers appointed by an authority other than his own.

It follows, too, from the existence of this distinction, that if an appointment was to be evidenced by any public act, other than the commission, the performance of such public act would create the officer ; and if he was not removable at the will of the president, would either give him a right to his commission, or enable him to perform the duties without it.

These observations are premised solely for the purpose of rendering more intelligible those which apply more directly to the particular case under consideration.

* *157*   * This is an appointment made by the president, by and with the advice and consent of the senate, and is evidenced by no act but the commission itself. In such a case, therefore, the commission and the appointment seem inseparable ; it being almost impossible to show an appointment otherwise than by proving the existence of a commission ; still the commission is not necessarily the appointment, though conclusive evidence of it.

But at what stage does it amount to this conclusive evidence ?

The answer to this question seems an obvious one. The appointment being the sole act of the president, must be completely evidenced, when it is shown that he has done everything to be performed by him.

Should the commission, instead of being evidence of an appointment, even be considered as constituting the appointment itself; still it would be made when the last act to be done by the president was performed, or, at furthest, when the commission was complete.

The last act to be done by the president is the signature of the commission. He has then acted on the advice and consent of the senate to his own nomination. The time for deliberation has then passed. He has decided. His judgment, on the advice and consent of the senate concurring with his nomination, has been made, and the officer is appointed. This appointment is evidenced by an open, unequivocal act; and being the last act required from the person making it, necessarily excludes the idea of its being, so far as respects the appointment, an inchoate and incomplete transaction.

Some point of time must be taken when the power of the executive over an officer, not removable at his will, must cease. That point of time must be when the constitutional power of appointment has been exercised. And this power has been exercised when the last act, required from the person possessing the power, has been performed. This last act is the signature of the commission. This idea seems to * *158* have prevailed with the legislature, when the act passed converting the department * of foreign affairs into the department of state. By that act it is enacted, that the secretary of state shall keep the seal of the United States, "and shall make out and record, and shall affix the said seal to all civil commissions to officers of the United States, to be appointed by the president;" "Provided, that the said seal shall not be affixed to any commission before the same shall have been signed by the President of the United States; nor to any other instrument or act, without the special warrant of the president therefor."

The signature is a warrant for affixing the great seal to the commission; and the great seal is only to be affixed to an instrument which is complete. It attests, by an act supposed to be of public notoriety, the verity of the presidential signature.

It is never to be affixed till the commission is signed, because the signature, which gives force and effect to the commission, is conclusive evidence that the appointment is made.

The commission being signed, the subsequent duty of the secretary of state is prescribed by law, and not to be guided by the will of the president. He is to affix the seal of the United States to the commission, and is to record it.

This is not a proceeding which may be varied, if the judgment of the executive shall suggest one more eligible; but is a precise course accurately marked out by law, and is to be strictly pursued. It is the duty of the secretary of state to conform to the law, and in this he is an officer of the United States, bound to obey the laws. He acts, in this respect, as has been very properly stated at the bar, under the authority of law, and not by the instructions of the president. It is a ministerial act which the law enjoins on a particular officer for a particular purpose.

If it should be supposed, that the solemnity of affixing the seal is necessary not only to the validity of the commission, but even to the completion of an * *159* appointment, still when the seal is affixed the appointment is made, and * the commission is valid. No other solemnity is required by law ; no other act is to be performed on the part of the government. All that the executive can do to invest the person with his office is done ; and unless the appointment be then made, the executive cannot make one without the co-operation of others.

After searching anxiously for the principles on which a contrary opinion may be supported, none have been found which appear of sufficient force to maintain the opposite doctrine.

Such as the imagination of the court could suggest, have been very deliberately examined, and after allowing them all the weight which it appears possible to give them, they do not shake the opinion which has been formed.

In considering this question, it has been conjectured that the commission may have been assimilated to a deed, to the validity of which delivery is essential.

This idea is founded on the supposition that the commission is not merely evidence of an appointment, but is itself the actual appointment ; a supposition by no means unquestionable. But for the purpose of examining this objection fairly ; let it be conceded, that the principle claimed for its support is estab- lished.

The appointment being, under the constitution, to be made by the president personally, the delivery of the deed of appointment, if necessary to its comple- tion, must be made by the president also. It is not necessary that the delivery should be made person- ally to the grantee of the office ; it never is so made. The law would seem to contemplate that it should be made to the Secretary of State, since it directs the secretary to affix the seal to the commission after it shall have been signed by the President. If, then, the act of delivery be necessary to give validity to the commission, it has been delivered when executed and given to the secretary for the purpose of being sealed, recorded, and transmitted to the party.

But in all cases of letters patent, certain solemnities are required by law, which solemnities are the evi- dences * of the validity of the instrument. * *160* A formal delivery to the person is not among them. In cases of commissions, the sign manual of the President, and the seal of the United States, are those solemnities. This objection, therefore, does not touch the case.

It has also occurred as possible, and barely possible, that the transmission of the commission, and the acceptance thereof, might be deemed necessary to complete the right of the plaintiff.

The transmission of the commission is a practice directed by convenience, but not by law. It cannot, therefore, be necessary to constitute the appointment which must precede it, and which is the mere act of the President. If the executive required that every person appointed to an office should himself take means to procure his commission, the appointment would not be the less valid on that account. The appointment is the sole act of the President; the transmission of the commission is the sole act of the officer to whom that duty is assigned, and may be accelerated or retarded by circumstances which can have no influence on the appointment. A commission is transmitted to a person already appointed; not to a person to be appointed or not, as the letter enclosing the commission should happen to get into the post office and reach him in safety, or to miscarry.

It may have some tendency to elucidate this point, to inquire whether the possession of the original commission be indispensably necessary to authorize a person, appointed to any office, to perform the duties of that office. If it was necessary, then a loss of the commission would lose the office. Not only negligence, but accident or fraud, fire or theft, might deprive an individual of his office. In such a case, I presume it could not be doubted but that a copy from the record of the office of the Secretary of State would be, to every intent and purpose, equal to the original. The act of congress has expressly made it so. To give that copy validity, it would not be necessary to prove that the original had been transmitted and afterwards lost. The copy would be complete evidence that the original had existed, and that the appointment had been made, but not that the original had been transmitted. If indeed it should ap-

* *161*   pear that * the original had been mislaid in the office of state, that circumstance would not affect the operation of the copy. When all the requisites have been performed which authorize a recording officer to record any instrument whatever, and the order for that purpose has been given, the instrument is, in law, considered as recorded, although the manual labor of inserting it in a book kept for that purpose may not have been performed.

In the case of commissions, the law orders the Secretary of State to record them. When, therefore, they are signed and sealed, the order for their being recorded is given; and whether inserted in the book or not, they are in law recorded.

A copy of this record is declared equal to the original, and the fees to be paid by a person requiring a copy are ascertained by law. Can a keeper of a public record erase therefrom a commission which has been recorded? Or can he refuse a copy thereof to a person demanding it on the terms prescribed by law?

Such a copy would, equally with the original, authorize the justice of peace to proceed in the performance of his duty, because it would, equally with the original, attest his appointment.

If the transmission of a commission be not considered as necessary to give validity to an appointment, still less is its acceptance. The appointment is the sole act of the President; the acceptance is the sole

act of the officer, and is, in plain common sense, pos-
terior to the appointment.   As he may resign, so may
he refuse to accept : but neither the one nor the other
is capable of rendering the appointment a nonentity.

That this is the understanding of the government,
is apparent from the whole tenor of its conduct.

A commission bears date, and the salary of the
officer commences, from his appointment; not from
the transmission or acceptance of his commission.
When a person appointed to any office refuses to
*162   accept that office, the successor is nominated
        in the place of the person who * has declined
to accept, and not in the place of the person who had
been previously in office, and had created the original
vacancy.

It is, therefore, decidedly the opinion of the court,
that when a commission has been signed by the President, the appointment is made ; and that the commission is complete when the seal of the United States
has been affixed to it by the Secretary of State.

When an officer is removable at the will of the
executive, the circumstance which completes his appointment is of no concern ; because the act is at any
time revocable ; and the commission may be arrested,
if still in the office.   But when the officer is not removable at the will of the executive, the appointment
is not revocable, and cannot be annulled.   It has
conferred legal rights which cannot be resumed.

The discretion of the executive is to be exercised
until the appointment has been made.   But having
once made the appointment, his power over the office

is terminated in all cases, where by law the officer is not removable by him. The right to the office is then in the person appointed, and he has the absolute, unconditional power of accepting or rejecting it.

Mr. Marbury, then, since his commission was signed by the President, and sealed by the Secretary of State, was appointed; and as the law creating the office, gave the officer a right to hold for five years, independent of the executive, the appointment was not revocable, but vested in the officer legal rights, which are protected by the laws of his country.

To withhold his commission, therefore, is an act deemed by the court not warranted by law, but violative of a vested legal right.

This brings us to the second inquiry; which is,

2d. If he has a right, and that right has been violated, do the laws of his country afford him a remedy?

* *163*   *The very essence of civil liberty certainly consists in the right of every individual to claim the protection of the laws, whenever he receives an injury. One of the first duties of government is to afford that protection. In Great Britain the king himself is sued in the respectful form of a petition, and he never fails to comply with the judgment of his court.

In the 3d vol. of his Commentaries, p. 23, Blackstone states two cases in which a remedy is afforded by mere operation of law.

" In all other cases," he says, " it is a general and indisputable rule, that where there is a legal right, there is also a legal remedy by suit, or action at law, whenever that right is invaded."

And afterwards, p. 109, of the same vol. he says, " I am next to consider such injuries as are cognizable by the courts of the common law. And herein I shall for the present only remark, that all possible injuries whatsoever, that did not fall within the exclusive cognizance of either the ecclesiastical, military, or maritime tribunals, are, for that very reason, within the cognizance of the common law courts of justice; for it is a settled and invariable principle in the laws of England, that every right, when withheld, must have a remedy, and every injury its proper redress."

The government of the United States has been emphatically termed a government of laws, and not of men. It will certainly cease to deserve this high appellation, if the laws furnish no remedy for the violation of a vested legal right.

If this obloquy is to be cast on the jurisprudence of our country, it must arise from the peculiar character of the case.

It behooves us, then, to inquire whether there be in its composition any ingredient which shall exempt it from legal investigation, or exclude the injured party from legal redress. In pursuing this inquiry the first question which presents itself is, whether
* *164* this can be arranged *with that class of cases which come under the description of *damnum absque injuria ;* a loss without an injury.

This description of cases never has been considered, and it is believed never can be considered, as comprehending offices of trust, of honor, or of profit. The office of justice of peace in the District of Columbia is such an office ; it is therefore worthy of the attention and guardianship of the laws. It has received that attention and guardianship. It has been created by special act of congress, and has been secured, so far as the laws can give security, to the person appointed to fill it, for five years. It is not, then, on account of the worthlessness of the thing pursued, that the injured party can be alleged to be without remedy.

Is it in the nature of the transaction ? Is the act of delivering or withholding a commission to be considered as a mere political act, belonging to the executive department alone, for the performance of which entire confidence is placed by our constitution in the supreme executive ; and for any misconduct respecting which, the injured individual has no remedy ?

That there may be such cases is not to be questioned : but that every act of duty, to be performed in any of the great departments of government, constitutes such a case, is not to be admitted.

By the act concerning invalids, passed in June, 1794, *vol. 3, p. 112*, the Secretary of War is ordered to place on the pension list all persons whose names are contained in a report previously made by him to congress. If he should refuse to do so, would the wounded veteran be without remedy ? Is it to be contended that where the law in precise term, directs the performance of an act, in which an individual is interested, the law is incapable of securing obedience to its mandate?   Is it on account of the character of the person against whom the complaint is made?   Is it to be contended that the heads of departments are not amenable to the laws of their country?

Whatever the practice on particular occasions may be, the theory of this principle will certainly ** 165*   never be maintained.   * No act of the legislature confers so extraordinary a privilege, nor can it derive countenance from the doctrines of the common law.   After stating that personal injury from the king to a subject is presumed to be impossible, *Blackstone, vol. 3, p. 255,* says, " but injuries to the rights of property can scarcely be committed by the crown without the intervention of its officers; for whom the law, in matters of right, entertains no respect or delicacy : but furnishes various methods of detecting the errors and misconduct of those agents, by whom the king has been deceived and induced to do a temporary injustice."

By the act passed in 1796, authorizing the sale of the lands above the mouth of Kentucky river, (*vol. 3, p. 299,*) the purchaser, on paying his purchase money, becomes completely entitled to the property purchased; and on producing to the Secretary of State the receipt of the treasurer upon a certificate required by the law, the President of the United States is authorized to grant him a patent.   It is further enacted that all patents shall be countersigned by the Secretary of State, and recorded in his office.   If the Secretary of State should choose to withhold this patent ; or, the patent being lost, should refuse a copy of it ; can it be imagined that the law furnishes to the injured person no remedy ?

It is not believed that any person whatever would attempt to maintain such a proposition.

It follows, then, that the question, whether the legality of an act of the head of a department be examinable in a court of justice or not, must always depend on the nature of that act.

If some acts be examinable, and others not, there must be some rule of law to guide the court in the exercise of its jurisdiction.

In some instances there may be difficulty in applying the rule to particular cases; but there cannot, it is believed, be much difficulty in laying down the rule.

By the constitution of the United States, the President is invested with certain important political *166   powers, in the * exercise of which he is to use his own discretion, and is accountable only to his country in his political character and to his own conscience.   To aid him in the performance of these duties, he is authorized to appoint certain officers, who act by his authority, and in conformity with his orders.

In such cases, their acts are his acts ; and whatever opinion may be entertained of the manner in which executive discretion may be used, still there exists, and can exist, no power to control that discretion. The subjects are political.   They respect the nation, not individual rights, and being intrusted to the executive, the decision of the executive is conclusive. The application of this remark will be perceived by adverting to the act of congress for establishing the department of foreign affairs. This officer, as his duties were prescribed by that act, is to conform precisely to the will of the President. He is the mere organ by whom that will is communicated. The acts of such an officer, as an officer, can never be examinable by the courts.

But when the legislature proceeds to impose on that officer other duties; when he is directed peremptorily to perform certain acts; when the rights of individuals are dependent on the performance of those acts; he is so far the officer of the law; is amenable to the laws for his conduct; and cannot at his discretion sport away the vested rights of others.

The conclusion from this reasoning is, that where the heads of departments are the political or confidential agents of the executive, merely to execute the will of the President, or rather to act in cases in which the executive possesses a constitutional or legal discretion, nothing can be more perfectly clear than that their acts are only politically examinable. But where a specific duty is assigned by law, and individual rights depend upon the performance of that duty, it seems equally clear that the individual who considers himself injured, has a right to resort to the laws of his country for a remedy.

If this be the rule, let us inquire how it applies to the case under the consideration of the court.

*167   * The power of nominating to the senate, and the power of appointing the person nominated, are political powers, to be exercised by the President according to his discretion. When he has made an appointment, he has exercised his whole power and his discretion has been completely applied to the case.   If, by law, the officer be removable at the will of the President, then a new appointment may be immediately made, and the rights of the officer are terminated.   But as a fact which has existed cannot be made never to have existed, the appointment cannot be annihilated; and consequently, if the officer is by law not removable at the will of the President, the rights he has acquired are protected by the law, and are not resumable by the President.   They can not be extinguished by executive authority, and he has the privilege of asserting them in like manner as if they had been derived from any other source.

The question whether a right has vested or not, is, in its nature, judicial, and must be tried by the judicial authority.   If, for example, Mr. Marbury had taken the oaths of a magistrate, and proceeded to act as one; in consequence of which a suit had been instituted against him, in which his defence had depended on his being a magistrate, the validity of his appointment must have been determined by judicial authority.

So, if he conceives that, by virtue of his appointment, he has a legal right either to the commission which has been made out for him, or to a copy of that commission, it is equally a question examinable in a court, and the decision of the court upon it must depend on the opinion entertained of his appointment.

That question has been discussed, and the opinion is, that the latest point of time which can be taken as that at which the appointment was complete, and evidenced, was when, after the signature of the President, the seal of the United States was affixed to the commission.

It is, then, the opinion of the Court,

1st.   That by signing the commission of Mr. Marbury, the President of the United States appointed

*168   him a justice * of peace for the county of Washington, in the District of Columbia; and that the seal of the United States, affixed thereto by the Secretary of State, is conclusive testimony of the verity of the signature, and of the completion of the appointment; and that the appointment conferred on him a legal right to the office for the space of five years.

2d.   That, having this legal title to the office, he has a consequent right to the commission; a refusal to deliver which is a plain violation of that right, for which the laws of his country afford him a remedy.

It remains to be inquired whether,

3d.   He is entitled to the remedy for which he applies.   This depends on,

1st.   The nature of the writ applied for; and,

2d.   The power of this court.

1st.   The nature of the writ.

Blackstone, in the 3d volume of his Commentaries, page 110, defines a mandamus to be "a command issuing in the king's name from the court of king's bench, and directed to any person, corporation, or inferior court of judicature within the king's dominions, requiring them to do some particular thing therein specified, which appertains to their office and duty, and which the court of king's bench has previously determined, or at least supposes, to be consonant to right and justice."

Lord Mansfield, in *3 Burrow, 1266,* in the case of *The King v. Baker et al.,* states, with much precision and explicitness, the cases in which this writ may be used.

"Whenever," says that very able judge, "there is a right to execute an office, perform a service, or exercise a franchise, (more especially if it be in a matter of public concern, or attended with profit,) and a person is kept out of possession, or dispossessed of such right, and * has no other specific legal remedy, this court ought to assist by mandamus, upon reasons of justice, as the writ expresses, and upon reasons of public policy, to preserve peace, order and good government." In the same case he says, "this writ ought to be used upon all occasions where the law has established no specific remedy, and where in justice and good government there ought to be one."

* *169*

In addition to the authorities now particularly cited, many others were relied on at the bar, which show how far the practice has conformed to the general doctrines that have been just quoted.

This writ, if awarded, would be directed to an officer of government, and its mandate to him would be, to use the words of Blackstone, "to do a particular thing therein specified, which appertains to his office and duty, and which the court has previously determined, or at least supposes, to be consonant to right and justice." Or, in the words of Lord Mansfield, the applicant, in this case, has a right to execute an office of public concern, and is kept out of possession of that right.

These circumstances certainly concur in this case.

Still, to render the mandamus a proper remedy, the officer to whom it is to be directed, must be one to whom, on legal principles, such writ may be directed; and the person applying for it must be without any other specific and legal remedy.

1st. With respect to the officer to whom it would be directed. The intimate political relation subsisting between the President of the United States and the heads of departments, necessarily renders any legal investigation of the acts of one of those high officers peculiarly irksome, as well as delicate; and excites some hesitation with respect to the propriety of entering into such investigation. Impressions are often received without much reflection or examination, and it is not wonderful that in such a case as this the assertion, by an individual, of his legal claims in a court of justice, to which claims it is the duty of that

* *170*   court to attend, should at first view be considered * by some, as an attempt to intrude into the cabinet, and to intermeddle with the prerogatives of the executive.

It is scarcely necessary for the court to disclaim all pretensions to such jurisdiction. An extravagance, so absurd and excessive, could not have been entertained for a moment. The province of the court is, solely, to decide on the rights of individuals, not to inquire how the executive, or executive officers, perform duties in which they have a discretion. Questions in their nature political, or which are, by the constitution and laws, submitted to the executive, can never be made in this court.

But, if this be not such a question; if, so far from being an intrusion into the secrets of the cabinet, it respects a paper which, according to law, is upon record, and to a copy of which the law gives a right, on the payment of ten cents; if it be no intermeddling with a subject over which the executive can be considered as having exercised any control; what is there in the exalted station of the officer, which shall bar a citizen from asserting, in a court of justice, his legal rights, or shall forbid a court to listen to the claim, or to issue a mandamus directing the performance of a duty, not depending on executive discretion, but on particular acts of congress, and the general principles of law?

If one of the heads of departments commits any illegal act, under colour of his office, by which an individual sustains an injury, it cannot be pretended that his office alone exempts him from being sued in the ordinary mode of proceeding, and being compelled to obey the judgment of the law. How, then, can his office exempt him from this particular mode of deciding on the legality of his conduct, if the case be such a case as would, were any other individual the party complained of, authorize the process?

It is not by the office of the person to whom the writ is directed, but the nature of the thing to be done, that the propriety or impropriety of issuing a mandamus is to be determined. Where the head of a department acts in a case, in which executive dis-

*171 cretion is to be exercised; in which he is the mere organ of executive will; it is *again repeated, that any application to a court to control, in any respect, his conduct would be rejected without hesitation.

But where he is directed by law to do a certain act affecting the absolute rights of individuals, in the performance of which he is not placed under the particular direction of the President, and the performance of which the President cannot lawfully forbid, and therefore is never presumed to have forbidden; as for example, to record a commission, or a patent for land, which has received all the legal solemnities; or to give a copy of such record; in such cases, it is not perceived on what ground the courts of the country are further excused from the duty of giving judgment that right be done to an injured individual, than if the same services were to be performed by a person not the head of a department.

This opinion seems not now, for the first time, to be taken up in this country.

It must be well recollected that in 1792, an act passed, directing the Secretary of War to place on

the pension list such disabled officers and soldiers as
should be reported to him, by the circuit courts, which
act, so far as the duty was imposed on the courts, was
deemed unconstitutional; but some of the judges
thinking that the law might be executed by them in
the character of commissioners, proceeded to act, and
to report in that character.

This law being deemed unconstitutional at the circuits, was repealed, and a different system was established; but the question whether those persons who
have been reported by the judges, as commissioners,
were entitled, in consequence of that report, to be
placed on the pension list, was a legal question, properly determinable in the courts, although the act of
placing such persons on the list was to be performed
by the head of a department.

That this question might be properly settled, congress passed an act in February, 1793, making it the
duty of the secretary of War, in conjunction with the
attorney general, to take such measures as might be
* *172*   necessary to obtain an adjudication of the
Supreme Court of the United * States on
the validity of any such rights, claimed under the act
aforesaid.

After the passage of this act, a mandamus was
moved for, to be directed to the Secretary of War,
commanding him to place on the pension list, a person stating himself to be on the report of the judges.

There is, therefore, much reason to believe, that
this mode of trying the legal right of the com-
plainant was deemed by the head of a department,

and by the highest law officer of the United States, the most proper which could be selected for the purpose.

When the subject was brought before the court, the decision was, not that a mandamus would not lie to the head of a department directing him to perform an act, enjoined by law, in the performance of which an individual had a vested interest; but that a mandamus ought not to issue in that case; the decision necessarily to be made of the report of the commissioners did not confer on the applicant a legal right.

The judgment, in that case, is understood to have decided the merits of all claims of that description; and the persons, on the report of the commissioners, found it necessary to pursue the mode prescribed by the law subsequent to that which had been deemed unconstitutional, in order to place themselves on the pension list.

The doctrine, therefore, now advanced, is by no means a novel one.

It is true that the mandamus, now moved for, is not for the performance of an act expressly enjoined by statute.

It is to deliver a commission; on which subject the acts of congress are silent. This difference is not considered as affecting the case. It has already been stated that the applicant has, to that commission, a vested legal right, of which the executive cannot deprive him. He has been appointed to an office, from

* *173*   which he is not removable at the will of the executive; and being so * appointed, he has a right to the commission which the secretary has received from the President for his use. The act of congress does not indeed order the Secretary of State to send it to him, but it is placed in his hands for the person entitled to it; and cannot be more lawfully withheld by him than by any other person.

It was at first doubted whether the action of *detinue* was not a specific legal remedy for the commission which has been withheld from Mr. Marbury; in which case a mandamus would be improper. But this doubt has yielded to the consideration that the judgment in *detinue* is for the thing itself, or its value. The value of a public office not to be sold is incapable of being ascertained; and the applicant has a right to the office itself, or to nothing. He will obtain the office by obtaining the commission, or a copy of it from the record.

This, then, is a plain case for a mandamus, either to deliver the commission, or a copy of it from the record; and it only remains to be inquired,

Whether it can issue from this court.

The act to establish the judicial courts of the United States authorizes the Supreme Court " to issue writs of mandamus in cases warranted by the principles and usages of law, to any courts appointed, or persons holding office, under the authority of the United States."

The Secretary of State, being a person holding an office under the authority of the United States, is precisely within the letter of the description, and if this court is not authorized to issue a writ of mandamus to such an officer, it must be because the law

is unconstitutional, and therefore absolutely incapable
of conferring the authority, and assigning the duties
which its words purport to confer and assign.

The constitution vests the whole judicial power of
the United States in one Supreme Court, and such
inferior courts as congress shall, from time to time,
ordain and establish. This power is expressly extended to all cases arising under the laws of the
United States; and, consequently, in some form, may
*174   be exercised over the present * case; be-
cause the right claimed is given by a law of
the United States.

In the distribution of this power it is declared that
"the Supreme Court shall have original jurisdiction
in all cases affecting ambassadors, other public ministers and consuls, and those in which a state shall be a
party. In all other cases, the Supreme Court shall
have appellate jurisdiction."

It has been insisted, at the bar, that as the original
grant of jurisdiction, to the Supreme and inferior
courts, is general, and the clause, assigning original
jurisdiction to the Supreme Court, contains no negative or restrictive words, the power remains to the
legislature, to assign original jurisdiction to that court
in other cases than those specified in the article which
has been recited; provided those cases belong to the
judicial power of the United States.

If it had been intended to leave it in the discretion of
the legislature to apportion the judicial power between
the supreme and inferior courts according to the will
of that body, it would certainly have been useless to

have proceeded further than to have defined the judicial power, and the tribunals in which it should be vested. The subsequent part of the section is mere surplusage, is entirely without meaning, if such is to be the construction. If congress remains at liberty to give this court appellate jurisdiction, where the constitution has declared their jurisdiction shall be original; and original jurisdiction where the constitution has declared it shall be appellate; the distribution of jurisdiction, made in the constitution, is form without substance.

Affirmative words are often, in their operation, negative of other objects than those affirmed; and in this case, a negative or exclusive sense must be given to them, or they have no operation at all.

It cannot be presumed that any clause in the constitution is intended to be without effect; and, therefore, such a construction is inadmissible, unless the words require it.

*175   * If the solicitude of the convention, respecting our peace with foreign powers, induced a provision that the Supreme Court should take original jurisdiction in cases which might be supposed to affect them; yet the clause would have proceeded no further than to provide for such cases, if no further restriction on the powers of congress had been intended. That they should have appellate jurisdiction in all other cases, with such exceptions as congress might make, is no restriction; unless the words be deemed exclusive of original jurisdiction.

When an instrument organizing fundamentally a

judicial system, divides it into one supreme, and so
many inferior courts as the legislature may ordain
and establish; then enumerates its powers, and proceeds so far to distribute them, as to define the jurisdiction of the Supreme Court by declaring the cases
in which it shall take original jurisdiction, and that in
others it shall take appellate jurisdiction; the plain
import of the words seems to be, that in one class of
cases its jurisdiction is original, and not appellate; in
the other it is appellate, and not original. If any
other construction would render the clause inoperative, that is an additional reason for rejecting such
other construction, and for adhering to their obvious
meaning.

To enable this court, then, to issue a mandamus, it
must be shown to be an exercise of appellate jurisdiction, or to be necessary to enable them to exercise
appellate jurisdiction.

It has been stated at the bar that the appellate
jurisdiction may be exercised in a variety of forms,
and that if it be the will of the legislature that a mandamus should be used for that purpose, that will must
be obeyed. This is true, yet the jurisdiction must be
appellate, not original.

It is the essential criterion of appellate jurisdiction,
that it revises and corrects the proceedings in a cause
already instituted, and does not create that cause.
Although, therefore, a mandamus may be directed to
courts, yet to issue such a writ to an officer for the
delivery of a paper, is in effect the same as to sustain
an original action for that paper, and, therefore,

*176   seems not to belong to *appellate, but to original jurisdiction.   Neither is it necessary in such a case as this, to enable the court to exercise its appellate jurisdiction.

The authority, therefore, given to the Supreme Court, by the act establishing the judicial courts of the United States, to issue writs of mandamus to public officers, appears not to be warranted by the constitution; and it becomes necessary to inquire whether a jurisdiction so conferred can be exercised.

The question, whether an act, repugnant to the constitution, can become the law of the land, is a question deeply interesting to the United States; but, happily, not of an intricacy proportioned to its interest.   It seems only necessary to recognize certain principles, supposed to have been long and well established, to decide it.

That the people have an original right to establish, for their future government, such principles, as, in their opinion, shall most conduce to their own happiness is the basis on which the whole American fabric has been erected.   The exercise of this original right is a very great exertion; nor can it, nor ought it, to be frequently repeated.   The principles, therefore, so established, are deemed fundamental.   And as the authority from which they proceed is supreme, and can seldom act, they are designed to be permanent.

This original and supreme will organizes the government, and assigns to different departments their respective powers.   It may either stop here, or establish certain limits not to be transcended by those departments.

The government of the United States is of the latter description. The powers of the legislature are defined and limited ; and that those limits may not be mistaken, or forgotten, the constitution is written. To what purpose are powers limited, and to what purpose is that limitation committed to writing, if these limits may, at any time, be passed by those intended to be restrained ?   The distinction between a government with limited and unlimited powers is abolished, if those limits do not confine the persons on whom they are imposed, and if acts prohibited * and acts allowed, are of equal obligation.   It is a proposition too plain to be contested, that the constitution controls any legislative act repugnant to it ; or, that the legislature may alter the constitution by an ordinary act.

* *177*

Between these alternatives there is no middle ground.   The constitution is either a superior paramount law, unchangeable by ordinary means, or it is on a level with ordinary legislative acts, and, like other acts, is alterable when the legislature shall please to alter it.

If the former part of the alternative be true, then a legislative act contrary to the constitution is not law : if the latter part be true, then written constitutions are absurd attempts, on the part of the people, to limit a power in its own nature illimitable.

Certainly all those who have framed written constitutions contemplate them as forming the fundamental and paramount law of the nation, and, consequently, the theory of every such government must be, that an act of the legislature, repugnant to the constitution, is void.

This theory is essentially attached to a written constitution, and, is consequently, to be considered, by this court, as one of the fundamental principles of our society. It is not therefore to be lost sight of in the further consideration of this subject.

If an act of the legislature, repugnant to the constitution, is void, does it, notwithstanding its invalidity, bind the courts, and oblige them to give it effect? Or, in other words, though it be not law, does it constitute a rule as operative as if it was a law? This would be to overthrow in fact what was established in theory; and would seem, at first view, an absurdity too gross to be insisted on. It shall, however, receive a more attentive consideration.

It is emphatically the province and duty of the judicial department to say what the law is. Those who apply the rule to particular cases, must of necessity expound and interpret that rule. If two laws conflict with each other, the courts must decide on the operation of each.

* *178*   * So if a law be in opposition to the constitution; if both the law and the constitution apply to a particular case, so that the court must either decide that case conformably to the law, disregarding the constitution; or conformably to the constitution, disregarding the law; the court must determine which of these conflicting rules governs the case. This is of the very essence of judicial duty.

If, then, the courts are to regard the constitution, and the constitution is superior to any ordinary act of the legislature, the constitution, and not such ordinary act, must govern the case to which they both apply.

Those, then, who controvert the principle that the constitution is to be considered, in court, as a paramount law, are reduced to the necessity of maintaining that courts must close their eyes on the constitution, and see only the law.

This doctrine would subvert the very foundation of all written constitutions. It would declare that an act which, according to the principles and theory of our government, is entirely void, is yet, in practice, completely obligatory. It would declare that if the legislature shall do what is expressly forbidden, such act, notwithstanding the express prohibition, is in reality effectual. It would be giving to the legislature a practical and real omnipotence, with the same breath which professes to restrict their powers within narrow limits. It is prescribing limits, and declaring that those limits may be passed at pleasure.

That it thus reduces to nothing what we have deemed the greatest improvement on political institutions, a written constitution, would of itself be sufficient, in America, where written constitutions have been viewed with so much reverence, for rejecting the construction. But the peculiar expressions of the constitution of the United States furnish additional arguments in favour of its rejection.

The judicial power of the United States is extended to all cases arising under the constitution.

* *179*   * Could it be the intention of those who gave this power, to say that in using it the constitution should not be looked into? That a case arising under the constitution should be decided without examining the instrument under which it arises?

This is too extravagant to be maintained.

In some cases, then, the constitution must be looked into by the judges. And if they can open it at all, what part of it are they forbidden to read or to obey?

There are many other parts of the constitution which serve to illustrate this subject.

It is declared that " no tax or duty shall be laid on articles exported from any state." Suppose a duty on the export of cotton, of tobacco, or of flour; and a suit instituted to recover it. Ought judgment to be rendered in such a case? ought the judges to close their eyes on the constitution, and only see the law?

The constitution declares " that no bill of attainder or ex post facto law shall be passed."

If, however, such a bill should be passed, and a person should be prosecuted under it; must the court condemn to death those victims whom the constitution endeavours to preserve?

" No person," says the constitution, " shall be convicted of treason unless on the testimony of two witnesses to the same overt act, or on confession in open court."

Here the language of the constitution is addressed

especially to the courts.   It prescribes, directly for
them, a rule of evidence not to be departed from.   If
the legislature should change that rule, and declare
one witness, or a confession out of court, sufficient
for conviction, must the constitutional principle yield
to the legislative act?

From these, and many other selections which might
be made, it is apparent, that the framers of the constitution * contemplated that instrument as
* *180*   a rule for the government of courts, as well
as of the legislature.

Why otherwise does it direct the judges to take an
oath to support it?   This oath certainly applies in
an especial manner, to their conduct in their official
character.   How immoral to impose it on them, if
they were to be used as the instruments, and the knowing instruments, for violating what they swear to
support!

The oath of office, too, imposed by the legislature,
is completely demonstrative of the legislative opinion
on this subject.   It is in these words : " I do solemnly
swear that I will administer justice without respect to
persons, and do equal right to the poor and to the
rich ; and that I will faithfully and impartially discharge all the duties incumbent on me as   ,
according to the best of my abilities and understanding, agreeably to the constitution and laws of the
United States."

Why does a judge swear to discharge his duties
agreeably to the constitution of the United States, if
that constitution forms no rule for his government?

if it is closed upon him, and cannot be inspected by him?

If such be the real state of things, this is worse than solemn mockery. To prescribe, or to take this oath, becomes equally a crime.

It is also not entirely unworthy of observation, that in declaring what shall be the supreme law of the land, the constitution itself is first mentioned; and not the laws of the United States generally, but those only which shall be made in pursuance of the constitution, have that rank.

Thus, the particular phraseology of the constitution of the United States confirms and strengthens the principle, supposed to be essential to all written constitutions, that a law repugnant to the constitution is void; and that courts, as well as other departments, are bound by that instrument.

The rule must be discharged.

The United States *v.* Fisher *et al.*

NOTE.

THIS case arose on certain questions certified by the Circuit Court of Pennsylvania in regard to the right of the United States, in case of the insolvency or bankruptcy of a debtor, to enforce, without regard to his other creditors, priority of payment out of his effects. The main point which counsel made against the claim of the United States, the consideration of which occupies by far the major part of the opinion, was that the statute under which the United States claimed that right did not apply to the specific case at bar. The constitutional point, as to whether Congress could create such a priority, was, however, definitely and strongly raised by Mr. Ingersoll (of counsel for Fisher). It was rather summarily and brusquely disposed of by Marshall in his opinion, and his decision settled the law, yet, as an original question, it is hard to see why the point was not of real difficulty. There was no particular clause in the Constitution giving this priority to the United States,—as Mr. Ingersoll in the argument said : " How strange and improbable is it, that Congress should give the United States a preference so much exceeding the royal prerogative of England," and again: " Under what clause of the Constitution is such a power given to Congress ? Is it under the general power to make all laws necessary or proper for carrying into execution the particular powers specified ? If so, where is the necessity or the propriety of such a provision, and to the exercise of what other power is it necessary ? " Such a power, Mr. Ingersoll argued, would produce a collision between the prerogative of the United States and the prerogative of the several states. " Suppose," he said, " the treasurer of a state should become indebted to the United States, the latter would take his whole property in opposition to any law of the state which had passed, to secure herself against the default of her officers."

To answer this Marshall in his opinion gives one brief sentence on the doctrine of implied powers. "Congress must possess the choice of means and must be empowered to use any means which are in fact conducive to the exercise of a power granted by the Constitution." That sentence contains in a nutshell the whole doctrine of implied powers under the Constitution that was later put forth so strongly in *McCulloch* v. *Maryland*, 4 Wheat, 316; it would seem the point which was later so bitterly contested deserved a more extensive justification. The implied power of the United States to secure its finances by this priority is hardly more clear than its right to secure its finances by the agency of a national bank; each was historically a power of sovereignty, neither a natural attribute of a federated republic. The slightness of the opinion on the constitutional point may be easily explained. The point was little pressed in argument, the attorneys against the United States were federalists,— Harper was obliged to break off his argument to appear before the Senate to oppose the impeachment of Justice Chase which Jefferson and the Republicans sought,—again the priority of the United States in such cases was a natural and convenient power, and the question could never become a political one. But surely the opinion interprets the Constitution very broadly without a hint that the question presented any difficulty, — as Mr. Henry Adams says: "Constructive power could hardly go further." [1]

---

[1] *History of the United States*, vol. iv., p. 270. Mr. Adams was speaking of the failure of the opponents of the embargo to raise the question of its constitutionality.

The United States

v.

Fisher *et al.*, Assignees of Blight, a Bankrupt.

[2 Cranch, 358.]

1804.

Mr. Dallas (Attorney of the United States) for the Plaintiffs in Error.

Mr. Harper, Mr. Ingersoll, Mr. Lewis, Mr. C. Lee, contra.

ERROR FROM THE CIRCUIT COURT FOR THE DISTRICT OF
PENNSYLVANIA.

Marshall, Ch. J., delivered the opinion of the
Court. The question in this case is, whether the
United States, as holders of a protested bill of exchange, which has been negotiated in the ordinary
course of trade, are entitled to be preferred to the
general creditors, where the debtor becomes bankrupt.

The claim to this preference is founded on the 5th
section of the act, entitled " An act to provide more
effectually for the settlement of accounts between
the United States and receivers of public money."
Vol. 3, p. 423. The section is in these words : " And
be it further enacted, that where any revenue officer,
or other person, hereafter becoming indebted to the
United States, by bond or otherwise, shall become

insolvent, or where the estate of any deceased debtor, in the hands of executors or administrators, shall be insufficient to pay all the debts due from the deceased, the debt due to the United States shall be first satisfied; and the priority hereby established shall be deemed to extend, as well to cases in which a debtor, not having sufficient property to pay all his debts, shall make a voluntary assignment thereof, or in which the estate and effects of an absconding, concealed, or absent debtor, shall be attached by process of law, as to cases in which an act of legal bankruptcy shall be committed."

That these words, taken in their natural and usual sense, would embrace the case before the court, seems not to be controverted. "Any revenue officer, or other person, hereafter becoming indebted to the United States by bond or otherwise," is a description of persons, which, if neither explained nor restricted by other words or circumstances, would comprehend every debtor of the public, however his debt might have been contracted.

* *386   * But other parts of the act involve this question in much embarrassment.

It is undoubtedly a well established principle in the exposition of statutes, that every part is to be considered, and the intention of the legislature to be extracted from the whole. It is also true, that where great inconvenience will result from a particular construction, that construction is to be avoided, unless the meaning of the legislature be plain; in which case it must be obeyed.

On the abstract principles which govern courts in construing legislative acts, no difference of opinion can exist.   It is only in the application of those principles that the difference discovers itself.

As the enacting clause in this case would plainly give the United States the preference they claim, it is incumbent on those who oppose that preference, to show an intent varying from that which the words import.   In doing this, the whole act has been critically examined; and it has been contended with great ingenuity, that every part of it demonstrates the legislative mind to have been directed towards a class of debtors, entirely different from those who become so by drawing or indorsing bills, in the ordinary course of business.

The first part which has been resorted to is the title.

On the influence which the title ought to have in construing the enacting clauses, much has been said : and yet it is not easy to discern the point of difference between the opposing counsel in this respect. Neither party contends that the title of an act can control plain words in the body of the statute; and neither denies that, taken with other parts, it may assist in removing ambiguities.   Where the intent is plain, nothing is left to construction.   Where the mind labors to discover the design of the legislature, it seizes everything from which aid can be derived ; and in such case the title claims a degree of notice, and will have its due share of consideration.

The title of the act is unquestionably limited to

*387   "receivers * of public money;" a term which undoubtedly excludes the defendants in the present case.

The counsel for the defendants have also completely succeeded in demonstrating, that the four first sections of this act relate only to particular classes of debtors, among whom the drawer and indorser of a protested bill of exchange would not be comprehended. Wherever general words have been used in these sections, they are restrained by the subject to which they relate, and by other words frequently in the same sentence, to particular objects, so as to make it apparent that they were employed by the legislature in a limited sense. Hence it has been argued with strength of a great reasoning, that the same restricted interpretation ought to be given to the fifth section likewise.

If the same reason for that interpretation exists; if the words of the act generally, or the particular provisions of this section, afford the same reason for limiting its operation which is afforded with respect to those which precede it, then its operation must be limited to the same objects.

The 5th section relates entirely to the priority claimed by the United States in the payment of debts.

On the phraseology of this act it has been observed, that there is a circuity of expression, which would not have been used if the intention of the legislature had been to establish its priority in all cases whatever. Instead of saying "any revenue

officer, or other person hereafter becoming indebted
to the United States," the natural mode of expressing
such an intent would have been, "any person indebted to the United States;" and hence it has been
inferred that debtors of a particular description only
were in the mind of the legislature.

It is true the mode of expression which has been
suggested, is at least as appropriate as that which
has been used; but between the two there is no difference of meaning, and it cannot be pretended that the
natural sense of words is to be disregarded, because
that which they import might have been better, or
more directly expressed.

*388   *As a branch of this argument, it has also
            been said that the description commences
with the very words which are used in the beginning
of the first section; and from that circumstance it
has been inferred that the same class of cases was
still in view. The commencing words of each section are, "any revenue officer, or other person." But
the argument drawn from this source, if the subject
be pursued further, seems to operate against the defendants. In the first section the words are, "Any
revenue officer, or other person accountable for public money." With this expression completely in view,
and having used it in part, the description would
probably have been adopted throughout, had it been
the intention of the legislature to describe the same
class of debtors. But it is immediately dropped, and
more comprehensive words are employed. For persons "accountable for public money," persons "here-

after becoming indebted to the United States, by bond or otherwise," are substituted. This change of language strongly implies an intent to change the object of legislation.

But the great effort on the part of the defendants is to connect the fifth with the four preceding sections; and to prove that as the general words in those sections are restricted to debtors of a particular description, the general words of the 5th section ought also to be restricted to debtors of the same description. On this point lies the stress of the cause.

In the analysis of the foregoing parts of the act, the counsel for the defendants have shown that the general terms which have been used are uniformly connected with other words in the same section, and frequently in the same sentence, which necessarily restrict them. They have also shown that the provisions of those parts of the act are of such a nature that the words, taking the natural import of the whole sentence together, plainly form provisions only adapted to a class of cases which those words describe if used in a limited sense.

It may be added that the four first sections of the act are connected with each other, and plainly contain provisions on the same subject. They all relate *389 to the *mode of proceeding on suits instituted in courts, and each section regulates a particular branch of that proceeding. Where the class of suits is described in the first section, it is natural to suppose that the subsequent regulations respecting suits apply to those which have been described.

The first section directs that suits shall be instituted against revenue officers, and other persons accountable for public money, and imposes a penalty on delinquents, where a suit shall be commenced and prosecuted to judgment.

The second section directs that certain testimony shall be admitted at the trial of the cause.

The third section prescribes the condition under which a continuance may be granted : and

The fourth section respects the testimony which may be produced by the defendant. These are all parts of the same subject ; and there is strong reason, independent of the language of the act, to suppose that the provisions respecting them were designed to be co-extensive with each other.

But the fifth section is totally unconnected with those which precede it. Regulations of a suit in court no longer employ the mind of the legislature. The preference of the United States to other creditors becomes the subject of legislation ; and as this subject is unconnected with that which had been disposed of in the foregoing sections, so is the language employed upon it without reference to that which had been previously used. If this language was ambiguous, all the means recommended by the counsel for the defendants would be resorted to in order to remove the ambiguity. But it appears, to the majority of the court, to be too explicit to require the application of those principles which are useful in doubtful cases.

The mischiefs to result from the construction on

which the United States insist, have been stated as
strong motives for overruling that construction.   That

*390 the consequences * are to be considered in
expounding laws, where the intent is doubtful, is a principle not to be controverted; but it is
also true that it is a principle which must be applied
with caution, and which has a degree of influence
dependent on the nature of the case to which it is
applied.   Where rights are infringed, where fundamental principles are overthrown, where the general
system of the laws is departed from, the legislative
intention must be expressed with irresistible clearness
to induce a court of justice to suppose a design to
effect such objects.   But where only a political regulation is made, which is inconvenient, if the intention of
the legislature be expressed in terms which are sufficiently intelligible to leave no doubt in the mind
when the words are taken in their ordinary sense, it
would be going a great way to say that a constrained
interpretation must be put upon them, to avoid an
inconvenience which ought to have been contemplated in the legislature when the act was passed, and
which, in their opinion, was probably overbalanced by
the particular advantages it was calculated to produce.

Of, the latter description of inconveniences are
those occasioned by the act in question.   It is for the
legislature to appreciate them.   They are not of such
magnitude as to induce an opinion that the legislature
could not intend to expose the citizens of the United
States to them, when words are used which manifest
that intent.

On this subject it is to be remarked, that no lien is created by this law. No bona fide transfer of property in the ordinary course of business is overreached. It is only a priority in payment, which, under different modifications, is a regulation in common use ; and this priority is limited to a particular state of things when the debtor is living ; though it takes effect generally if he be dead.[1]

Passing from a consideration of the act itself, and the consequences which flow from it, the counsel on each side have sought to strengthen their construction by other acts in *pari materia.* * The act of the 3d of March, 1797, has been supposed to be a continuation of legislative proceeding on the subject, which was commenced on the third of March, 1795, (*vol. 3, p. 225,*) by the act " For the more effectual recovery of debts due from individuals to the United States," which relates exclusively to the receivers of public money.

*391

Admitting the opinion, that the act of 1797 was particularly designed to supply the defects of that of 1795, to be correct, it does not seem to follow, that a substantive and independent section, having no connection with the provisions made in 1795, should be restricted by it.

The act of 1795 contains nothing relative to the priority of the United States, and, therefore, will not

---

[1] The *Ch. J.* in delivering the opinion, observed as follows: " I only say for myself, as the point has not been submitted to the court, that it does not appear to me to create a *devastavit* in the administration of effects, and would require notice in order to bind the executor, or administrator, or assignee."

explain the 5th section of the act of 1797, which relates exclusively to that subject. But the act of 1797, neither in its title nor its enacting clauses, contains any words of reference to the act of 1795. The words which are supposed to imply this reference are, "to provide more effectually." But these words have relation to the existing state of the law, on all the subjects to which the act of 1797 relates, not to those alone which are comprehended in the act of 1795. The title of the act of 1795 is also, "for the more effectual recovery of debts," and, consequently, refers to certain pre-existing laws. The act of 1797, therefore, may be supposed to have in view the act of 1795, when providing for the objects contemplated in that act; but must be supposed to have other acts in view, when providing for objects not contemplated in that act.

As, therefore, the act of 1795 contains nothing respecting the priority of the United States, but is limited to provisions respecting suits in court, the act of 1797 may be considered in connection with that act, while on the subject of suits in court; but when on the subject of preference, must be considered in connection with act. which relate to the preference of the United States.

The first act on this subject passed on the 31st of July, 1789, *s. 21*, and gave the United States a preference only in the case of bonds for duties.

*392   *On the 4th of August, 1790, *vol. 1, p. 221*, an act was passed on the same subject with that of 1789, which repeals all former acts, and re-enacts, in substance, the 21st section, relative to the priority of the United States.

On the 2d of May, 1792, *vol. 2, p. 78,* the priority previously given to the United States is transferred to the sureties on duty bonds, who shall themselves pay the debt ; and the cases of insolvency, in which this priority is to take place, are explained to comprehend the case of a voluntary assignment, and the attached effects of an absconding, concealed, or absent debtor.

Such was the title of the United States to a preference in the payment of debts previous to the passage of the act of 1797. It was limited to bonds for the payment of duties on imported goods, and on the tonnage of vessels. An internal revenue had been established, and extensive transactions had taken place; in the course of which, many persons had necessarily become indebted to the United States. But no attempt to give them a preference in the collection of such debts had been made.

This subject is taken up in the 5th section of the act of 1797. The term "revenue officer," which is used in that act, would certainly comprehend any persons employed in the collection of the internal revenue; yet it may be well doubted whether those persons are contemplated in the foregoing sections of the act. They relate to a suit in court, and are perhaps restricted to those receivers of public money who have accounts on the books of the treasury. The head of the department in each state most probably accounts with the treasury, and the sub-collectors account with him.

If this be correct, a class of debtors would be introduced into the 5th section by the term "revenue
officer," who are indeed within the title, but not
within the preceding enacting clauses of the law.

But passing over this term, the succeeding words
seem, to the majority of the court, certainly to produce this effect. They are, "or other person hereafter becoming indebted to the United States, by
bond or otherwise." If this section was designed to
place * the collection of the internal revenue
*393   on the same footing of security with the ex-
ternal revenue, as has been argued by one of the
counsel for the defendants, a design so reasonable
that it would naturally be attributed to the legislature, then the debtors for excise duties would be
comprehended within it; yet those debtors cannot
be brought within the title, or the previous enacting
clauses of the bill.

The 5th section, then, would introduce a new class
of debtors, and if it does so in any case, the act furnishes no principle which shall restrain the words of
that section to every case to which they apply.

Three acts of Congress have passed, subsequent
to that under particular consideration, which have
been supposed to bear upon the case.

The first passed on the 11th of July, 1798, and is
entitled "An act to regulate and fix the compensation of the officers employed in collecting the internal revenues of the United States, and to insure
more effectually the settlement of their accounts."
The 13th section of this act (*vol. 4, p. 196,*) refers

expressly to the provisions of the act of March, 1797, on the subject of suits to be instituted on the bonds given by the officers collecting the internal revenue, and shows conclusively that in the opinion of the legislature the four first sections of that act did not extend to the case of those officers; consequently, if the 5th section extends to them, it introduces a class of debtors distinct from those contemplated in the clauses which respect suits in court. The 15th section of this act takes up the subject which is supposed to be contemplated by the 5th section of the act of 1797, and declares the debt due from these revenue officers to the United States to be a lien on their real estates, and on the real estates of their sureties, from the institution of suit thereon. It can scarcely be supposed that the legislature would have given a lien on the real estate without providing for a preference out of the personal estate, especially where there was no real estate, unless that preference was understood to be secured by a previous law.

The same observation applies to a subsequent act of the same session for laying a direct tax. A lien is

*394   reserved * on the real estate of the collector, without mentioning any claim to preference out of his personal estate.

The last law which contains any provision on the subject of preference passed on the 2d of March, 1799. The 65th section of that act has been considered as repealing the 5th section of the act of 1797, or of manifesting the limited sense in which it is to be understood.

It must be admitted that this section involves the subject in additional perplexity; but it is the opinion of the Court, that on fair construction, it can apply only to bonds taken for those duties on imports and tonnage, which are the subject of the act.

From the first law passed on this subject, every law respecting the collection of those duties, had contained a section giving a preference to the United States, in case of the insolvency of the collectors of them.

The act of 1797, if construed as the United States would construe it, would extend to those collectors if there was no other provision in any other act giving a priority to the United States in these cases. As there was such a previous act, it might be supposed that its repeal by a subsequent law would create a doubt whether the act of 1797 would comprehend the case, and, therefore, from abundant caution, it might be deemed necessary still to retain the section in the new act respecting those duties. The general repealing clause of the act of 1799 cannot be construed to repeal the act of 1797, unless it provides for the cases to which that act extends.

It has also been argued that the bankrupt law itself affords ground for the opinion that the United States do not claim a general preference. (*Vol. 5, p. 82.*) The words of the 62d section of that law apply to debts generally as secured by prior acts. But as that section was not upon the subject of preference, but was merely designed to retain the right of the United States in their existing situation, whatever that situation might be, the question may well be supposed not to have been investigated at that time, and the expressions of the section were probably not considered with a view to any influence they might have on those rights.

* *395*   * After maturely considering this doubtful statute, and comparing it with other acts in *pari materia*, it is the opinion of the majority of the court, that the preference given to the United States by the 5th section is not confined to revenue officers and persons accountable for public money, but extends to debtors generally.

Supposing this distinction not to exist, it is contended that this priority of the United States cannot take effect in any case where suit has not been instituted; and in support of this opinion several decisions of the English judges with respect to the prerogative of the crown have been quoted.

To this argument the express words of the act of Congress seem to be opposed. The legislature has declared the time when this priority shall have its commencement; and the court think those words conclusive on the point. The cases certainly show that a bona fide alienation of property before the right of priority attaches will be good, but that does not affect the present case. From the decisions on this subject a very ingenious argument was drawn by the counsel who made this point. The bankrupt law, he says, does not bind the king because he is not named in it; yet it has been adjudged that the effects of a bankrupt are placed beyond the reach of the

king by the assignment made under that law, unless
they shall have been previously bound. He argues,
that according to the understanding of the legislature,
as proved by their acts relative to insolvent debtors,
and according to the decisions in some of the inferior
courts, the bankrupt law would not bind the United
States although the 62d section had not been inserted.
That section, therefore, is only an expression of what
would be law without it, and, consequently, is an immaterial section; as the king, though not bound by
the bankrupt law, is bound by the assignment made
under it; so, he contended, that the United States,
though not bound by the law, are bound by the assignment.

But the assignment is made under and by the
direction of the law; and a proviso that nothing contained in the law shall affect the right of preference
claimed by the United States, is equivalent to a proviso that the assignment shall not affect the right of
preference claimed by the United States.

* *396*   * If the act has attempted to give the
United States a preference in the case
before the court, it remains to inquire whether the
constitution obstructs its operation.

To the general observations made on this subject, it
will only be observed, that as the court can never be
unmindful of the solemn duty imposed on the judicial
department when a claim is supported by an act
which conflicts with the constitution, so the court can
never be unmindful of its duty to obey laws which
are authorized by that instrument.

In the case at bar, the preference claimed by the United States is not prohibited ; but it has been truly said that under a constitution conferring specific powers, the power contended for must be granted, or it cannot be exercised.

It is claimed under the authority to make all laws which shall be necessary and proper to carry into execution the powers vested by the constitution in the government of the United States, or in any department or officer thereof.

In construing this clause it would be incorrect, and would produce endless difficulties, if the opinion should be maintained that no law was authorized which was not indispensably necessary to give effect to a specified power.

Where various systems might be adopted for that purpose, it might be said with respect to each, that it was not necessary, because the end might be obtained by other means. Congress must possess the choice of means, and must be empowered to use any means which are in fact conducive to the exercise of a power granted by the constitution.

The government is to pay the debt of the union, and must be authorized to use the means which appear to itself most eligible to effect that object. It has, consequently, a right to make remittances by bills or otherwise, and to take those precautions which will render the transaction safe.

This claim of priority on the part of the United States * will, it has been said, interfere with the right of the state sovereignties respect-

* 397

ing the dignity of debts, and will defeat the measures they have a right to adopt to secure themselves against delinquencies on the part of their own revenue officers.

But this is an objection to the constitution itself. The mischief suggested, so far as it can really happen, is the necessary consequence of the supremacy of the laws of the United States on all subjects to which the legislative power of Congress extends.

As the opinion given in the court below was, that the plaintiffs did not maintain their action on the whole testimony exhibited, it is necessary to examine that testimony.

It appears that the plaintiffs have proceeded on the transcripts from the books of the treasury, under the idea that this suit is maintainable under the act of 1797. The Court does not mean to sanction that opinion; but, as no objection was taken to the testimony, it is understood to have been admitted. It is also understood that there is no question to be made respecting notice; but that the existence of the debt is admitted, and the right of the United States to priority of payment is the only real point in the cause.

The majority of this court is of opinion that the United States are entitled to that priority, and, therefore, the judgment of the circuit court is to be reversed, and the cause to be remanded for further proceedings.

Judgment reversed.

Hepburn and Dundas *v.* Ellzey.

NOTE.

THIS case decided that under the Judiciary Act a citizen of the District of Columbia had no right to bring an action in the federal courts against a citizen of a state. The decision, very briefly, is that the word "state" in the Constitution and the Judiciary Act means a member of the union only. The case is clear law and has been generally followed ; with *New Orleans* v. *Winter*, 1 Wheat., 94, which declares that a territory is not a "state" for the purpose of suing in the United States Courts; it created the law on the subject. The doctrine was lately affirmed in *Hooe* v. *Jamieson*, 166 W. S., 395, and again recognized in the recent insular cases, where in the opinion of the court in *Downes* v. *Bidwell*, 182 W. S., 244, 259, it is cited as an authority for the broader proposition that the Constitution does not extend *ex proprio vigore* to the territorial possessions of the United States. Grouping the case with other cognate decisions by Marshall, *New Orleans* v. *Winter supra*, *Loughborough* v. *Blake*, 5 Wheat., 317, and *American Ins. Co.* v. *Canter*, 1 Pet., 511 (all reprinted in these volumes), the case surely has a bearing on that point, but the weight and authority given to these opinions of Marshall in the recent cases before the Supreme Court, notwithstanding their remoteness from the actual question at issue, is a notable example of the magical power of Marshall's name in the courts to-day.

Hepburn and Dundas

v.

Ellzey.

[2 Cranch, 445.]

1804.

Mr. E. J. Lee for the plaintiffs,

Mr. C. Lee, contra.

Marshall, Ch. J., delivered the opinion of the Court.

The question in this case is, whether the plaintiffs, as residents of the District of Columbia, can maintain an action in the circuit court of the United States for the district of Virginia.

This depends on the act of Congress describing the jurisdiction of that court. That act gives jurisdiction to the circuit courts in cases between a citizen of the state in which the suit is brought, and a citizen of another state. To support the jurisdiction in this case, therefore, it must appear that Columbia is a state.

On the part of the plaintiffs it has been urged that Columbia is a distinct political society; and is, therefore, "a state" according to the definitions of writers on general law.

This is true.   But as the act of Congress obviously uses the word " state" in reference to that term as used in the constitution, it becomes necessary to inquire whether Columbia is a state in the sense of that instrument.   The result of that examination is a conviction that the members of the American confederacy only are the states contemplated in the constitution.

The house of representatives is to be composed of members chosen by the people of the several states ; and each state shall have at least one representative.

The senate of the United States shall be composed of two senators from each state.

Each state shall appoint, for the election of the executive, a number of electors equal to its whole number of senators and representatives.

These clauses show that the word state is used in the constitution as designating a member of the * *453* union, and excludes *from the term the signification attached to it by writers on the law of nations.   When the same term which has been used plainly in this limited sense in the articles respecting the legislative and executive departments, is also employed in that which respects the judicial department, it must be understood as retaining the sense originally given to it.

Other passages from the constitution have been cited by the plaintiffs to show that the term state is sometimes used in its more enlarged sense.   But on examining the passages quoted, they do not prove what was to be shown by them.

It is true that as citizens of the United States, and of that particular district which is subject to the jurisdiction of Congress, it is extraordinary that the courts of the United States, which are open to aliens, and to the citizens of every state in the union, should be closed upon them.   But this is a subject for legislative, not for judicial consideration.

The opinion to be certified to the circuit court is, that that court has no jurisdiction in the case.

Ex parte Bollman and *ex parte* Swartwout.

NOTE.

THIS case arose on a motion before the Supreme Court of the United States for writs of *habeas corpus* to the marshal of the District of Columbia to produce Bollman and Swartwout, then committed by the Circuit Court of the District on a charge of treason, and for writs of *certiorari* to review the proceedings of that court. Bollman and Swartwout were confidential followers of Aaron Burr who acted as emissaries for him to General Wilkinson for the carrying out of his alleged treasonable plans.

The Supreme Court gave two opinions on these motions : the first is on the technical question whether under the Constitution the court had the power to issue the writ asked, the court holding that such writs were issuable under the appellate jurisdiction of the court and were not, like the writ asked in *Marbury* v. *Madison*, an exercise of original jurisdiction ; the second opinion decides that there was no evidence of treason justifying the commitment of the two prisoners. This second opinion and the doctrines it decides are commented on at length in the note preceding the opinion in the case of the *United States* v. *Aaron Burr.* See *infra*, page 100.

Ex parte Bollman and *ex parte* Swartwout.

[4 Cranch, 75.]

February, 1807.

Messrs. Charles Lee, Harper, F. S. Key, and Luther Martin for Bollman and Swartwout.
Rodney, Attorney-General, and Mr. Jones, contra.

February 13. *Marshall, Ch. J.,*[1] delivered the opinion of the court.

As preliminary to any investigation of the merits of this motion, this court deems it proper to declare that it disclaims all jurisdiction not given by the constitution, or by the laws of the United States.

Courts which originate in the common law possess a jurisdiction which must be regulated by the common law, until some statute shall change their established principles ; but courts which are created by written law, and whose jurisdiction is defined by written law, cannot transcend that jurisdiction. It is unnecessary to state the reasoning on which this opinion is founded, because it has been repeatedly given by this court ; and with the decisions heretofore rendered on

---

[1] The only judges present when these opinions were given were, Marshall, Ch. J. ; Washington, Johnson, and Livingston, Justices. Cushing, J., and Chase, J., were prevented by ill health from attending.

this point, no member of the bench has, even for an instant, been dissatisfied. The reasoning from the bar, in relation to it, may be answered by the single observation, that for the meaning * of the term habeas corpus, resort may unquestionably be had to the common law; but the power to award the writ by any of the courts of the United States, must be given by written law.

*94

This opinion is not to be considered as abridging the power of courts over their own officers, or to protect themselves, and their members, from being disturbed in the exercise of their functions. It extends only to the power of taking cognizance of any question between individuals, or between the government and individuals.

To enable the court to decide on such question, the power to determine it must be given by written law.

The inquiry, therefore, on this motion will be, whether by any statute compatible with the constitution of the United States, the power to award a writ of habeas corpus, in such a case as that of Erick Bollman and Samuel Swartwout, has been given to this court.

The 14th section of the judiciary act (*Laws U. S.*, *vol. 1, p. 58*,) has been considered as containing a substantive grant of this power.

It is in these words: "That all the before-mentioned courts of the United States shall have power to issue writs of *scire facias*, habeas corpus, and all other writs, not specially provided for by statute, which may be necessary for the exercise of their respective jurisdictions, and agreeable to the principles and usages of law.   And that either of the justices of the Supreme Court, as well as judges of the district courts, shall have power to grant writs of habeas corpus, for the purpose of an inquiry into the cause of commitment.   Provided, that writs of habeas corpus shall in no case extend to prisoners in gaol, unless where they are in custody under or by color of the authority of the United States, or are committed for trial before some court of the same, or are necessary to be brought into court to testify."

*95   *The only doubt of which this section can be susceptible is, whether the restrictive words of the first sentence limit the power to the award of such writs of habeas corpus as are necessary to enable the courts of the United States to exercise their respective jurisdictions in some causes which they are capable of finally deciding.

It has been urged, that in strict grammatical construction, these words refer to the last antecedent, which is, "all other writs not specially provided for by statute."

This criticism may be correct, and is not entirely without its influence; but the sound construction which the court thinks it safer to adopt, is, that the true sense of the words is to be determined by the nature of the provision, and by the context.

It may be worthy of remark, that this act was passed by the first Congress of the United States, sitting under a constitution which had declared "that the privilege of the writ of habeas corpus should not be

suspended, unless when, in cases of rebellion or invasion, the public safety might require it."

Acting under the immediate influence of this injunction, they must have felt, with peculiar force, the
obligation of providing efficient means by which this
great constitutional privilege should receive life and
activity; for if the means be not in existence, the
privilege itself would be lost, although no law for its
suspension should be enacted.   Under the impression
of this obligation, they give to all the courts the
power of awarding writs of habeas corpus.

It has been truly said that this is a generic term,
and includes every species of that writ.   To this it
may be added, that when used singly — when we say
the writ of habeas corpus, without addition, we most
generally mean that great writ which is now applied
for; and in that sense it is used in the constitution.

* 96　　　　　* The section proceeds to say, that " either
of the justices of the Supreme Court, as
well as judges of the district courts, shall have power
to grant writs of habeas corpus for the purpose of an
inquiry into the cause of commitment."

It has been argued that Congress could never
intend to give a power of this kind to one of the
judges of this court, which is refused to all of them
when assembled.

There is certainly much force in this argument, and
it receives additional strength from the consideration,
that if the power be denied to this court, it is denied
to every other court of the United States; the right
to grant this important writ is given, in this sentence,

to every judge of the circuit, or district court, but can neither be exercised by the circuit nor district court. It would be strange if the judge, sitting on the bench, should be unable to hear a motion for this writ where it might be openly made, and openly discussed, and might yet retire to his chamber, and in private receive and decide upon the motion. This is not consistent with the genius of our legislation, nor with the course of our judicial proceedings. It would be much more consonant with both, that the power of the judge at his chambers should be suspended during his term, than that it should be exercised only in secret.

Whatever motives might induce the legislature to withhold from the Supreme Court the power to award the great writ of habeas corpus, there could be none which would induce them to withhold it from every court in the United States; and as it is granted to all in the same sentence and by the same words, the sound construction would seem to be, that the first sentence vests this power in all the courts of the United States: but as those courts are not always in session, the second sentence vests it in every justice or judge of the United States.

The doubt which has been raised on this subject may be further explained by examining the character of the various writs of habeas corpus, and selecting those to which this general grant of power must be restricted, if taken in the limited sense of being merely
*97   used to enable * the court to exercise its
jurisdiction in causes which it is enabled to decide finally.

The various writs of habeas corpus, as stated and accurately defined by Judge Blackstone, (*3 Bl. Com. 129,*) are 1st. The writ of *habeas corpus ad respondendum*, "When a man hath a cause of action against one who is confined by the process of some inferior court; in order to remove the prisoner and charge him with this new action in the court above."

This case may occur when a party, having a right to sue in this court, (as a state at the time of the passage of this act, or a foreign minister,) wishes to institute a suit against a person who is already confined by the process of an inferior court. This confinement may be either by the process of a court of the United States, or of a state court. If it be in a court of the United States, this writ would be inapplicable, because perfectly useless, and, consequently, could not be contemplated by the legislature. It would not be required, in such case, to bring the body of the defendant actually into court, and he would already be in the charge of the person who, under an original writ from this court, would be directed to take him into custody, and would already be confined in the same gaol in which he would be confined under the process of this court, if he should be unable to give bail.

If the party should be confined by process from a state court, there are many additional reasons against the use of this writ in such a case.

The state courts are not, in any sense of the word, inferior courts, except in the particular cases in which an appeal lies from their judgment to this court; and in these cases the mode of proceeding is particularly

prescribed, and is not by habeas corpus.   They are
not inferior courts, because they emanate from a different authority, and are the creatures of a distinct
government.

2d. The writ of *habeas corpus ad satisfaciendum*,
" When a prisoner hath had judgment against him in
an action, and the plaintiff is desirous to bring him

*98   up to * some superior court to charge him
with process of execution."

This case can never occur in the courts of the
United States.   One court never awards execution on
the judgment of another.   Our whole juridical system
forbids it.

3d. *Ad prosequendum, testificandum, deliberandum*,
&c., " Which issue when it is necessary to remove a
prisoner, in order to prosecute, or bear testimony, in
any court, or to be tried in the proper jurisdiction
wherein the fact was committed."

This writ might unquestionably be employed to
bring up a prisoner to bear testimony in a court, consistently with the most limited construction of the
words in the act of Congress ; but the power to bring
a person up that he may be tried in the proper jurisdiction, is understood to be the very question now
before the court.

4th, and last. The common writ *ad faciendum et
recipiendum*, " Which issues out of any of the courts
of Westminster Hall, when a person is sued in some
inferior jurisdiction, and is desirous to remove the
action into the superior court, commanding the inferior
judges to produce the body of the defendant, together

with the day and cause of his caption and detainer, (whence the writ is frequently denominated a *habeas corpus cum causâ,*) to do and receive whatever the king's court shall consider in that behalf. This writ is grantable of common right, without any motion in court, and it instantly supersedes all proceedings in the court below."

Can a solemn grant of power to a court to award a writ be considered as applicable to a case in which that writ, if issuable at all, issues by law without the leave of the court?

It would not be difficult to demonstrate that the writ of *habeas corpus cum causâ* cannot be the particular writ contemplated by the legislature in the section under consideration ; but it will be sufficient to observe generally, that the same act prescribes a different mode for bringing into the courts of the United States suits brought in a *state court against a person having a right to claim the jurisdiction of the courts of the United States. He may, on his first appearance, file his petition and authenticate the fact, upon which the cause is *ipso facto* removed into the courts of the United States.

The only power, then, which, on this limited construction, would be granted by the section under consideration, would be that of issuing writs of *habeas corpus ad testificandum.* The section itself proves that this was not the intention of the legislature. It concludes with the following proviso, " That writs of habeas corpus shall in no case extend to prisoners in gaol, unless where they are in custody under or by

*99

color of the authority of the United States, or are committed for trial before some court of the same, or are necessary to be brought into court to testify."

This proviso extends to the whole section. It limits the powers previously granted to the courts, because it specifies a case in which it is particularly applicable to the use of the power by courts — where the person is necessary to be brought into court to testify. That construction cannot be a fair one which would make the legislature except from the operation of a proviso, limiting the express grant of a power, the whole power intended to be granted.

From this review of the extent of the power of awarding writs of habeas corpus, if the section be construed in its restricted sense; from a comparison of the nature of the writ which the courts of the United States would, on that view of the subject, be enabled to issue; from a comparison of the power so granted with the other parts of the section, it is apparent that this limited sense of the term cannot be that which was contemplated by the legislature.

But the 33d section throws much light upon this question. It contains these words: "And upon all arrests in criminal cases, bail shall be admitted, except where the punishment may be death; in which cases it shall not be admitted but by the Supreme or a circuit court, or by a justice of the Supreme Court, or a judge of a district * court who shall
* *100*   exercise their discretion therein, regarding the nature and circumstances of the offense, and of the evidence, and of the usages of law."

The appropriate process of bringing up a prisoner, not committed by the court itself, to be bailed, is by the writ now applied for. Of consequence, a court possessing the power to bail prisoners not committed by itself, may award a writ of habeas corpus for the exercise of that power. The clause under consideration obviously proceeds on the supposition that this power was previously given, and is explanatory of the 14th section.

If, by the sound construction of the act of Congress, the power to award writs of habeas corpus in order to examine into the cause of commitment is given to this court, it remains to inquire whether this be a case in which the writ ought to be granted.

The only objection is, that the commitment has been made by a court having power to commit and to bail.

Against this objection the argument from the bar has been so conclusive that nothing can be added to it.

If, then, this were *res integra*, the court would decide in favor of the motion. But the question is considered as long since decided. The case of Hamilton is expressly in point in all its parts; and although the question of jurisdiction was not made at the bar, the case was several days under advisement, and this question could not have escaped the attention of the court. From that decision the court would not lightly depart. (*United States v. Hamilton, 3 Dall. 17.*)

If the act of Congress gives this court the power to award a writ of habeas corpus in the present case, it remains to inquire whether that act be compatible with the constitution.

In the mandamus case, (*ante, vol. 1, p. 175, Marbury v. Madison,*) it was decided that this Court would not exercise original jurisdiction except so far as that jurisdiction was given by the constitution.

*101   But so far as that case has * distinguished between original and appellate jurisdiction, that which the court is now asked to exercise is clearly appellate.   It is the revision of a decision of an inferior court, by which a citizen has been committed to gaol.

It has been demonstrated at the bar, that the question brought forward on a habeas corpus, is always distinct from that which is involved in the cause itself. The question whether the individual shall be imprisoned is always distinct from the question whether he shall be convicted or acquitted of the charge on which he is to be tried, and, therefore, these questions are separated, and may be decided in different courts.

The decision that the individual shall be imprisoned must always precede the application for a writ of habeas corpus, and this writ must always be for the purpose of revising that decision, and, therefore, appellate in its nature.

But this point also is decided in *Hamilton's Case* and in *Burford's Case.*[1]

If at any time the public safety should require the suspension of the powers vested by this act in the courts of the United States, it is for the legislature to say so.

---

[1] At February term, 1806, in this court.

That question depends on political considerations, on which the legislature is to decide. Until the legislative will be expressed, this Court can only see its duty, and must obey the laws.

The motion, therefore, must be granted.

OPINION OF COURT ON THE SECOND ARGUMENT.

* *125*   * February 21. *Marshall, Ch. J.,*[1] delivered the opinion of the court.

The prisoners having been brought before this court on a writ of habeas corpus, and the testimony on which they were committed having been fully examined and attentively considered, the court is now to declare the law upon their case.

This being a mere inquiry, which, without deciding upon guilt, precedes the institution of a prosecution, the question to be determined is, whether the accused shall be discharged or held to trial; and if the latter, in what place they are to be tried, and whether they shall be confined or admitted to bail. " If," says a very learned and accurate commentator, "upon this inquiry it manifestly appears that no such crime has been committed, or that the suspicion entertained of the prisoner was wholly groundless, in such cases only is it lawful totally to discharge him. Otherwise he must either be committed to prison or give bail."

The specific charge brought against the prisoners is treason in levying war against the United States.

As there is no crime which can more excite and

---

[1] The other judges present were Chase, Washington, and Johnson.

agitate the passions of men than treason, no charge demands more from the tribunal before which it is made a deliberate and temperate inquiry. Whether this inquiry be directed to the fact or to the law, none can be more solemn, none more important to the citizen or to the government; none can more affect the safety of both.

To prevent the possibility of those calamities which result from the extension of treason to offenses of minor * importance, that great fundamental
* *126*
law which defines and limits the various departments of our government has given a rule on the subject both to the legislature and the courts of America, which neither can be permitted to transcend.

" Treason against the United States shall consist only in levying war against them, or in adhering to their enemies, giving them aid and comfort."

To constitute that specific crime for which the prisoners now before the court have been committed, war must be actually levied against the United States. However flagitious may be the crime of conspiring to subvert by force the government of our country, such conspiracy is not treason. To conspire to levy war, and actually to levy war, are distinct offenses. The first must be brought into open action by the assemblage of men for a purpose treasonable in itself, or the fact of levying war cannot have been committed. So far has this principle been carried, that, in a case reported by Ventris, and mentioned in some modern treatises on criminal law, it has been determined that the actual enlistment of men to serve against the government does not amount to levying war. It is true that in that case the soldiers enlisted were to serve without the realm, but they were enlisted within it, and if the enlistment for a treasonable purpose could amount to levying war, then war had been actually levied.

It is not the intention of the court to say that no individual can be guilty of this crime who has not appeared in arms against his country. On the contrary, if war be actually levied, that is, if a body of men be actually assembled for the purpose of effecting by force a treasonable purpose, all those who perform any part, however minute, or however remote from the scene of action, and who are actually leagued in the general conspiracy, are to be considered as traitors. But there must be an actual assembling of men for the treasonable purpose, to constitute a levying of war.

Crimes so atrocious as those which have for their object the subversion by violence of those laws and

* *127*

those* institutions which have been ordained in order to secure the peace and happiness of society, are not to escape punishment because they have not ripened into treason. The wisdom of the legislature is competent to provide for the case; and the framers of our constitution, who not only defined and limited the crime, but with jealous circumspection attempted to protect their limitation by providing that no person should be convicted of it, unless on the testimony of two witnesses to the same overt act, or on confession in open court, must have conceived it more safe that punishment in such cases should be ordained by general laws, formed upon deliberation, under the influence of no resentments, and without knowing on whom they were to operate, than that it should be inflicted under the influence of those passions which the occasion seldom fails to excite, and which a flexible definition of the crime, or a construction which would render it flexible, might bring into operation. It is, therefore, more safe as well as more consonant to the principles of our constitution, that the crime of treason should not be extended by construction to doubtful cases ; and that crimes not clearly within the constitutional definition, should receive such punishment as the legislature in its wisdom may provide.

To complete the crime of levying war against the United States, there must be an actual assemblage of men for the purpose of executing a treasonable design. In the case now before the court, a design to overturn the government of the United States in New Orleans by force, would have been unquestionably a design which, if carried into execution, would have been treason, and the assemblage of a body of men for the purpose of carrying it into execution would amount to levying of war against the United States ; but no conspiracy for this object, no enlisting of men to effect it, would be an actual levying of war.

In conformity with the principles now laid down, have been the decisions heretofore made by the judges of the United States.

*128   * The opinions given by Judge Paterson
and Judge Iredell, in cases before them, imply an actual assembling of men, though they rather
designed to remark on the purpose to which the force
was to be applied than on the nature of the force
itself.   Their opinions, however, contemplate the
actual employment of force.

Judge Chase, in the trial of Fries, was more explicit.

He stated the opinion of the court to be, "that if
a body of people conspire and meditate an insurrection to resist or oppose the execution of any statute
of the United States by force, they are only guilty of
a high misdemeanor; but if they proceed to carry
such intention into execution by force, that they are
guilty of the treason of levying war; and the quantum
of the force employed neither lessens nor increases
the crime: whether by one hundred, or one thousand
persons, is wholly immaterial." "The court are of
opinion," continued Judge Chase, on that occasion,
"that a combination or conspiracy to levy war against
the United States is not treason, unless combined
with an attempt to carry such combination or conspiracy into execution; some actual force or violence
must be used in pursuance of such design to levy
war; but it is altogether immaterial whether the force
used is sufficient to effectuate the object; any force
connected with the intention will constitute the crime
of levying war."

The application of these general principles to the
particular case before the court will depend on the

testimony which has been exhibited against the accused.

The first deposition to be considered is that of General Eaton. This gentleman connects in one statement the purport of numerous conversations held with Col. Burr throughout the last winter. In the course of these conversations were communicated various criminal projects which seem to have been revolving in the mind of the projector. An expedition against Mexico seems to have been the first and most matured part of his plan, if indeed it did not constitute a distinct and separate plan, upon * the success of which other schemes still more culpable, but not yet well digested, might depend. Maps and other information preparatory to its execution, and which would rather indicate that it was the immediate object, had been procured, and for a considerable time, in repeated conversations, the whole efforts of Col. Burr were directed to prove to the witness, who was to have held a high command under him, the practicability of the enterprise, and in explaining to him the means by which it was to be effected.

129

This deposition exhibits the various schemes of Col. Burr, and its materiality depends on connecting the prisoners at the bar in such of those schemes as were treasonable. For this purpose the affidavit of General Wilkinson, comprehending in its body the substance of a letter from Col. Burr, has been offered, and was received by the circuit court. To the admission of this testimony great and serious objections

have been made. It has been urged that it is a
voluntary or rather an extrajudicial affidavit, made
before a person not appearing to be a magistrate, and
contains the substance only of a letter, of which the
original is retained by the person who made the
affidavit.

The objection that the affidavit is extrajudicial
resolves itself into the question whether one magistrate may commit on an affidavit taken before another
magistrate. For if he may, an affidavit made as the
foundation of a commitment ceases to be extrajudicial,
and the person who makes it would be as liable to a
prosecution for perjury as if the warrant of commitment had been issued by the magistrate before whom
the affidavit was made.

To decide that an affidavit made before one magistrate would not justify a commitment by another,
might in many cases be productive of great inconvenience, and does not appear susceptible of abuse if
the verity of the certificate be established.   Such an
affidavit seems admissible on the principle that before
the accused is put upon his trial all the proceedings
are *ex parte*. The court, therefore, overrule this
objection.

* *130*   * That which questions the character of
the person who has on this occasion ad-
ministered the oath is next to be considered.

The certificate from the office of the department of
state has been deemed insufficient by the counsel for
the prisoners, because the law does not require the
appointment of magistrates for the territory of New

Orleans to be certified to that office; because the certificate is in itself informal, and because it does not appear that the magistrates had taken the oath required by the act of Congress.

The first of these objections is not supported by the law of the case, and the second may be so readily corrected, that the court has proceeded to consider the subject as if it were corrected, retaining, however, any final decision, if against the prisoners, until the correction shall be made. With regard to the third, the magistrate must be presumed to have taken the requisite oaths, since he is found acting as a magistrate.

On the admissibility of that part of the affidavit which purports to be as near the substance of the letter from Col. Burr to General Wilkinson as the latter could interpret it, a division of opinion has taken place in the Court. Two judges are of opinion that as such testimony delivered in the presence of the prisoner on his trial would be totally inadmissible, neither can it be considered as a foundation for a commitment. Although in making a commitment the magistrate does not decide on the guilt of the prisoner, yet he does decide on the probable cause, and a long and painful imprisonment may be the consequence of his decision. This probable cause, therefore, ought to be proved by testimony in itself legal, and which, though from the nature of the case it must be *ex parte*, ought in most other respects to be such as a Court and jury might hear.

Two judges are of opinion that in this incipient

stage of the prosecution, an affidavit stating the general purport of a letter may be read, particularly where the person in possession of it is at too great a distance to admit of * its being obtained, and that a commitment may be founded on it.

* *131*

Under this embarrassment it was deemed necessary to look into the affidavit for the purpose of discovering whether, if admitted, it contains matter which would justify the commitment of the prisoners at the bar on the charge of treason.

That the letter from Col. Burr to General Wilkinson relates to a military enterprise meditated by the former, has not been questioned. If this enterprise was against Mexico, it would amount to a high misdemeanor; if against any of the territories of the United States, or if in its progress the subversion of the government of the United States in any of their territories was a mean clearly and necessarily to be employed, if such mean formed a substantive part of the plan, the assemblage of a body of men to effect it would be levying war against the United States.

The letter is in language which furnishes no distinct view of the design of the writer. The co-operation, however, which is stated to have been secured, points strongly to some expedition against the territories of Spain. After making these general statements, the writer becomes rather more explicit, and says, " Burr's plan of operations is to move down rapidly from the falls on the 15th of November, with the first 500 or 1,000 men in light boats now constructing for that purpose, to be at Natchez between the 5th and 15th of December, there to meet Wilkinson ; then to determine whether it will be expedient in the first instance to seize on, or to pass by, Baton Rouge.   The people of the country to which we are going are prepared to receive us.   Their agents now with Burr say that if we will protect their religion, and will not subject them to a foreign power, in three weeks all will be settled."

There is no expression in these sentences which would justify a suspicion that any territory of the United States was the object of the expedition.

* *132*   * For what purpose seize on Baton Rouge ? why engage Spain against this enterprise, if it was designed against the United States ?

" The people of the country to which we are going are prepared to receive us."   This language is peculiarly appropriate to a foreign country.   It will not be contended that the terms would be inapplicable to a territory of the United States, but other terms would more aptly convey the idea, and Burr seems to consider himself as giving information of which Wilkinson was not possessed.   When it is recollected that he was the governor of a territory adjoining that which must have been threatened, if a territory of the United States was threatened, and that he commanded the army, a part of which was stationed in that territory, the probability that the information communicated related to a foreign country, it must be admitted, gains strength.

" Their agents now with Burr say, that if we will protect their religion, and will not subject them to a foreign power, in three weeks all will be settled."

This is apparently the language of a people who, from the contemplated change in their political situation, feared for their religion, and feared that they would be made the subjects of a foreign power. That the Mexicans should entertain these apprehensions was natural, and would readily be believed. They were, if the representation made of their dispositions be correct, about to place themselves much in the power of men who professed a different faith from theirs, and who, by making them dependent on England or the United States, would subject them to a foreign power.

That the people of New Orleans, as a people, if really engaged in the conspiracy, should feel the same apprehensions, and require assurances on the same points, is by no means so obvious.

There certainly is not in the letter delivered to General Wilkinson, so far as the letter is laid before *133 the court, one syllable which has a necessary or a natural reference * to an enterprise against any territory of the United States.

That the bearer of this letter must be considered as acquainted with its contents is not to be controverted. The letter and his own declarations evince the fact.

After stating himself to have passed through New York, and the western states and territories, without insinuating that he had performed on his route any act whatever which was connected with the enterprise, he states their object to be, "to carry an expedition to the Mexican provinces."

This statement may be considered as explanatory

of the letter of Col. Burr, if the expressions of that
letter could be thought ambiguous.

But there are other declarations made by Mr.
Swartwout, which constitute the difficulty of this case.
On an inquiry from General Wilkinson, he said,
"this territory would be revolutionized where the
people were ready to join them, and that there would
be some seizing, he supposed at New Orleans."

If these words import that the government established by the United States in any of its territories,
was to be revolutionized by force, although merely as
a step to, or a means of executing some greater projects, the design was unquestionably treasonable, and
any assemblage of men for that purpose would amount
to a levying of war.   But on the import of the words
a difference of opinion exists.   Some of the judges
suppose they refer to the territory against which the
expedition was intended ; others to that in which the
conversation was held.   Some consider the words, if
even applicable to a territory of the United States, as
alluding to a revolution to be effected by the people,
rather than by the party conducted by Col. Burr.

But whether this treasonable intention be really
imputable to the plan or not, it is admitted that it
must have been carried into execution by an open
*134   assemblage of * men for that purpose, pre-
vious to the arrest of the prisoner, in order
to consummate the crime as to him ; and a majority
of the court is of opinion that the conversation of
Mr. Swartwout affords no sufficient proof of such
assembling.

The prisoner stated that " Col. Burr, with the support of a powerful association extending from New York to New Orleans, was levying an armed body of 7,000 men from the state of New York and the western states and territories, with a view to carry an expedition to the Mexican territories."

That the association, whatever may be its purpose, is not treason, has been already stated. That levying an army may or may not be treason, and that this depends on the intention with which it is levied, and on the point to which the parties have advanced, has been also stated. The mere enlisting of men, without assembling them, is not levying war. The question, then, is, whether this evidence proves Col. Burr to have advanced so far in levying an army as actually to have assembled them.

It is argued that since it cannot be necessary that the whole 7,000 men should have assembled, their commencing their march by detachments to the place of rendezvous must be sufficient to constitute the crime.

This position is correct, with some qualification. It cannot be necessary that the whole army should assemble, and that the various parts which are to compose it should have combined. But it is necessary that there should be an actual assemblage, and, therefore, the evidence should make the fact unequivocal.

The traveling of individuals to the place of rendezvous would perhaps not be sufficient. This would be an equivocal act, and has no warlike appearance.

The meeting of particular bodies of men, and their marching from places of partial to a place of general rendezvous, would be such an assemblage.

The particular words used by Mr. Swartwout are, that Col. Burr " was levying an armed body of 7,000 men." * If the term levying in this place, *135 imports that they were assembled, then such fact would amount, if the intention be against the United States, to levying war. If it barely imports that he was enlisting or engaging them in his service, the fact would not amount to levying war. It is thought sufficiently apparent that the latter is the sense in which the term was used. The fact alluded to, if taken in the former sense, is of a nature so to force itself upon the public view, that if the army had then actually assembled, either together or in detachments, some evidence of such assembling would have been laid before the court.

The words used by the prisoner in reference to seizing at New Orleans, and borrowing perhaps by force from the bank, though indicating a design to rob, and consequently importing a high offense, do not designate the specific crime of levying war against the United States.

It is, therefore, the opinion of a majority of the court, that in the case of Samuel Swartwout there is not sufficient evidence of his levying war against the United States to justify his commitment on the charge of treason.

Against Erick Bollman there is still less testimony. Nothing has been said by him to support the charge that the enterprise in which he was engaged had any other object than was stated in the letter of Col. Burr. Against him, therefore, there is no evidence to support a charge of treason.

That both of the prisoners were engaged in a most culpable enterprise against the dominions of a power at peace with the United States, those who admit the affidavit of General Wilkinson cannot doubt. But that no part of this crime was committed in the District of Columbia is apparent. It is, therefore, the unanimous opinion of the court that they cannot be tried in this district.

*136   * The law read on the part of the prosecution is understood to apply only to offenses committed on the high seas, or in any river, haven, basin or bay, not within the jurisdiction of any particular state. In those cases there is no court which has particular cognizance of the crime, and, therefore, the place in which the criminal shall be apprehended, or, if he be apprehended where no court has exclusive jurisdiction, that to which he shall be first brought, is substituted for the place in which the offense was commited.

But in this case, a tribunal for the trial of the offense, wherever it may have been committed, had been provided by Congress; and at the place where the prisoners were seized by the authority of the commander in chief, there existed such a tribunal. It would, too, be extremely dangerous to say, that because the prisoners were apprehended, not by a civil magistrate, but by the military power, there could be given by law a right to try the person so seized in any place which the general might select, and to which he might direct them to be carried.

The act of Congress, which the prisoners are supposed to have violated, describes as offenders those who begin, or set on foot, or provide, or prepare, the means for any military expedition or enterprise to be carried on from thence against the dominions of a foreign prince or state with whom the United States are at peace.

There is a want of precision in the description of the offense which might produce some difficulty in deciding what cases would come within it. But several other questions arise, which a court consisting of four judges finds itself unable to decide, and, therefore, as the crime with which the prisoners stand charged has not been committed, the court can only direct them to be discharged. This is done with the less reluctance because the discharge does not acquit them from the offense which there is probable cause for supposing they have committed, and if those whose duty it is to protect the nation, by prosecuting offenders against the laws, shall suppose *those
*137   who have been charged with treason to be proper objects for punishment, they will, when possessed of less exceptionable testimony, and when able to say at what place the offense has been committed, institute fresh proceedings against them.

United States *v.* Aaron Burr.

NOTE.

AFTER his duel with Hamilton, discredited with his own political party and with the better element of the northern and eastern states, Aaron Burr, in the years 1805 and 1806, dreamed a dream as fantastic as that of any Elizabethan adventurer, to win for himself the crown of Mexico, and, adding to it the vast territories beyond the Mississippi, and perhaps New Orleans, and some part of the southern territory of the United States, to found a western empire. The exact limits of that scheme, and the means to be used for carrying it out, will, in all probability, never be known,—probably Burr himself had planned but vaguely. What he did was this : He travelled among and popularized himself with the communities along the Ohio and Mississippi,—communities that thought less harshly of the death of Hamilton and were but loosely bound to the federal union; he consorted with malcontents like Commodore Truxton and General Eaton, who had grievances against the government; he intrigued, or tried to intrigue, with General Wilkinson, then ranking officer of the United States army, in command at New Orleans, for the support of the army. Finally, in the fall of 1806 he inspired a small gathering of men, who bore arms, on Blennerhassett's Island in the Ohio, who finally started down the Ohio in boats, an apparently peaceful vanguard for a settlement beyond the Mississippi preparatory to a descent on Mexico or on New Orleans. Just what they meant to do is not clear. But the collapse of Burr's house of cards was brought on by a sudden access of virtue that bore every appearance of cowardly treachery on the part of General Wilkinson. Wilkinson communicated to President Jefferson, with translations, certain cipher messages which Burr had sent him, which set out Burr's plan to move down the Mississippi in force and evidently refer to an expediiton into

Mexico and a new empire in the southwest in which " Wilkinson shall be second to Burr *only.*"   General Wilkinson never adequately explained how he came to be in cipher correspondence with Burr on affairs of state.

After the receipt of this information, on January 22, 1807, Jefferson issued a special presidential message denouncing Burr. As soon as the news spread the whole country was at a high pitch of excitement and Burr became a fugitive from justice.   Two of his emissaries, Bollman and Swartwout, who had been go-betweens to Wilkinson, were arrested for treason.   (The affidavits of General Wilkinson and General Eaton, on which Bollman and Swartwout were arrested and which were attached to Jefferson's message, are set out in a note at at the end of opinion, *infra.*)

Bollman and Swartwout were both discharged on writs of *habeas corpus* before the Supreme Court of the United States. (See opinion *Ex parte Bollman and Swartwout,* 4 Cranch 75, and *supra,* page 69.)   In February, 1807, a month later, Burr was arrested in Alabama, brought east, and indicted for treason in Virginia, and his case came on for trial at Richmond before Chief Justice Marshall, sitting on circuit with District Judge Cyrus Griffin.

That trial is famous.   The country at large seems to have demanded the conviction of Burr.   The President himself was behind the prosecution and made every effort for a conviction. So strong was the local sentiment against the prisoner that it was impossible to obtain a jury not predisposed against him.   At such a trial Marshall held the scales of justice to determine whether Burr was guilty of treason, as treason was defined in the statutes and the Constitution.

The framers of the Constitution of the United States, remembering, and fearing, the doctrine of constructive treason which had proved so apt a tool of tyranny in England, had written in it: " Treason against the United States shall consist only in levying war against them, or in adhering to their enemies, giving them aid and comfort "; (these were almost the words of the act of 25 Edward III., chapter 2, passed to define the crime of treason); and the Constitution further provided, " No person shall be convicted of treason unless on the testimony of two witnesses to the same overt act or on confession in open court." The question of what constituted treason came up for the first time in the United States in the cases of Burr's two emissaries, Bollman and Swartwout, *supra.* In those cases the principle was squarely laid down, by Marshall and the Supreme Court, that to complete the crime of levying war against the United States there must be "an actual assemblage of men for the purpose of executing a treasonable design." In the case of Bollman and Swartwout the Court found evidence of a heinous plot, which was, perhaps, aimed against Mexico and not against the United States at all. The Court again found in the enlistment of occasional armed men only an equivocal act which was not necessarily an assemblage of men for levying war, and so not levying war. That opinion contained a further statement,—clearly *obiter,*—that was interpreted by the prosecution in the Burr case to mean that a meeting under arms of conspirators against the government, as such, was a levying of war within the meaning of the Constitution. That was the theory of the prosecution against Burr.

The indictment charged Burr with levying war on Blennerhassett Island, although Burr was not present at the time that the troops were assembled. The theory of the prosecution was that inasmuch as Burr had planned the assemblage he should be regarded as present and taking part in it. Testimony was first introduced at the trial to show the levying of an armed force on Blennerhassett Island, and then was offered to show Burr's connection with that force. The defendant objected to that testimony, and on its motion to exclude it, which went to the root of the whole question, Marshall delivered the main opinion in the case. The opinion, full of technicalities and at great length, is to the effect that the assemblage was not clearly a levying of war, that the connection of Burr with the overt act of levying war on Blennerhassett Island, if an overt act was proved, was not sufficiently made out to charge him as one taking part in it, and in any case was not proved by two witnesses as required by the Constitution, and further, that he could not be considered as constructively present as an accessory or otherwise, even if under such a doctrine a conviction could be reached without the previous conviction of a principal in the crime.

Marshall discussed at length the meaning of the statements in the cases of Bollman and Swartwout as to what was necessary to constitute a levying of war, and construed them as going no farther than the previous English and American decisions, and interpreted the constitutional provision as requiring some act of war, not necessarily actual violence, but some act further than plotting and gathering arms and detached levies of men. Yet that plotting and those levies were all the prosecution could prove. The decision on the motion practically threw out all the evidence that the prosecution had to offer, and left to the jury no other course but to bring in a verdict of not guilty, or, as that Virginian jury chose to phrase it, "not proved guilty."

It is significant of Marshall's power that no later commentator —the question has not been later raised in any important case— has criticised adversely the doctrines there laid down, and they are accepted law. It is notable again how closely and how strictly Marshall followed the constitutional requirements in the face of the national outcry for a conviction. Not less notable are the firmness, the dignity, and moderation with which he presided at the trial.

One point has been frequently adversely criticised in the conduct of the case. At one stage of it Marshall saw fit to issue a subpœna to President Jefferson to produce at the trial certain official documents. This Jefferson, with sufficient dignity but considerable heat, refused to do. The course of recent criticism has usually been to support Marshall in this matter of the subpœna. It is confessed that the court had no authority to enforce this command against the President, and it must be admitted that the issuing of futile orders is not conducive to the dignity of the court. And again, it seems a curious conception of the judicial function to call the head of the nation from his official duties to give testimony. The incident seems best explained as an honest mistake of judgment, and the course of recent criticism is to be attributed to the great awe of Marshall's reputation. The matter is hardly of first importance.

United States

v.

Aaron Burr.

*OPINION ON THE MOTION TO INTRODUCE CERTAIN
EVIDENCE IN THE TRIAL OF AARON BURR,
FOR TREASON. PRONOUNCED MON-
DAY, AUGUST 31.

The question now to be decided has been argued
in a manner worthy of its importance, and with an
earnestness evincing the strong conviction felt by the
counsel on each side that the law is with them.

A degree of eloquence seldom displayed on any
occasion has embellished a solidity of argument, and
a depth of research, by which the court has been
greatly aided in forming the opinion it is about to
deliver.

The testimony adduced on the part of the United
States, to prove the overt act laid in the indictment,
having shown, and the attorney for the United States
having admitted, that the prisoner was not present
when the act, whatever may be its character, was committed, and there being no reason to doubt but that
he was at a great distance and in a different state, it
is objected to the testimony offered on the part of
the United States to connect him with those who

committed the overt act, that such testimony is totally
irrelevant, and must, therefore, be rejected.

The arguments in support of this motion respect in
part the merits of the case as it may be supposed to
stand independent of the pleadings, and in part as
exhibited by the pleadings.

On the first division of the subject two points are
made.

1st. That conformably to the constitution of the
United States, no man can be convicted of treason
who was not present when the war was levied.

2d. That if this construction be erroneous, no testimony can be received to charge one man with the
overt acts of others, until those overt acts, as laid in
the indictment, be proved to the satisfaction of the
court.

The question which arises on the construction of
the constitution, in every point of view in which it
can be contemplated, is of infinite moment to the people of this country and to their government, and
requires the most temperate and the most deliberate
consideration.

" Treason against the United States shall consist
only in levying war against them."

What is the natural import of the words "levying
war"? And who * may be said to levy it?

* 470

Had their first application to treason been
made by our constitution, they would certainly have
admitted of some latitude of construction. Taken
most literally, they are, perhaps, of the same import
with the words raising or creating war, but as those

who join after the commencement are equally the
object of punishment, there would probably be a general admission, that the term also comprehended
making war, or carrying on war.   In the construction
which courts would be required to give these words,
it is not improbable that those who should raise,
create, make, or carry on war, might be comprehended.   The various acts which would be considered
as coming within the term, would be settled by a
course of decisions, and it would be affirming boldly,
to say that those only who actually constituted a portion of the military force appearing in arms could be
considered as levying war.   There is no difficulty in
affirming that there must be a war, or the crime of
levying it cannot exist ; but there would often be
considerable difficulty in affirming that a particular
act did or did not involve the person committing it
in the guilt, and in the fact of levying war.   If, for
example, an army should be actually raised for the
avowed purpose of carrying on open war against
the United States and subverting their government, the
point must be weighed very deliberately before a judge
would venture to decide that an overt act of levying
war had not been committed by a commissary of pur-
chases, who never saw the army, but who, knowing its
object, and leaguing himself with the rebels, supplied
that army with provisions, or by a recruiting officer
holding a commission in the rebel service, who, though
never in camp, executed the particular duty assigned
to him.

But the term is not for the first time applied to

treason by the constitution of the United States.   It is a technical term.   It is used in a very old statute of that country, whose language is our language, and whose laws form the substratum of our laws.   It is scarcely conceivable that the term was not employed by the framers of our constitution in the sense which had been affixed to it by those from whom we borrowed it.   So far as the meaning of any terms, particularly terms of art, is completely ascertained, those by whom they are employed must be considered as employing them in that ascertained meaning, unless the contrary be proved by the context.   It is, therefore, reasonable to suppose, unless it be incompatible with other expressions of the constitution, that the term "levying war," is used in that instrument in the same sense in which it was understood in England, and in this country, to have been used in the statute of the 25th of Edward III. from which it was borrowed.

It is said that this meaning is to be collected only from adjudged cases.   But this position cannot be conceded to the extent in which it is laid down.   The superior authority of adjudged cases will never be controverted.   But those celebrated elementary writers who have stated the principles of the law, whose statements have received the common approbation of legal men, are not to be disregarded.   Principles laid down by such writers as Coke, Hale, Foster and Black-

* *471*

stone, are not * lightly to be rejected.   These books are in the hands of every student. Legal opinions are formed upon them, and those opinions are afterwards carried to the bar, the bench, and the legislature. In the exposition of terms, therefore, used in instruments of the present day, the definitions and the dicta of those authors, if not contradicted by adjudications, and if compatible with the words of the statute, are entitled to respect. It is to be regretted that they do not shed as much light on this part of the subject as is to be wished.

Coke does not give a complete definition of the term, but puts cases which amount to levying war. "An actual rebellion or insurrection," he says, "is a levying of war." In whom? Coke does not say whether in those only who appear in arms, or in all those who take part in the rebellion or insurrection by real open deed.

Hale, in treating on the same subject, puts many cases which shall constitute a levying of war, without which no act can amount to treason, but he does not particularize the parts to be performed by the different persons concerned in that war, which shall be sufficient to fix on each the guilt of levying it.

Foster says, "The joining with rebels in an act of rebellion, or with enemies in acts of hostility, will make a man a traitor." "Furnishing rebels or enemies with money, arms, ammunition, or other necessaries, will prima facie make a man a traitor."

Foster does not say that he would be a traitor under the words of the statute, independent of the legal rule which attaches the guilt of the principal to an accessory, nor that his treason is occasioned by that rule. In England, this discrimination need not be made except for the purpose of framing the indictment, and, therefore, in the English books we do not perceive any effort to make it.   Thus, surrendering a castle to rebels, being in confederacy with them, is said, by Hale and Foster, to be treason under the clause of levying war; but whether it be levying war in fact, or aiding those who levy it, is not said.   Upon this point Blackstone is not more satisfactory.   Although we may find among the commentators upon treason enough to satisfy the inquiry, what is a state of internal war, yet no precise information can be acquired from them, which would enable us to decide, with clearness, whether persons not in arms, but taking part in a rebellion, could be said to levy war independent of that doctrine which attaches to the accessory the guilt of his principal.

If in adjudged cases this question has been taken up and directly decided, the court has not seen those cases.   The arguments which may be drawn from the form of the indictment, though strong, are not conclusive.   In the precedent found in Tremaine, Mary Speake, who was indicted for furnishing provisions to the party of the Duke of Monmouth, is indicted for furnishing provisions to those who were levying war, not for levying war herself.   It may correctly be argued, that had this act amounted to levying war, she would have been indicted for levying war, and the furnishing of provisions would have been laid as the *overt act.   The court felt
*472   this when the precedent was produced. But the argument, though strong, is not conclusive, because, in England, the inquiry whether he had

become a traitor by levying war, or by giving aid and comfort to those who were levying war, was unimportant, and because, too, it does not appear from the indictment that she was actually concerned in the rebellion, that she belonged to the rebel party, or was guilty of anything further than a criminal speculation in selling them provisions.

It is not deemed necessary to trace the doctrine that in treason all are principals, to its source. Its origin is most probably stated correctly by Judge Tucker, in a work, the merit of which is with pleasure acknowledged. But if a spurious doctrine has been introduced into the common law, and has for centuries been admitted as genuine, it would require great hardihood in a judge to reject it. Accordingly, we find those of the English jurists, who seem to disapprove the principle, declaring that it is now too firmly settled to be shaken.

It is unnecessary to trace this doctrine to its source for another reason. The terms of the constitution comprise no question respecting principal and accessory, so far as either may be truly and in fact said to levy war. Whether in England a person would be indicted in express terms for levying war, or for assisting others in levying war, yet if, in correct and legal language, he can be said to have levied war, and if it has never been decided that the act would not amount to levying war, his case may, without violent construction, be brought within the letter and the plain meaning of the constitution.

In examining these words, the argument which
may be drawn from felonies, as for example, from
murder, is not more conclusive.   Murder is the single
act of killing with malice aforethought.   But war is
a complex operation composed of many parts, co-
operating with each other.   No one man, or body of
men, can perform them all, if the war be of any continuance.   Although, then, in correct and in law
language, he alone is said to have murdered another
who has perpetrated the fact of killing, or has been
present aiding that fact, it does not follow that he
alone can have levied war who has borne arms.
All those who perform the various and essential military parts of prosecuting the war which must be
assigned to different persons, may with correctness
and accuracy be said to levy war.

Taking this view of the subject, it appears to the
court, that those who perform a part in the prosecution of the war may correctly be said to levy war,
and to commit treason under the constitution.   It
will be observed that this opinion does not extend to
the case of a person who performs no act in the
prosecution of the war, who counsels and advises it,
or who, being engaged in the conspiracy, fails to
perform his part.   Whether such persons may be
implicated by the doctrine, that whatever would make
a man an accessory in felony makes him a principal
in treason, or are excluded, because that doctrine is
inapplicable to the United States, the constitution
having declared that treason shall consist only in
levying war, and having made the proof of overt

*473 acts necessary to *conviction, is a question of vast importance, which it would be proper for the Supreme Court to take a fit occasion to decide, but which an inferior tribunal would not willingly determine, unless the case before them should require it.

It may now be proper to notice the opinion of the Supreme Court in the case of the *United States against Bollman and Swartwout.* It is said that this opinion, in declaring that those who do not bear arms may yet be guilty of treason, is contrary to law, and is not obligatory, because it is extrajudicial, and was delivered on a point not argued. This court is, therefore, required to depart from the principle there laid down.

It is true, that in that case, after forming the opinion that no treason could be committed, because no treasonable assemblage had taken place, the court might have dispensed with proceeding further in the doctrines of treason. But it is to be remembered, that the judges might act separately, and, perhaps, at the same time, on the various prosecutions which might be instituted, and that no appeal lay from their decisions. Opposite judgments on the point would have presented a state of things infinitely to be deplored by all. It was not surprising, then, that they should have made some attempt to settle principles which would probably occur, and which were in some degree connected with the point before them.

The court had employed some reasoning to show that without the actual embodying of men, war could not be levied. It might have been inferred from this, that those only who were so embodied could be guilty of treason. Not only to exclude this inference, but also to affirm the contrary, the court proceeded to observe, "It is not the intention of the court to say that no individual can be guilty of this crime who has not appeared in arms against his country. On the contrary, if war be actually levied; that is, if a body of men be actually assembled for the purpose of effecting by force a treasonable object, all those who perform any part, however minute, or however remote from the scene of action, and who are actually leagued in the general conspiracy, are to be considered as traitors."

This court is told that if this opinion be incorrect it ought not to be obeyed, because it was extrajudicial. For myself, I can say that I could not lightly be prevailed on to disobey it, were I even convinced that it was erroneous, but I would certainly use any means which the law placed in my power to carry the question again before the supreme court, for reconsideration, in a case in which it would directly occur and be fully argued.

The court which gave this opinion was composed of four judges. At the time I thought them unanimous, but I have since had reason to suspect that one of them, whose opinion is entitled to great respect, and whose indisposition prevented his entering into the discussions, on some of those points which were not essential to the decision of the very case under consideration, did not concur in this particular

point with his brethren.   Had the opinion been
unanimous it would have *been given by
474   a majority of the judges.   But should the
three who were absent concur with that judge who
was present, and who, perhaps, dissents from what
was then the opinion of the court, a majority of the
judges may overrule this decision.   I should, therefore, feel no objection, although I then thought, and
still think, the opinion perfectly correct, to carry the
point, if possible, again before the supreme court, if
the case should depend upon it.

In saying that I still think the opinion perfectly
correct, I do not consider myself as going further
than the preceding reasoning goes.   Some gentlemen have argued as if the Supreme Court had
adopted the whole doctrine of the English books on
the subject of accessories to treason.   But certainly
such is not the fact.   Those only who perform a
part, and who are leagued in the conspiracy, are
declared to be traitors.   To complete the definition
both circumstances must concur.   They must "perform a part," which will furnish the overt act, and
they must be "leagued in the conspiracy."   The
person who comes within this description, in the
opinion of the court, levies war.   The present motion, however, does not rest upon this point ; for, if
under this indictment the United States might be let
in to prove the part performed by the prisoner, if he
did perform any part, the court could not stop the
testimony in its present stage.

2d. The second point involves the character of the

overt act which has been given in evidence, and calls
upon the court to declare whether that act can
amount to levying war.   Although the court ought
now to avoid any analysis of the testimony which has
been offered in this case, provided the decision of
the motion should not rest upon it, yet many reasons
concur in giving peculiar propriety to a delivery, in
the course of these trials, of a detailed opinion on
the question, what is levying war?   As this question
has been argued at great length, it may probably
save much trouble to the counsel now to give that
opinion.

In opening the case it was contended by the attorney for the United States, and has since been
maintained on the part of the prosecution, that
neither arms, nor the application of force or violence,
are indispensably necessary to constitute the fact of
levying war.   To illustrate these positions, several
cases have been stated, many of which would clearly
amount to treason.   In all of them, except that which
was probably intended to be this case, and on which
no observation will be made, the object of the assemblage was clearly treasonable ; its character was
unequivocal, and was demonstrated by evidence
furnished by the assemblage itself ; there was no
necessity to rely upon information drawn from extrinsic sources, or in order to understand the fact, to
pursue a course of intricate reasoning, and to conjecture motives.   A force is supposed to be collected
for an avowed treasonable object, in a condition to
attempt that object, and to have commenced the

attempt by moving towards it. I state these par-
ticulars, because, although the cases put may establish
the doctrine they are intended to support, may prove
that the absence of arms, or the failure to apply force
to sensible objects by the actual commission of violence on those objects, may be *supplied
*475   by other circumstances, yet, they also serve
to show that the mind requires those circumstances
to be satisfied that war is levied.

Their construction of the opinion of the Supreme
Court is, I think, thus far correct. It is certainly the
opinion which was at the time entertained by myself,
and which is still entertained. If a rebel army,
avowing its hostility to the sovereign power, should
front that of the government, should march and
countermarch before it, should manœuvre in its face,
and should then disperse, from any cause whatever,
without firing a gun, I confess I could not, without
some surprise, hear gentlemen seriously contend that
this could not amount to an act of levying war. A
case equally strong may be put with respect to the
absence of military weapons. If the party be in a
condition to execute the purposed treason without
the usual implements of war, I can perceive no
reason for requiring those implements in order to
constitute the crime.

It is argued that no adjudged case can be produced
from the English books where actual violence has not
been committed. Suppose this were true. No adjudged case has, or, it is believed, can be, produced
from those books in which it has been laid down, that

war cannot be levied without the actual application
of violence to external objects. The silence of the
reporters on this point may be readily accounted for.
In cases of actual rebellion against the government,
the most active and influential leaders are generally
most actively engaged in the war, and as the object
can never be to extend punishment to extermination,
a sufficient number are found among those who have
committed actual hostilities, to satisfy the avenging
arm of justice. In cases of constructive treason, such
as pulling down meeting-houses, where the direct and
avowed object is not the destruction of the sovereign
power, some act of violence might be generally required to give the crime a sufficient degree of malig-
nity to convert it into treason, to render the guilt of
an individual unequivocal.

But *Vaughan's Case* is a case where there was no
real application of violence, and where the act was
adjudged to be treason. Gentlemen argue that
Vaughan was only guilty of adhering to the king's
enemies, but they have not the authority of the court
for so saying. The judges unquestionably treat the
cruising of Vaughan as an overt act of levying war.

The opinions of the best elementary writers concur
in declaring, that where a body of men are assembled
for the purpose of making war against the government, and are in a condition to make that war, the
assemblage is an act of levying war. These opinions
are contradicted by no adjudged case, and are supported by *Vaughan's Case.* This court is not inclined to controvert them.

But although, in this respect, the opinion of the Supreme Court has not been misunderstood on the part of the prosecution, that opinion seems not to have been fully adverted to in a very essential point in which it is said to have been misconceived by others.

* *476*   * The opinion, I am informed, has been construed to mean that any assemblage whatever for a treasonable purpose, whether in force, or not in force, whether in a condition to use violence, or not in that condition, is a levying of war. It is this construction, which has not, indeed, been expressly advanced at the bar, but which is said to have been adopted elsewhere, that the court deems it necessary to examine.

Independent of authority, trusting only to the dictates of reason, and expounding terms according to their ordinary signification, we should probably all concur in the declaration that war could not be levied without the employment and exhibition of force. War is an appeal from reason to the sword, and he who makes the appeal evidences the fact by the use of the means. His intention to go to war may be proved by words, but the actual going to war is a fact which is to be proved by open deed. The end is to be effected by force, and it would seem that in cases where no declaration is to be made, the state of actual war could only be created by the employment of force, or being in a condition to employ it.

But the term having been adopted by our constitution, must be understood in that sense in which it was

universally received in this country, when the constitution was framed.   The sense in which it was received
is to be collected from the most approved authorities
of that nation from which we have borrowed the term.

Lord Coke says that levying war against the king
was treason at the common law.   "A compassing or
conspiracy to levy war," he adds, "is no treason, for
there must be a levying of war in fact."   He proceeds
to state cases of constructive levying war, where the
direct design is not to overturn the government, but
to effect some general object by force.   The terms
he employs in stating these cases are such as indicate
an impression on his mind that actual ivolence is
a necessary ingredient in constituting the fact of levying war.   He then proceeds to say, "An actual rebellion, or insurrection, is a levying of war within this
act."   "If any with strength and weapons invasive
and defensive, doth hold and defend a castle or fort
against the king and his power, this is levying of war
against the king."   These cases are put to illustrate
what he denominates "a war in fact."   It is not easy
to conceive "an actual invasion or insurrection" unconnected with force, nor can "a castle or fort be
defended with strength and weapons invasive and
defensive" without the employment of actual force.
It would seem, then, to have been the opinion of
Lord Coke, that to levy war there must be an assemblage of men in a condition, and with an intention, to
employ force.   He certainly puts no case of a different
description.

Lord Hale says (*149 6.*)   "What shall be said a

levying of war is partly a question of fact, for it is not every unlawful or riotous assembly of many persons to do an unlawful act, though *de facto* they commit the act they intend, that makes a levying of war ; for then every riot would be treason," &c., "but it must be such an assembly as carries with it *speciem belli,* the appearance of war, as if they ride or march, *vexil-*

* *477*   *lis explicatis,* * with colors flying, or if they be formed into companies, or furnished with military officers, or if they are armed with military weapons, as swords, guns, bills, halberds, pikes, and are so circumstanced that it may be reasonably concluded they are in a posture of war, which circumstances are so various that it is hard to describe them all particularly."

"Only the general expressions in all the indictments of this nature that I have seen are more *guerrino arraiati,* arrayed in a warlike manner."

He afterwards adds, " If there be a war levied as is above declared, viz., an assembly arrayed in warlike manner, and so in the posture of war for any treasonable attempt, it is *bellum levatum,* but not *percussum.*"

It is obvious that Lord Hale supposed an assemblage of men in force, in a military posture, to be necessary to constitute the fact of levying war. The idea he appears to suggest, that the apparatus of war is necessary, has been very justly combated by an able judge who has written a valuable treatise on the subject of treason ; but it is not recollected that his position, that the assembly should be in a posture of war for any treasonable attempt, has ever been denied.

Hawk. c. 17. s. 23, says, "That not only those who rebel against the king, and take up arms to dethrone him, but also in many other cases, those who in a violent and forcible manner withstand his lawful authority, are said to levy war against him, and, therefore, those that hold a fort or castle against the king's forces, or keep together armed numbers of men against the king's express command, have been adjudged to levy war against him."

The cases put by Hawkins are all cases of actual force and violence. "Those who rebel against the king and take up arms to dethrone him;" in many other cases those "who in a violent and forcible manner withstand his lawful authority." "Those that hold a fort or castle against his forces, or keep together armed numbers of men against his express command."

These cases are obviously cases of force and violence.

Hawkins next proceeds to describe cases in which war is understood to be levied under the statute, although it was not directly made against the government. This Lord Hale terms an interpretative or constructive levying of war, and it will be perceived that he puts no case in which actual force is dispensed with.

"Those also," he says, "who make an insurrection in order to redress a public grievance, whether it be a real or pretended one, and of their own authority attempt with force to redress it, are said to levy war against the king, although they have no direct design

against his person, inasmuch as they insolently invade
his prerogative, by attempting to do that by private
authority which he by public justice ought to do,
which manifestly tends to a downright rebellion. As
where great numbers by force attempt to remove certain persons from the king," &c. The cases here put
by Hawkins, of a constructive levying of war, do in
terms require force as a constituent part of the
description of the offense.

* 478   * Judge Foster, in his valuable treatise on
treason, states the opinion which has been
quoted from Lord Hale, and differs from that writer
so far as the latter might seem to require swords,
drums, colors, &c., what he terms the pomp and
pageantry of war, as essential circumstances to constitute the fact of levying war. In the cases of
Damaree and Purchase he says, "The want of those
circumstances weighed nothing with the court, although the prisoners' counsel insisted much on that
matter." But he adds, "The number of the insurgents supplied the want of military weapons; and
they were provided with axes, crows, and other tools
of the like nature, proper for the mischief they intended
to effect. *Furor arma ministrat.*"

It is apparent that Judge Foster here alludes to an
assemblage in force, or, as Lord Hale terms it, "in a
warlike posture;" that is, in a condition to attempt
or proceed upon the treason which had been contemplated. The same author afterwards states at large
the cases of Damaree and Purchase, from 8th State
Trials, and they are cases where the insurgents not

only assembled in force, in the posture of war, or in a condition to execute the treasonable design, but they did actually carry it into execution, and did resist the guards who were sent to disperse them.

Judge Foster states, *s. 4*, all insurrections to effect certain innovations of a public and general concern by an armed force, to be, in construction of law, high treason within the clause of levying war.

The cases put by Foster of constructive levying of war, all contain, as a material ingredient, the actual employment of force. After going through this branch of his subject, he proceeds to state the law in a case of actual levying war, that is, where the war is intended directly against the government.

He says, *s. 9*. " An assembly armed and arrayed in a warlike manner for a treasonable purpose, is *bellum levatum*, though not *bellum percussum*. Listing and marching are sufficient overt acts without coming to a battle or action. So cruising on the king's subjects under a French commission, France being then at war with us, was held to be adhering to the king's enemies, though no other act of hostility be proved."

"An assembly armed and arrayed in a warlike manner for any treasonable purpose " is certainly in a state of force ; in a condition to execute the treason for which they assembled. The words "enlisting and marching," which are overt acts of levying war, do, in the arrangement of the sentence, also imply a state of force, though that state is not expressed in terms, for the succeeding words, which state a

particular event as not having happened, prove that
event to have been the next circumstance to those
which had happened; they are, "without coming to a
battle or action." "If men be enlisted and march,"
(that is, if they march prepared for battle, or in a
condition for action, for marching is a technical term
applied to the movement of a military corps,) it is an
overt act of levying war, though they do not come to
a battle or action. This exposition is rendered the

* 479   stronger by what * seems to be put in the
same sentence as a parallel case with respect to adhering to an enemy. It is cruising under a
commission from an enemy, without committing any
other act of hostility. Cruising is the act of sailing
in warlike form, and in a condition to assail those
of whom the cruiser is in quest.

This exposition, which seems to be that intended
by Judge Foster, is rendered the more certain by a
reference to the case in the State Trials from which
the extracts are taken. The words used by the chief
justice are, "When men form themselves into a body,
and march rank and file with weapons offensive and
defensive, this is levying of war with open force, if
the design be public." Mr. Phipps, the counsel for
the prisoner, afterwards observed, "Intending to levy
war is not treason, unless a war be actually levied."
To this the chief justice answered, "Is it not actually
levying of war, if they actually provide arms and levy
men, and in a warlike manner set out and cruise, and
come with a design to destroy our ships?" Mr.
Phipps still insisted, "it would not be an actual levy-

ing of war unless they committed some act of hostility." "Yes, indeed," said the chief justice, "the going on board and being in a posture to attack the king's ships." Mr. Baron Powis added, "But for you to say that because they did not actually fight it is not a levying of war, is it not plain what they did intend? That they came with that intention, that they came in that posture, that they came armed, and had guns and blunderbusses, and surrounded the ship twice ; they came with an armed force, that is a strong evidence of the design."

The point insisted on by counsel in the case of Vaughan, as in this case, was, that war could not be levied without actual fighting. In this the counsel was very properly overruled ; but it is apparent that the judges proceeded entirely on the idea that a warlike posture was indispensable to the fact of levying war.

Judge Foster proceeds to give other instances of levying war. "Attacking the king's forces in opposition to his authority upon a march, or in quarters, is levying war." "Holding a castle or fort against the king or his forces, if actual force be used in order to keep possession, is levying war. But a bare detainer, as suppose by shutting the gates against the king or his forces, without any other force from within, Lord Hale conceiveth will not amount to treason."

The whole doctrine of Judge Foster on this subject, seems to demonstrate a clear opinion that a state of force and violence, a posture of war, must exist to constitute technically, as well as really, the fact of levying war.

Judge Blackstone seems to concur with his predecessors. Speaking of levying war, he says, " This may be done by taking arms not only to dethrone the king, but under pretense to reform religion, or the laws, or to remove evil counsellors, or other grievances, whether real or pretended. For the law does not, neither can it, permit any private man or set of men to interfere forcibly in matters of such high importance."

* *480*   * He proceeds to give examples of levying war, which show that he contemplated actual force as a necessary ingredient in the composition of this crime.

It would seem, then, from the English authorities, that the words " levying war," have not received a technical, different from their natural meaning, so far as respects the character of the assemblage of men which may constitute the fact. It must be a warlike assemblage, carrying the appearance of force, and in a situation to practice hostility.

Several judges of the United States have given opinions at their circuits on this subject, all of which deserve and will receive the particular attention of this court.

In his charge to the grand jury, when John Fries was indicted, in consequence of a forcible opposition to the direct tax, Judge Iredell is understood to have said, " I think I am warranted in saying, that if in the case of the insurgents who may come under your consideration, the intention was to prevent by force of arms the execution of any act of the Congress of the United States altogether, any forcible opposition calculated to carry that intention into effect was a levying of war against the United States, and of course an act of treason."   To levy war, then, according to this opinion of Judge Iredell, required the actual exertion of force.

Judge Paterson, in his opinions delivered in two different cases, seems not to differ from Judge Iredell. He does not, indeed, precisely state the employment of force as necessary to constitute a levying of war, but in giving his opinion in cases in which force was actually employed, he considers the crime in one case as dependent on the intention, and in the other case he says, "Combining these facts, with this design," (that is, combining actual force with a treasonable design,) "the crime is high treason."

Judge Peters has also indicated the opinion that force was necessary to constitute the crime of levying war.

Judge Chase has been particularly clear and explicit. In an opinion which he appears to have prepared on great consideration, he says, "The court are of opinion, that if a body of people conspire and meditate an insurrection to resist or oppose the execution of a statute of the United States by force, that they are only guilty of a high misdemeanor ; but if they proceed to carry such intention into execution by force, that they are guilty of the treason of levying war ; and the *quantum* of the force employed neither increases nor diminishes the crime ; whether by one hundred or one thousand persons, is wholly immaterial.

"The court are of opinion, that a combination or

conspiracy to levy war against the United States is not treason, unless combined with an attempt to carry such combination or conspiracy into execution : some actual force or violence must be used in pursuance of such design to levy war ; but that it is altogether immaterial whether the force used be sufficient to effectuate the object. Any force connected with the intention will constitute the crime of levying of war."

In various parts of the opinion delivered by Judge Chase, in the case * of *Fries*, the same sentiments are to be found. It is to be observed, that these judges are not content that troops should be assembled in a condition to employ force ; according to them, some degree of force must have been actually employed.

* *481*

The judges of the United States, then, so far as their opinions have been quoted, seem to have required still more to constitute the fact of levying war, than has been required by the English books. Our judges seem to have required the actual exercise of force, the actual employment of some degree of violence. This, however, may be, and probably is, because in the cases in which their opinions were given, the design not having been to overturn the government, but to resist the execution of a law, such an assemblage would be sufficient for the purpose, as to require the actual employment of force to render the object unequivocal.

But it is said, all these authorities have been overruled by the decision of the Supreme Court in the case of the *United States against Swartwout and Bollman.*

If the Supreme Court have indeed extended the doctrine of treason further than it has heretofore been carried by the judges of England, or of this country, their decision would be submitted to. At least, this court could go no further than to endeavor again to bring the point directly before them. It would, however, be expected that an opinion which is to overrule all former precedents, and to establish a principle never before recognized, should be expressed in plain and explicit terms. A mere implication ought not to prostrate a principle which seems to have been so well established. Had the intention been entertained to make so material a change in this respect, the court ought to have expressly declared, that any assemblage of men whatever, who had formed a treasonable design, whether in force or not, whether in a condition to attempt the design or not, whether attended with warlike appearances or not, constitutes the fact of levying war. Yet no declaration to this amount is made. Not an expression of the kind is to be found in the opinion of the Supreme Court. The foundation on which this argument rests is the omission of the court to state, that the assemblage which constitutes the fact of levying war ought to be in force, and some passages which show that the question respecting the nature of the assemblage was not in the mind of the court when the opinion was drawn, which passages are mingled with others, which at least show that there was no intention to depart from the course of the precedents in cases of treason by levying war.

Every opinion, to be correctly understood, ought

to be considered with a view to the case in which it was delivered. In the case of the *United States against Bollman and Swartwout,* there was no evidence that even two men had ever met for the purpose of executing the plan, in which those persons were charged with having participated. It was, therefore, sufficient for the court to say, that unless men were assembled, war could not be levied. That case was decided by this declaration. The court might, indeed, have defined the species of assemblage *which would amount to levying of war; *but, as this opinion was not a treatise on treason, but a decision of a particular case, expressions of doubtful import should be construed in reference to the case itself; and the mere omission to state that a particular circumstance was necessary to the consummation of the crime, ought not to be construed into a declaration that the circumstance was unimportant. General expressions ought not to be considered as overruling settled principles, without a direct declaration to that effect. After these preliminary observations the court will proceed to examine the opinion which has occasioned them.

* 482

The first expression in it bearing on the present question is, "To constitute that specific crime for which the prisoner now before the court has been committed, war must be actually levied against the United States. However flagitious may be the crime of conspiracy to subvert by force the government of our country, such conspiracy is not treason. To conspire to levy war, and actually to levy war, are distinct offences.   The first must be brought into operation by the assemblage of men for a purpose treasonable in itself, or the fact of levying war cannot have been committed."

Although it is not expressly stated that the assemblage of men for the purpose of carrying into operation the treasonable intent, which will amount to levying war, must be an assemblage in force, yet it is fairly to be inferred from the context, and nothing like dispensing with force appears in this paragraph. The expressions are, "To constitute the crime, war must be actually levied."   A conspiracy to levy war is spoken of as "a conspiracy to subvert by force the government of our country."   Speaking in general terms of an assemblage of men for this, or for any other purpose, a person would naturally be understood as speaking of an assemblage in some degree adapted to the purpose.   An assemblage to subvert by force the government of our country, and amounting to a levying of war, should be an assemblage in force.

In a subsequent paragraph, the court says, "It is not the intention of the court to say, that no individual can be guilty of this crime who has not appeared in arms against his country.   On the contrary, if war be actually levied, that is, if a body of men be actually assembled in order to effect by force a treasonable purpose, all those who perform any part, however minute, etc., and who are actually, leagued in the general conspiracy, are traitors.   But there must be an actual assembling of men for the treasonable purpose, to constitute a levying of war.

The observations made on the preceding paragraph apply to this. " A body of men actually assembled, in order to effect by force a treasonable purpose," must be a body assembled with such appearance of force as would warrant the opinion that they were assembled for the particular purpose ; an assemblage to constitute an actual levying of war, should be an assemblage with such appearance of force as would justify the opinion that they met for the purpose.

This explanation, which is believed to be the natural, certainly not a strained, explanation of the words, derives some additional aid from the * *483* *terms in which the paragraph last quoted commences. " It is not the intention of the court to say that no individual can be guilty of treason who has not appeared in arms against his country." These words seem to obviate an inference which might otherwise have been drawn from the preceding paragraph. They indicate that in the mind of the court the assemblage stated in that paragraph was an assemblage in arms. That the individuals who composed it had appeared in arms against their country. That is, in other words, that the assemblage was a military, a warlike assemblage.

The succeeding paragraph in the opinion relates to a conspiracy, and serves to show that force and violence were in the mind of the court, and that there was no idea of extending the crime of treason by construction beyond the constitutional definition which had been given of it.

Returning to the case actually before the court, it

is said, "A design to overturn the government of the United States in New Orleans by force, would have been unquestionably a design which, if carried into execution, would have been treason, and the assemblage of a body of men for the purpose of carrying it into execution would amount to levying of war against the United States."

Now what could reasonably be said to be an assemblage of a body of men for the purpose of overturning the government of the United States in New Orleans by force? Certainly an assemblage in force; an assemblage prepared and intending to act with force; a military assemblage.

The decisions theretofore made by the judges of the United States, are then declared to be in conformity with the principles laid down by the Supreme Court. Is this declaration compatible with the idea of departing from those opinions on a point within the contemplation of the court? The opinions of Judge Paterson and Judge Iredell are said "to imply an actual assembling of men, though they rather designed to remark on the purpose to which the force was to be applied than on the nature of the force itself." This observation certainly indicates that the necessity of an assemblage of men was the particular point the court meant to establish, and that the idea of force was never separated from this assemblage.

The opinion of Judge Chase is next quoted with approbation. This opinion, in terms, requires the employment of force.

After stating the verbal communications said to

have been made by Mr. Swartwout to General Wilkinson, the court says, "If these words import that the government of New Orleans was to be revolutionized by force, although merely as a step to, or a means of, executing some greater projects, the design was unquestionably treasonable, and any assemblage of men for that purpose would amount to a levying of war."

The words "any assemblage of men," if construed to affirm that any two or three of the conspirators who might be found together after this plan had been formed, would be the act of levying war, would certainly be misconstrued. The sense of the expression *484 "any assemblage of * men," is restricted by the words "for this purpose." Now, could it be in the contemplation of the court that a body of men would assemble for the purpose of revolutionizing New Orleans by force, who should not themselves be in force?

After noticing some difference of opinion among the judges respecting the import of the words said to have been used by Mr. Swartwout, the court proceeds to observe, "But whether this treasonable intention be really imputable to the plan or not, it is admitted that it must have been carried into execution by an open assemblage for that purpose, previous to the arrest of the prisoner, in order to consummate the crime as to him."

Could the court have conceived "an open assemblage," "for the purpose of overturning the government of New Orleans by force," "to be only equivalent to a secret furtive assemblage without the appearance of force."

After quoting the words of Mr. Swartwout, from the affidavit, in which it was stated that Mr. Burr was levying an army of 7,000 men, and observing, that the treason to be inferred from these words would depend on the intention with which it was levied, and on the progress which had been made in levying it, the court say, "The question, then, is, whether this evidence proves Colonel Burr to have advanced so far in levying an army as actually to have assembled them."

Actually to assemble an army of 7,000 men is unquestionably to place those who are so assembled in a state of open force.

But as the mode of expression used in this passage might be misconstrued so far as to countenance the opinion that it would be necessary to assemble the whole army in order to constitute the fact of levying war, the court proceeds to say, "It is argued that since it cannot be necessary that the whole 7,000 men should be assembled, their commencing their march by detachments to the place of rendezvous must be sufficient to constitute the crime."

"This position is correct with some qualification. It cannot be necessary that the whole army should assemble, and that the various parts which are to compose it should have combined. But it is necessary there should be an actual assemblage ; and, therefore, this evidence should make the fact unequivocal.

"The traveling of individuals to the place of rendez-

vous would, perhaps, not be sufficient. This would
be an equivocal act, and has no warlike appearance.
The meeting of particular bodies of men, and their
marching from places of partial to a place of general
rendezvous, would be such an assemblage."

The position here stated by the counsel for the
prosecution is, that the army "commencing its march
by detachments to the place of rendezvous (that is,
of the army), must be sufficient to constitute the
crime."

This position is not admitted by the court to be
universally correct. It is said to be "correct with
some qualification." What is that qualification?

*485   * "The traveling of individuals to the
place of rendezvous" (and by this term is
not to be understood one individual by himself, but
several individuals, either separately or together, but
not in military form) "would, perhaps, not be sufficient." Why not sufficient? "Because," says the
court, "this would be an equivocal act, and has no
warlike appearance." The act, then, should be unequivocal, and should have a warlike appearance.
It must exhibit, in the words of Sir Mathew Hale,
speciem belli, the appearance of war.

This construction is rendered in some measure
necessary when we observe that the court in qualify-
ing the position, "That the army commencing their
march by detachments to the place of rendezvous
must be sufficient to constitute the crime." In quali-
fying this position they say, "The traveling of
individuals would, perhaps, not be sufficient." Now

a solitary individual traveling to any point, with any intent, could not, without a total disregard of language, be termed a marching detachment. The court, therefore, must have contemplated several individuals traveling together ; and the words being used in reference to the position they were intended to qualify, would seem to indicate the distinction between the appearances attending the usual movement of a company of men for civil purposes, and that military movement which might, in correct language, be denominated " marching by detachments."

The court then proceeded to say, " The meeting of particular bodies of men, and their marching from places of partial to a place of general rendezvous, would be such an assemblage."

It is obvious, from the context, that the court must have intended to state a case which would in itself be unequivocal, because it would have a warlike appearance. The case stated is that of distinct bodies of men assembling at different places, and marching from these places of partial to a place of general rendezvous. When this has been done, an assemblage is produced which would in itself be unequivocal. But when is it done ? what is the assemblage here described ? The assemblage formed of the different bodies of partial at a general place of rendezvous. In describing the mode of coming to this assemblage, the civil term " traveling" is dropped, and the military term " marching " is employed. If this was intended as a definition of an assemblage which would amount to levying war, the definition requires an assemblage at a general place of rendezvous composed of bodies of men who had previously assembled at places of partial rendezvous. But this is not intended as a definition, for clearly if there should be no places of partial rendezvous, if troops should embody in the first instance, in great force for the purpose of subverting the government by violence, the act would be unequivocal, it would have a warlike appearance, and it would, according to the opinion of the Supreme Court, properly construed, and according to the English authorities, amount to levying war. But this, though not a definition, is put as an example; and surely it may be safely taken as an example. If different bodies of men, in pursuance of a treasonable design, plainly proved, should assemble in warlike appearance at places of partial rendezvous, and should march from those places to

*486

a place of general rendezvous, it is difficult * to conceive how such a transaction could take place without exhibiting the appearance of war, without an obvious display of force. At any rate, a court in stating generally such a military assemblage as would amount to levying war, and having a case before them in which there was no assemblage whatever, cannot reasonably be understood, in putting such an example, to dispense with those appearances of war which seem to be required by the general current of authorities. Certainly they ought not to be so understood when they say, in express terms, that " it is more safe, as well as more consonant to the principles of our constitution, that

the crime of treason should not be extended by construction to doubtful cases ; and that crimes not
already within the constitutional definition, should
receive such punishment as the legislature in its
wisdom may provide."

After this analysis of the opinion of the Supreme
Court, it will be observed, that the direct question,
whether an assemblage of men which might be construed to amount to a levying of war, must appear in
force or in military form, was not in argument or in
fact before the court, and does not appear to have
been in terms decided.   The opinion seems to have
been drawn without particularly adverting to this
question, and, therefore, upon a transient view of
particular expressions, might inspire the idea that a
display of force, that appearances of war, were not
necessary ingredients to constitute the fact of levying
war.   But upon a more intent and more accurate
investigation of this opinion, although the terms
force and violence are not employed as descriptive of
the assemblage, such requisites are declared to be
indispensable as can scarcely exist without the appearance of war, and the existence of real force.   It is
said that war must be levied in fact; that the object
must be one which is to be effected by force ; that
the assemblage must be such as to prove that this is
its object ; that it must not be an equivocal act, without a warlike appearance ; that it must be an open
assemblage for the purpose of force.   In the course
of this opinion, decisions are quoted and approved,
which require the employment of force to constitute

the crime. It seems extremely difficult, if not impossible, to reconcile these various declarations with the idea that the Supreme Court considered a secret, unarmed meeting, although that meeting be of conspirators, and although it met with a treasonable intent, as an actual levying of war. Without saying that the assemblage must be in force or in warlike form, they express themselves so as to show that this idea was never discarded, and they use terms which cannot be otherwise satisfied.

The opinion of a single judge certainly weighs as nothing if opposed to that of the Supreme Court; but if he was one of the judges who assisted in framing that opinion, if while the impression under which it was framed was yet fresh upon his mind, he delivered an opinion on the same testimony, not contradictory to that which had been given by all the judges together, but showing the sense in which he understood terms that might be differently expounded, it may fairly be said to be in some measure explanatory of the opinion itself.

*487   * To the judge before whom the charge against the prisoner at the bar was first brought, the same testimony was offered with that which had been exhibited before the Supreme Court, and he was required to give an opinion in almost the same case. Upon this occasion, he said, " War can only be levied by the employment of actual force. Troops must be embodied; men must be assembled in order to levy war." Again, he observed, " The fact to be proved in this case, is an act of public

notoriety. It must exist in the view of the world, or
it cannot exist at all. The assembling of forces to
levy war is a visible transaction, and numbers must
witness it."

It is not easy to doubt what kind of assemblage
was in the mind of the judge who used these expressions, and it is to be recollected that he had just
returned from the Supreme Court, and was speaking
on the very facts on which the opinion of that court
was delivered.

The same judge, in his charge to the grand jury
who found this bill, observed, " To constitute the
fact of levying war, it is not necessary that hostilities
shall have actually commenced by engaging the military force of the United States, or that measures of
violence against the government shall have been carried into execution. But levying war is a fact, in the
constitution of which force is an indispensable ingredient. Any combination to subvert, by force, the
government of the United States, violently to dismember the union, to compel a change in the administration, to coerce the repeal or adoption of a general
law, is a conspiracy to levy war, and if the conspiracy
be carried into effect by the actual employment of
force, by the embodying and assembling of men for
the purpose of executing the treasonable design
which was previously conceived, it amounts to levying of war. It has been held that arms are not
essential to levying war provided the force assembled
be sufficient to attain, or perhaps to justify attempting, the object without them." This paragraph is

immediately followed by a reference to the opinion.
of the Supreme Court.

It requires no commentary upon these words to
show that, in the opinion of the judge who uttered
them, an assemblage of men which should constitute
the fact of levying war must be an assemblage in
force, and that he so understood the opinion of the
Supreme Court. If in that opinion there may be
found in some passages, a want of precision, and in-
definiteness of expression, which has occasioned it to
be differently understood by different persons, that
may well be accounted for, when it is recollected that
in the particular case there was no assemblage whatever. In expounding that opinion the whole should
be taken together, and in reference to the particular
case in which it was delivered. It is, however, not
improbable that the misunderstanding has arisen
from this circumstance. The court, unquestionably,
did not consider arms as an indispensable requisite to
levying war; an assemblage adapted to the object
might be in a condition to effect or to attempt it
without them. Nor did the court consider the actual
application * of the force to the object, at all
times, an indispensable requisite; for an assemblage might be in a condition to apply force,
might be in a state adapted to real war, without having made the actual application of that force. From
these positions, which are to be found in the opinion, it
may have been inferred, it is thought too hastily, that
the nature of the assemblage was unimportant,
and that war might be considered as actually levied

* 488

by any meeting of men, if a criminal intention can be imputed to them by testimony of any kind whatever.

It has been thought proper to discuss this question at large, and to review the opinion of the Supreme Court, although this court would be more disposed to leave the question of fact, whether an overt act of levying war was committed on Blennerhassett's island to the jury under this explanation of the law, and to instruct them, that unless the assemblage on Blennerhassett's island was an assemblage in force; was a military assemblage in a condition to make war, it was not a levying of war, and that they could not construe it into an act of war, than to arrest the further testimony which might be offered to connect the prisoner with that assemblage, or to prove the intention of those who assembled together at that place. This point, however, is not to be understood as decided. It will, perhaps, constitute an essential inquiry in another case.

Before leaving the opinion of the Supreme Court entirely on the question of the nature of the assemblage which will constitute an act of levying war, this court cannot forbear to ask, why is an assemblage absolutely required? Is it not to judge in some measure of the end by the proportion which the means bear to the end? Why is it that a single armed individual, entering a boat and sailing down the Ohio, for the avowed purpose of attacking New Orleans, could not be said to levy war? Is it not that he is apparently not in a condition to levy war? If this be so, ought not the assemblage to furnish some evidence of its intention and capacity to levy war before it can amount to levying war? And ought not the Supreme Court, when speaking of an assemblage for the purpose of effecting a treasonable object by force, be understood to indicate an assemblage exhibiting the appearance of force.

The definition of the attorney for the United States deserves notice in this respect. It is, "When there is an assemblage of men convened for the purpose of effecting by force a treasonable object, which force is meant to be employed before the assemblage disperses, this is treason."

To read this definition without adverting to the argument, we should infer that the assemblage was itself to effect by force the treasonable object, not to join itself to some other bodies of men, and then to effect the object by their combined force. Under this construction it would be expected the appearance of the assemblage would bear some proportion to the object, and would indicate the intention. At any rate, that it would be an assemblage in force. This construction is most certainly not that which was intended, but it serves to show that general * *489* phrases must always be understood in reference to the subject matter, and to the general principles of law.

On that division of the subject which respects the merits of the case connected with the pleadings, two points are also made.

1st. That this indictment, having charged the prisoner with levying war on Blennerhassett's island, and

containing no other overt act, cannot be supported
by proof that war was levied at that place by other
persons, in the absence of the prisoner, even admitting those persons to be connected with him in one
common treasonable conspiracy.

2d. That admitting such an indictment could be
supported by such evidence, the previous conviction
of some person who committed the act which is said
to amount to levying war, is indispensable to the conviction of a person who advised or procured that act.

As to the first point, the indictment contains two
counts, one of which charges that the prisoner, with
a number of persons unknown, levied war on Blennerhassett's island, in the county of Wood, in the district
of Virginia ; and the other adds the circumstance of
their proceeding from that island down the river, for
the purpose of seizing New Orleans by force.

In point of fact, the prisoner was not on Blennerhassett's island, nor in the county of Wood, nor in
the district of Virginia.

In considering this point the court is led first to
inquire whether an indictment for levying war must
specify an overt act, or would be sufficient if it
merely charged the prisoner in general terms with
having levied war, omitting the expression of place
or circumstance.

The place in which a crime was committed is essential to an indictment, were it only to show the jurisdiction of the court. It is also essential for the
purpose of enabling the prisoner to make his defense.
That, at common law, an indictment would have been

defective which did not mention the place in which
the crime was committed, can scarcely be doubted.
For this, it is sufficient to refer to *Hawkins, b. 2, c. 25,
sect. 84,* and *c. 23, sect. 91.*   This necessity is rendered
the stronger by the constitutional provision that the
offender "shall be tried in the state and district
wherein the crime shall have been committed," and
by the act of Congress which requires that twelve
petty jurors at least shall be summoned from the
county where the offense was committed.

A description of the particular manner in which the
war was levied seems also essential to enable the accused to make his defense.   The law does not expect
a man to be prepared to defend every act of his life
which may be suddenly and without notice alleged
against him.   In common justice, the particular fact
with which he is charged ought to be stated, and
stated in such a manner as to afford a reasonable cer-
tainty of the nature of the accusation, and the circumstances which will be adduced against him.   The
general doctrine on the subject of indictments is full
to this point.   *Foster, p. 149,* speaking of the treason
of compassing the King's death, says, " From what
has been said it followeth that in every indictment
*490   for this species of treason, and indeed * for
          levying war and adhering to the King's ene-
mies, an overt act must be alleged and proved.   For
the overt act is the charge to which the prisoner must
apply his defense."

In *p. 220,* Foster repeats this declaration.   It is
also laid down in *Hawk, b. 8, c. 17, sect. 29; 1 Hale,*

121; 1 East, 116, and by the other authorities cited, especially *Vaughan's Case.* In corroboration of this opinion, it may be observed, that treason can only be established by the proof of overt acts, and that by the common law as well as by the statute of 7 of William III. those overt acts only which are charged in the indictment can be given in evidence, unless, perhaps, as corroborative testimony after the overt acts are proved. That clause in the constitution, too, which says that in all criminal prosecutions the accused shall enjoy the right "to be informed of the nature and cause of the accusation," is considered as having a direct bearing on this point. It secures to him such information as will enable him to prepare for his defense.

It seems, then, to be perfectly clear, that it would not be sufficient for an indictment to allege generally that the accused had levied war against the United States. The charge must be more particularly specified by laying what is termed an overt act of levying war. The law relative to an appeal, as cited from Stamford, is strongly corroborative of this opinion.

If it be necessary to specify the charge in the indictment, it would seem to follow, irresistibly, that the charge must be proved as laid.

All the authorities which require an overt act, require also that this overt act should be proved. The decision in Vaughan's Case is particularly in point. Might it be otherwise, the charge of an overt act would be a mischief instead of an advantage to the accused. It would lead him from the true cause and nature of the accusation instead of informing him respecting it.

But it is contended on the part of the prosecution that, although the accused had never been with the party which assembled at Blennerhassett's island, and was, at the time, at a great distance, and in a different state, he was yet legally present, and, therefore, may properly be charged in the indictment as being present in fact.

It is, therefore, necessary to inquire whether in this case the doctrine of constructive presence can apply.

It is conceived by the court to be possible that a person may be concerned in a treasonable conspiracy, and yet be legally, as well as actually absent, while some one act of the treason is perpetrated. If a rebellion should be so extensive as to spread through every state in the union, it will scarcely be contended that every individual concerned in it is legally present at every overt act committed in the course of that rebellion. It would be a very violent presumption indeed, too violent to be made without clear authority, to presume that even the chief of the rebel army was legally present at every such overt act. If the main rebel army with the chief at its head, should be prosecuting war at one extremity of our territory, say in New Hampshire, if this chief should be there captured and sent to the other extremity for the purpose of *trial, if his indictment, instead of alleging

*491   an overt act which was true in point of fact, should allege that he had assembled some small party, which, in truth, he had not seen, and had levied war

by engaging in a skirmish in Georgia at a time when in reality he was fighting a battle in New Hampshire, if such evidence would support such an indictment, by the fiction that he was legally present though really absent, all would ask to what purpose are those provisions in the constitution which direct the place of trial, and ordain that the accused shall be informed of the nature and cause of the accusation?

But that a man may be legally absent who has counselled or procured a treasonable act, is proved by all those books which treat upon the subject, and which concur in declaring that such a person is a principal traitor, not because he was legally present, but because in treason all are principals. Yet the indictment, upon general principles, would charge him according to the truth of the case. Lord Coke says: "If many conspire to levy war, and some of them do levy the same according to the conspiracy, this is high treason in all." Why? Because all were legally present when the war was levied? No. "For in treason," continues Lord Coke, "all be principals, and war is levied." In this case the indictment, reasoning from analogy, would not charge that the absent conspirators were present, but would state the truth of the case. If the conspirator had done nothing which amounted to levying of war, and if, by our constitution, the doctrine that an accessory becomes a principal be not adopted, in consequence of which the conspirator could not be condemned under an indictment stating the truth of the case, it would be going very far to say that this defect, if it be termed one, may be cured by an indictment stating the case untruly.

This doctrine of Lord Coke has been adopted by all subsequent writers; and it is generally laid down in the English books, that whatever will make a man an accessory in felony, will make him a principal in treason; but it is nowhere suggested that he is by construction to be considered as present when in point of fact he was absent.

Foster has been particularly quoted, and certainly he is precisely in point. "It is well known," says Foster, "that in the language of the law there are no accessories in high treason; all are principals. Every instance of incitement, aid, or protection, which in the case of felony will render a man an accessory before or after the fact, in the case of high treason, whether it be treason at common law or by statute, will make him a principal in treason. The cases of incitement and aid are cases put as examples of a man's becoming a principal in treason, not because he was legally present, but by force of that maxim in the common law, that whatever will render a man an accessory to common law will render him a principal in treason." In other passages the words "command" or "procure" are used to indicate the same state of things, that is, a treasonable assemblage produced by a man who is not himself in that assemblage.

In point of law, then, the man who incites, aids, or
*492   procures a treasonable * act, is not, merely in consequence of that incitement, aid or procurement, legally present when that act is committed.

If it does not result from the nature of the crime, that all who are concerned in it are legally present at every overt act, then each case depends upon its own circumstances, and to judge how far the circumstances of any case can make him legally present who is in fact absent, the doctrine of constructive presence must be examined.

Hale, in his *1st vol. p. 615,* says : "Regularly no man can be a principal in felony unless he be present." In the same page he says : "An accessory before, is he that being absent at the time of the felony committed, doth yet procure, counsel, or command another to commit a felony." The books are full of passages which state this to be the law. Foster, in showing what acts of concurrence will make a man a principal, says, "He must be present at the perpetration, otherwise he can be no more than an accessory before the fact."

These strong distinctions would be idle, at any rate they would be inapplicable to treason, if they were to be entirely lost in the doctrine of constructive presence.

Foster adds, *p. 349 :* "When the law requireth the presence of the accomplice at the perpetration of the fact in order to render him a principal, it doth not require a strict actual immediate presence, such a presence as would make him an eye or ear witness of what passeth." The terms used by Foster are such as would be employed by a man intending to show the necessity that the absent person should be near at hand, although, from the nature of the thing, no

precise distance could be marked out.   An inspection
of the cases from which Foster drew this general principle will serve to illustrate it.   (See *Hale, 439.*)   In
all these cases, put by Hale, the whole party set out
together to commit the very fact charged in the indictment, or to commit some other unlawful act, in
which they are all to be personally concerned at the
same time and place, and are, at the very time when
the criminal fact is committed, near enough to give
actual personal aid and assistance to the man who
perpetrated it.   *Hale, in p. 449*, giving the reason for
the decision in the case of the *Lord Dacres*, says :
" They all came with an intent to steal the deer, and,
consequently, the law supposes that they came all
with the intent to oppose all that should hinder
them in that design."   The original case says this
was their resolution.   This opposition would be a
personal opposition.   This case, even as stated by
Hale, would clearly not comprehend any man who
entered into the combination, but who, instead of
going to the park where the murder was committed,
should not set out with the others, should go to a
different park, or should even lose his way.   (See
Hale, 534.)

In both the cases here stated, the persons actually
set out together, and were near enough to assist in
the commission of the fact.   That in the case of
Pudsy the felony was, as stated by Hale, a different
felony from that originally intended, is unimportant
in regard to the particular principle now under consideration, so far as respected distance ; as respected

capacity to assist in case of resistance, it is the same
as if the * robbery had been that which was
* 493   originally designed.   The case in the original report shows that the felony committed was in
fact in pursuance of that originally designed. *Foster,
350,* plainly supposes the same particular design, not
a general design composed of many particular distinct
facts.   He supposes them to be co-operating with
respect to that particular design.   This may be illustrated by a case which is perhaps common.   Suppose
a band of robbers confederated for the general purpose of robbing.   They set out together, or in parties,
to rob a particular individual, and each performs the
part assigned to him.   Some ride up to the individual
and demand his purse, others watch out of sight to
intercept those who might be coming to assist the
man on whom the robbery is to be committed.   If
murder or robbery actually take place, all are principals, and all, in construction of law, are present.   But
suppose they set out at the same time, or at different
times, by different roads, to attack and rob different
individuals or different companies ; to commit distinct
acts of robbery.   It has never been contended that
those who committed one act of robbery, or who failed
altogether, were constructively present at the act of
those who were associated with them in the common
object of robbery, who were to share the plunder, but
who did not assist at the particular fact.   They do
indeed belong to the general party, but they are not
of the particular party which committed this fact.
Foster concludes this subject by observing, that "in

order to render a person an accomplice and a principal in felony, he must be aiding and abetting at the
fact, or ready to afford assistance if necessary." That
is, at the particular fact which is charged, he must be
ready to render assistance to those who are committing that particular fact; he must, as is stated by
Hawkins, be ready to give immediate and direct
assistance.

All the cases to be found in the books go to the
same point. Let them be applied to that under
consideration.

The whole treason laid in this indictment is the
levying of war in Blennerhassett's island, and the
whole question to which the inquiry of the court is
now directed is, whether the prisoner was legally
present at that fact.

I say this is the whole question, because the prisoner can only be convicted on the overt act laid in
the indictment. With respect to this prosecution, it
is as if no other overt act existed. If other overt acts
can be inquired into, it is for the sole purpose of proving the particular fact charged; it is as evidence of
the crime consisting of this particular fact, not as
establishing the general crime by a distinct fact.

The counsel for the prosecution have charged those
engaged in the defense with considering the overt act
as the treason, whereas it ought to be considered
solely as the evidence of the treason; but the counsel
for the prosecution seem themselves not to have sufficiently adverted to this clear principle, that though
the overt act may not be itself the treason, it is the

sole act of that treason which can produce conviction.   It is the sole point in issue between the parties.
And the only division * of that point, if the
494   expression be allowed, which the court is
now examining, is the constructive presence of the
prisoner at the fact charged.

To return, then, to the application of the cases.

Had the prisoner set out with the party from
Beaver for Blennerhassett's island, or, perhaps, had
he set out for that place, though not from Beaver,
and had arrived in the island, he would have been
present at the fact; had he not arrived in the island,
but had taken a position near enough to co-operate
with those on the island, to assist them in any act of
hostility, or to aid them if attacked, the question
whether he was constructively present would be a
question compounded of law and fact, which would
be decided by the jury, with the aid of the court, so
far as respected the law.   In this case the accused
would have been of the particular party assembled on
the island, and would have been associated with them
in the particular act of levying war said to have been
committed on the island.

But if he was not with the party at any time before
they reached the island ; if he did not join them there,
or intend to join them there ; if his personal co-operation in the general plan was to be afforded elsewhere,
at a great distance, in a different state ; if the overt
acts of treason to be performed by him were to be
distinct overt acts, then he was not of the particular
party assembled at Blennerhassett's island, and was

not constructively present, aiding and assisting in the particular act which was there committed.

The testimony on this point, so far as it has been delivered, is not equivocal. There is not only no evidence that the accused was of the particular party which assembled on Blennerhassett's island, but the whole evidence shows he was not of that party.

In felony, then, admitting the crime to have been completed on the island, and to have been advised, procured, or commanded by the accused, he would have been incontestibly an accessory, and not a principal.

But in treason, it is said, the law is otherwise, because the theatre of action is more extensive.

This reasoning applies in England as strongly as in the United States. While in '15 and '45 the family of Stuart sought to regain the crown they had forfeited, the struggle was for the whole kingdom; yet no man was ever considered as legally present at one place, when actually at another; or as aiding in one transaction, while actually employed in another.

With the perfect knowledge that the whole nation may be the theatre of action, the English books unite in declaring, that he who counsels, procures, or aids treason, is guilty accessorily, and solely in virtue of the common law principle, that what will make a man an accessory in felony makes him a principal in treason. So far from considering a man as constructively present at every overt act of the general treason in which he may have been concerned, the whole doctrine of the books limits the proof against him to those particular overt acts of levying war with which he is charged.

* 495   * What would be the effect of a different doctrine? Clearly that which has been stated. If a person levying war in Kentucky may be said to be constructively present and assembled with a party carrying on war in Virginia, at a great distance from him, then he is present at every overt act performed anywhere; he may be tried in any state on the continent, where any overt act has been committed; he may be proved to be guilty of an overt act laid in the indictment in which he had no personal participation, by proving that he advised it, or that he committed other acts.

This is, perhaps, too extravagant to be in terms maintained. Certainly it cannot be supported by the doctrines of the English law.

The opinion of Judge Paterson, in *Mitchell's Case,* has been cited on this point. *2 Dall. 348.*

The indictment is not specially stated; but from the case as reported, it must have been either general for levying war in the county of Alleghany, and the overt act laid must have been the assemblage of men and levying of war in that county; or it must have given a particular detail of the treasonable transactions in that county. The first supposition is the most probable; but let the indictment be in the one form or the other, and the result is the same. The facts of the case are, that a large body of men, of whom Mitchell was one, assembled at Braddock's field, in the county of Alleghany, for the purpose of

committing acts of violence at Pittsburgh. That
there was also an assemblage at a different time at
Couches fort, at which the prisoner also attended.
The general and avowed object of that meeting was
to concert measures for resisting the execution of a
public law. At Couches fort the resolution was taken
to attack the house of the inspector, and the body
there assembled marched to that house and attacked
it. It was proved by the competent number of witnesses, that he was at Couches fort armed; that he
offered to reconnoitre the house to be attacked; that
he marched with the insurgents towards the house;
that he was with them after the action, attending the
body of one of his comrades who was killed in it;
one witness swore positively that he was present at
the burning of the house, and a second witness said
that "it ran in his head that he had seen him there."
That a doubt should exist in such a case as this, is
strong evidence of the necessity that the overt act
should be unequivocally proved by two witnesses.

But what was the opinion of the judge in this case?
Couches fort and Neville's house being in the same
county, the assemblage having been at Couches fort,
and the resolution to attack the house having been
there taken, the body having for the avowed purpose
moved in execution of that resolution towards the
house to be attacked, he inclined to think that the act
of marching was in itself levying war. If it was, then
the overt act laid in the indictment was consummated
by the assemblage at Couches, and the marching
from thence, and Mitchell was proved to be guilty by

more than two positive witnesses.   But without deciding this to be the law, he proceeded to consider
496   the meeting * at Couches, the immediate
     marching to Neville's house, and the attack
and burning of the house, as one transaction. Mitchell
was proved by more than two positive witnesses to
have been in that transaction, to have taken an active
part in it, and the judge declared it to be unnecessary
that all should have seen him at the same time and
place.

But suppose not a single witness had proved
Mitchell to have been at Couches, or on the march,
or at Neville's. Suppose he had been at the time
notoriously absent in a different state.   Can it be believed by any person who observes the caution with
which Judge Paterson required the constitutional
proof of two witnesses to the same overt act, that he
would have said Mitchell was constructively present,
and might, on that straining of a legal fiction, be
found guilty of treason?   Had he delivered such an
opinion, what would have been the language of this
country respecting it?   Had he given this opinion, it
would have required all the correctness of his life to
strike his name from that bloody list in which the
name of Jefferies is enrolled.

But to estimate the opinion in *Mitchell's Case,* let
its circumstances be transferred to *Burr's Case.* Suppose the body of men assembled in Blennerhassett's
island had previously met at some other place in the
same county, and that Burr had been proved to be
with them by four witnesses; that the resolution to

march to Blennerhassett's island for a treasonable
purpose had been there taken ; that he had been seen
on the march with them ; that one witness had seen
him on the island ; that another thought he had
seen him there ; that he had been seen with the party
directly after leaving the island ; that this indictment
had charged the levying of war in Wood county
generally ; the cases would then have been perfectly
parallel, and the decisions would have been the
same.

In conformity with principle and with authority,
then, the prisoner at the bar was neither legally nor
actually present at Blennerhassett's island ; and the
court is strongly inclined to the opinion, that, without
proving an actual or legal presence by two witnesses,
the overt act laid in this indictment cannot be proved.

But this opinion is controverted on two grounds.

The first is, that the indictment does not charge
the prisoner to have been present.

The second, that although he was absent, yet, if he
caused the assemblage, he may be indicted as being
present, and convicted on evidence that he caused the
treasonable act.

The first position is to be decided by the indictment itself.   The court understands the allegation
differently from the attorney for the United States.
The court understands it to be directly charged, that
the prisoner did assemble with the multitude, and did
march with them.   Nothing will more clearly test this
construction than putting the case into a shape which
it may possibly take.   Suppose the law to be that

the indictment would be defective unless it alleged
the presence of the * person indicted at the
*497   act of treason.   If upon a special verdict
facts should be found which amounted to a levying
of war by the accused, and his counsel should insist
that he could not be condemned because the indictment was defective in not charging that he was himself one of the assemblage which constituted the
treason, or because it alleged the procurement de-
fectively, would the attorney admit this construction
of his indictment to be correct?   I am persuaded
that he would not, and that he ought not to make
such a concession.   If, after a verdict, the indictment
ought to be construed to allege that the prisoner was
one of the assemblage at Blennerhassett's island, it
ought to be so construed now.   But this is unimportant, for if the indictment alleges that the prisoner
procured the assemblage, that procurement becomes
part of the overt act, and must be proved as will be
shown hereafter.

The second position is founded on *1 Hale, 214,
288*, and *1 East, 127.*

While I declare that this doctrine contradicts every
idea I had ever entertained on the subject of indictments, since it admits that one case may be stated,
and a very different case may be proved, I will
acknowledge that it is countenanced by the authorities adduced in its support.   To counsel or advise a
treasonable assemblage, and to be one of that assemblage, are certainly distinct acts, and, therefore,
ought not to be charged as the same act.   The great

objection to this mode of proceeding is, that the proof essentially varies from the charge in the character and essence of the offense, and in the testimony by which the accused is to defend himself. These *dicta* of Lord Hale, therefore, taken in the extent in which they are understood by the counsel of the United States, seem to be repugnant to the declarations we find everywhere, that an overt act must be laid, and must be proved. No case is cited by Hale in support of them, and I am strongly inclined to the opinion that, had the public received his corrected, instead of his original manuscript, they would, if not expunged, have been restrained in their application to cases of a particular description. Laid down generally, and applied to all cases of treason, they are repugnant to the principles for which Hale contends, for which all the elementary writers contend, and from which courts have in no case, either directly reported, or referred to in the books, ever departed. These principles are, that the indictment must give notice of the offense ; that the accused is only bound to answer the particular charge which the indictment contains, and that the overt act laid is that particular charge. Under such circumstances, it is only doing justice to Hale to examine his *dicta*, and if they will admit of being understood in a limited sense, not repugnant to his own doctrines, nor to the general principles of law, to understand them in that sense.

" If many conspire to counterfeit, or counsel or abet it, and one of them doth the fact upon that counselling or conspiracy, it is treason in all, and they may be all indicted for counterfeiting generally within the statute, for in such case, in treason, all are principals."

This is laid down as applicable singly to the treason of counterfeiting the coin, and is not applied by Hale to other treasons. Had * he designed *498 to apply the principle universally, he would have stated it as a general proposition ; he would have laid it down in treating on other branches of the statute, as well as in the chapter respecting the coin ; he would have laid it down when treating on indictments generally. But he has done neither. Every sentiment bearing in any manner on this point, which is to be found in Lord Hale, while on the doctrine of levying war, or on the general doctrine of indictments, militates against the opinion that he considered the proposition as more extensive than he has declared it to be. No court could be justified in extending the *dictum* of a judge beyond its terms, to cases in which he has expressly treated, to which he has not himself applied it, and on which he as well as others has delivered opinions which that *dictum* would overrule. This would be the less justifiable if there should be a clear legal distinction indicated by the very terms in which the judge has expressed himself between the particular case to which alone he has applied the *dictum*, and other cases to which the court is required to extend it.

There is this clear legal distinction. " They may," says Judge Hale, " be indicted for counterfeiting generally." But if many conspire to levy war, and some actually levy it, they may not be indicted for levying war generally. The books concur in declaring that they cannot be so indicted. A special overt act of levying war must be laid. This distinction between counterfeiting the coins, and that class of treasons among which levying war is placed, is taken in the statute of Edw. III. That statute requires an overt act of levying war to be laid in the indictment, and does not require an overt act of counterfeiting the coin to be laid. If in a particular case where a general indictment is sufficient, it be stated that the crime may be charged generally according to the legal effect of the act, it does not follow, that in other cases where a general indictment would be insufficient, where an overt act must be laid, that this overt act need not be laid according to the real fact. Hale, then, is to be reconciled with himself, and with the general principles of law, only by permitting the limits which he has himself given to his own *dictum*, to remain where he has placed them.

In *p. 238*, Hale is speaking generally of the receiver of a traitor, and is stating in what such receiver partakes of an accessory. 1st. His indictment must be special of the receipt, and not generally that he did the thing, which may be otherwise in case of one that is procurer, counsellor or consenter."

The words "may be otherwise," do not clearly convey the idea that it is universally otherwise. In all cases of a receiver the indictment must be special on the receipt, and not general. The words it "may be otherwise in case of a procurer," &c., signify that it may be otherwise in all treasons, or that it may be otherwise in some treasons. If it may be otherwise in some treasons without contradicting the doctrines of Hale himself, as well as of other writers, but cannot be otherwise in all treasons without such contradiction, the fair construction is, that Hale used these words in their restricted sense; that he used them in reference to treasons, in which a general indictment would lie, not to * treasons where *499 a general indictment would not lie, but an overt act of the treason must be charged. The two passages of Hale thus construed, may, perhaps, be law, and may leave him consistent with himself. It appears to the court to be the fair way of construing them.

These observations relative to the passages quoted from Hale, apply to that quoted from East, who obviously copies from Hale, and relies upon his authority.

Upon this point *Keeling, 26,* and *1 Hale, 626,* have also been relied upon. It is stated in both, that if a man be indicted as a principal and acquitted, he cannot afterwards be indicted as accessory before the fact. Whence it is inferred, not without reason, that evidence of accessorial guilt may be received on such an indictment. Yet no case is found in which the question has been made and decided. The objection has never been taken at a trial and overruled, nor do the books say it would be overruled. Were such a case produced, its application would be questionable. Keeling says, an accessory before the fact is *quodam modo*, in some manner guilty of the fact. The law may not require that the manner should be stated, for in felony it does not require that an overt act should be laid. The indictment, therefore, may be general. But an overt act of levying war must be laid. These cases, then, prove in their utmost extent, no more than the cases previously cited from Hale and East. This distinction between indictments which may state the fact generally, and those which must lay it specially, bear some analogy to a general and a special action on the case. In a general action, the declaration may lay the assumpsit according to the legal effect of the transaction, but in a special action on the case, the declaration must state the material circumstances truly, and they must be proved as stated. This distinction also derives some aid from a passage in *Hale, 625*, immediately preceding that which has been cited at the bar. He says, "If A. be indicted as principal, and B. as accessory before or after, and both be acquitted, yet B. may be indicted as principal, and the former acquittal as accessory is no bar."

The crimes, then, are not the same, and may not indifferently be tried under the same indictment. But why is it that an acquittal as principal may be pleaded in bar to an indictment as accessory, while an acquittal as accessory may not be pleaded in bar to an indictment as principal? If it be answered that the accessorial crime may be given in evidence on an indictment as principal, but that the principal crime may not be given in evidence on an indictment

as accessory, the question recurs, on what legal ground does this distinction stand? I can imagine only this. An accessory being *quodam modo* a principal, in indictments where the law does not require the manner to be stated, which need not be special, evidence of accessorial guilt, if the punishment be the same, may possibly be received; but every indictment as accessory must be special. The very allegation that he is an accessory must be a special allegation, and must show how he became an accessory. The charges of this special indictment, therefore, must be proved as laid, and no evidence which proves the crime in a form * substantially different can
*500 be received. If this be the legal reason for the distinction, it supports the exposition of these *dictā* which have been given. If it be not the legal reason, I can conceive no other.

But suppose the law to be as is contended by the counsel for the United States. Suppose an indictment, charging an individual with personally assembling among others, and thus levying war, may be satisfied with the proof that he caused the assemblage. What effect will this law have upon this case?

The guilt of the accused, if there be any guilt, does not consist in the assemblage, for he was not a member of it. The simple fact of assemblage no more affects one absent man than another. His guilt, then, consists in procuring the assemblage, and upon this fact depends his criminality. The proof relative to the character of an assemblage must be the same whether a man be present or absent. In the general, to charge any individual with the guilt of an assemblage, the fact of his presence must be proved. It constitutes an essential part of the overt act. If, then, the procurement be substituted in the place of presence, does it not also constitute an essential part of the overt act? Must it not also be proved? Must it not be proved in the same manner that presence must be proved? If in one case the presence of the individual makes the guilt of the assemblage his guilt, and in the other case the procurement by the individual makes the guilt of the assemblage his guilt, then presence and procurement are equally component parts of the overt act, and equally require two witnesses.

Collateral points may, say the books, be proved according to the course of the common law; but is this a collateral point? Is the fact, without which the accused does not participate in the guilt of the assemblage, if it was guilty, a collateral point? This cannot be. The presence of the party, where presence is necessary, being a part of the overt act, must be positively proved by two witnesses. No presumptive evidence, no facts from which presence may be conjectured or inferred, will satisfy the constitution and the law. If procurement take the place of presence, and become part of the overt act, then no presumptive evidence, no facts from which the procurement may be conjectured or inferred, can satisfy the constitution and the law. The mind is not to be led to the conclusion that the individual was present, by a train of conjectures or inferences, or of reasoning; the fact must be proved by two witnesses. Neither where procurement supplies the want of presence, is the mind to be conducted to the conclusion that the accused procured the assembly, by a train of conjectures or inferences, or of reasoning; the fact itself must be proved by two witnesses, and must have been committed within the district.

If it be said that the advising or procurement of treason is a secret transaction which can scarcely ever be proved in the manner required by this opinion; the answer which will readily suggest itself is, that the difficulty of proving a fact will not justify conviction without proof. Certainly it will not justify conviction without a direct and positive witness in a case where the constitution requires two. The more

*501   correct *inference from this circumstance would seem to be, that the advising of the fact is not within the constitutional definition of the crime. To advise or procure a treason is in the nature of conspiring or plotting treason, which is not treason in itself.

If, then, the doctrines of Keeling, Hale and East are to be understood in the sense in which they are pressed by the counsel for the prosecution, and are applicable in the United States, the fact that the accused procured the assemblage on Blennerhassett's island must be proved, not circumstantially, but positively by two witnesses, to charge him with that assemblage. But there are still other most important considerations, which must be well weighed before this doctrine can be applied to the United States.

The eighth amendment to the constitution has been pressed with great force, and it is impossible not to feel its application to this point. The accused cannot be truly said to be " informed of the nature and cause of the accusation," unless the indictment shall give him that notice which may reasonably suggest to him the point on which the accusation turns, so that he may know the course to be pursued in his defense.

It is also well worthy of consideration, that this doctrine, so far as it respects treason, is entirely supported by the operation of the common law, which is said to convert the accessory before the fact into the principal, and to make the act of the principal his act. The accessory before the fact is not said to have levied war. He is not said to be guilty under the statute. But the common law attaches to him the guilt of that fact which he has advised or procured, and, as contended, makes it his act. This is the operation of the common law, not the operation of the statute. It is an operation then, which can only be performed where the common law exists to perform it. It is the creature of the common law, and the creature presupposes its creator. To decide, then, that this doctrine is applicable to the United States, would seem to apply the decision that the United States, as a nation, have a common law which creates and defines the punishment of crimes accessorial in their nature. It would imply the further decisions that these accessorial crimes are not, in the case of treason, excluded by the definition of treason, given in the constitution. I will not pretend that I

have not individually an opinion on these points, but
it is one which I should give only in a case absolutely
requiring it, unless I could confer respecting it with
the judges of the Supreme Court.

I have said that this doctrine cannot apply to the
United States, without implying those decisions respecting the common law which I have stated, because,
should it be true, as is contended, that the constitutional definition of treason comprehends him who advises or procures an assemblage that levies war, it
would not follow that such adviser or procurer might
be charged as having been present at the assemblage.
If the adviser or procurer is within the definition of
levying war, and, independent of the agency of the
common law, does actually levy war, then the advisement or procurement is an overt act of levying war.

*502 * If it be the overt act on which he is to be
convicted, then it must be charged in the
indictment, for he can only be convicted on proof of
the overt acts which are charged.

To render this distinction more intelligible, let it be
recollected, that although it should be conceded that
since the statute of William and Mary, he who advises
or procures a treason may, in England, be charged as
having committed that treason, by virtue of the common law operation, which is said, so far as respects
the indictment, to unite the accessorial to the principal
offense, and permit them to be charged as one, yet it
can never be conceded that he who commits one overt
act under the statute of Edward, can be charged and
convicted on proof of another overt act. If, then,

procurement be an overt act of treason under the constitution, no man can be convicted for the procurement under an indictment charging him with actually assembling, whatever may be the doctrine of the common law in the case of an accessorial offender.

It may not be improper, in this place, again to advert to the opinion of the Supreme Court, and to show that it contains nothing contrary to the doctrine now laid down. That opinion is, that an individual may be guilty of treason "who has not appeared in arms against his country; that if war be actually levied, that is, if a body of men be actually assembled for the purpose of effecting by force a treasonable object, all those who perform any part, however minute, or however remote from the scene of action, and who are actually in the general conspiracy, are to be considered as traitors."

This opinion does not touch the case of a person who advises or procures an assemblage, and does nothing further. The advising certainly, and, perhaps, the procuring, is more in the nature of a conspiracy to levy war, than of the actual levying of war. According to the opinion, it is not enough to be leagued in the conspiracy, and that war be levied, but it is also necessary to perform a part; that part is the act of levying war. This part, it is true, may be minute; it may not be the actual appearance in arms, and it may be remote from the scene of action, that is, from the place where the army is assembled; but it must be a part, and that part must be performed by a person who is leagued in the conspiracy. This

part, however minute or remote, constitutes the overt
act on which alone the person who performs it can be
convicted.

The opinion does not declare that the person who
has performed this remote and minute part may be
indicted for a part which was in truth performed by
others, and convicted on their overt acts.   It amounts
to this and nothing more, that when war is actually
levied, not only those who bear arms, but those also
who are leagued in the conspiracy, and who perform
the various distinct parts which are necessary for the
prosecution of war, do, in the sense of the constitution, levy war.   It may possibly be the opinion of the
Supreme Court, that those who procure a treason,
and do nothing further, are guilty under the constitution ; I only say that opinion has not yet been given ;
still less has it * been indicated, that he
*503   who advises shall be indicted as having
performed the fact.

It is, then, the opinion of the court, that this indictment can be supported only by testimony which
proves the accused to have been actually or constructively present when the assemblage took place
on Blennerhassett's island, or by the admission of the
doctrine that he who procures an act may be indicted
as having performed that act.

It is further the opinion of the court, that there is
no testimony whatever which tends to prove that the
accused was actually or constructively present when
that assemblage did take place.   Indeed, the contrary
is most apparent.   With respect to admitting proof

of procurement to establish a charge of actual presence, the court is of opinion, that if this be admissible in England on an indictment for levying war, which is far from being conceded, it is admissible only by virtue of the operation of the common law upon the statute, and, therefore, is not admissible in this country unless by virtue of a similar operation ; a point far from being established, but on which, for the present, no opinion is given. If, however, this point be established, still the procurement must be proved in the same manner, and by the same kind of testimony, which would be required to prove actual presence.

The second point in this division of the subject is, the necessity of adducing the record of the previous conviction of some one person who committed the fact alleged to be treasonable.

This point presupposes the treason of the accused, if any has been committed, to be accessorial in its nature. Its being of this description, according to the British authorities, depends on the presence or absence of the accused at the time the fact was committed. The doctrine on this subject is well understood, has been most copiously explained, and need not be repeated. That there is no evidence of his actual or legal presence is a point already discussed and decided. It is, then, apparent that, but for the exception to the general principle which is made in cases of treason, those who assembled at Blennerhassett's island, if that assemblage was such as to constitute the crime, would be principals, and those who might really have caused that assemblage, although, in truth, the chief traitors would, in law, be accessories.

It is a settled principle in the law that the accessory cannot be guilty of a greater offense than his principal. The maxim is *accessorius sequitur naturam sui principalis;* the accessory follows the nature of his principal. Hence results the necessity of establishing the guilt of the principal before the accessory can be tried. For the degree of guilt which is incurred by counselling or commanding the commission of a crime depends upon the actual commission of that crime. No man is an accessory to murder unless the fact has been committed.

The fact can only be established in a prosecution against the person by whom a crime has been perpetrated. The law supposes a man more capable of defending his own conduct than any other person, and will not tolerate that the guilt of A. shall be established in a prosecution * against B. Consequently, if the guilt of B. depends on the guilt of A., A. must be convicted before B. can be tried. It would exhibit a monstrous deformity, indeed, in our system, if B. might be executed for being accessory to a murder committed by A. and A. should afterwards, upon a full trial, be acquitted of the fact. For this obvious reason, although the punishment of a principal and accessory was originally the same, and although in many instances it is still the same, the accessory could, in no case, be tried before the conviction of his principal, nor can he yet be tried

*504

previous to such conviction, unless he requires it, or unless a special provision to that effect be made by statute.

If, then, this was a felony, the prisoner at the bar could not be tried until the crime was established by the conviction of the person by whom it was actually perpetrated.

Is the law otherwise in this case, because, in treason all are principals?

Let this question be answered by reason and by authority.

Why is it that in felonies, however, atrocious, the trial of the accessory can never precede the conviction of the principal? Not because the one is denominated the principal and the other the accessory, for that would be ground on which a great law principle could never stand. Not because there was, in fact, a difference in the degree of moral guilt, for in the case of murder committed by a hardy villain for a bribe, the person plotting the murder and giving the bribe, is, perhaps, of the two the blacker criminal; and, were it otherwise, this would furnish no argument for precedence in trial.

What, then, is the reason?

It has been already given. The legal guilt of the accessory depends on the guilt of the principal; and the guilt of the principal can only be established in a prosecution against himself.

Does not this reason apply in full force to a case of treason?

The legal guilt of the person who planned the assemblage on Blennerhassett's island depends, not simply on the criminality of the previous conspiracy, but on the criminality of that assemblage.   If those who perpetrated the fact be not traitors, he who advised the fact cannot be a traitor.   His guilt, then, in contemplation of law, depends on theirs, and their guilt can only be established in a prosecution against themselves.   Whether the adviser of this assemblage be punishable with death as a principal or as an accessory, his liability to punishment depends on the degree of guilt attached to an act which has been perpetrated by others, and which, if it be a criminal act, renders them guilty also.   His guilt, therefore, depends on theirs, and their guilt cannot be legally established in a prosecution against him.

The whole reason of the law, then, relative to the principal and accessory, so far as respects the order of trial, seems to apply in full force to a case of treason committed by one body of men in conspiracy with others who are absent.

If from reason we pass to authority, we find it laid down by Hale, * Foster and East, in the ** 505*   most explicit terms, that the conviction of some one who has committed the treason must precede the trial of him who has advised or procured it. This position is also maintained by Leach, in his notes on Hawkins, and is not, so far as the court has discovered, anywhere contradicted.

These authorities have been read and commented on at such length, that it cannot be necessary for the court to bring them again into view.   It is the less necessary, because it is not understood that the law is controverted by the counsel for the United States.

It is, however, contended, that the prisoner has waived his right to demand the conviction of some one person who was present at the fact, by pleading to his indictment.

Had this indictment even charged the prisoner according to the truth of the case, the court would feel some difficulty in deciding that he had, by implication, waived his right to demand a specie of testimony essential to his conviction. The court is not prepared to say that the act which is to operate against his rights did not require that it should be performed with a full knowledge of its operations. It would seem consonant to the usual course of proceeding in other respects, in criminal cases, that the prisoner should be informed that he had a right to refuse to be tried until some person who committed the act should be convicted, and that he ought not to be considered as waiving the right to demand the record of conviction, unless with the full knowledge of that right he consented to be tried. The court, however, does not decide what the law would be in such a case. It is unnecessary to decide it, because pleading to an indictment in which a man is charged as having committed an act, cannot be construed to waive a right which he would have possessed, had he been charged with having advised the act. No person indicated as a principal can be expected to say, I am not a principal, I am an accessory ; I did not commit, I only advised the act.

The authority of the English cases on this subject depends in a great measure on the adoption of the common law doctrine of accessorial treasons. If that doctrine be excluded, this branch of it may not be directly applicable to treasons committed within the United States. If the crime of advising or procuring a levying of war be within the constitutional definition of treason, then he who advises or procures it must be indicted on the very fact, and the question whether the treasonableness of the act may be decided, in the first instance, in the trial of him who procured it, or must be decided in the trial of one who committed it, will depend upon the reason, as it respects the law of evidence, which produced the British decisions with regard to the trial of principal and accessory, rather than on the positive authority of those decisions.

This question is not essential in the present case, because, if the crime be within the constitutional definition, it is an overt act of levying war, and to produce a conviction ought to have been charged in the indictment.

*506   * The law of the case being thus far settled what ought to be the decision of the court on the present motion ? Ought the court to set and hear testimony which cannot effect the prisoner, or ought the court to arrest that testimony ? On this question much has been said ; much that may, perhaps, be ascribed to a misconception of the point really under consideration. The motion has been treated as a motion confessedly made to stop relevant testimony, and in the course of the argument, it has

been repeatedly stated by those who oppose the motion, that irrelevant testimony may, and ought to be
stopped.   That this statement is perfectly correct, is
one of those fundamental principles in judicial proceedings which is acknowledged by all, and is founded
in the absolute necessity of the thing.   No person will
contend that in a civil or criminal case, either party is
at liberty to introduce what testimony he pleases,
legal or illegal, and to consume the whole term in
details of facts unconnected with the particular case.
Some tribunal, then, must decide on the admissibility
of testimony.   The parties cannot constitute this
tribunal, for they do not agree.   The jury cannot
constitute it, for the question is, whether they shall
hear the testimony or not.   Who, then, but the court
can constitute it?   It is, of necessity, the peculiar
province of the court to judge of the admissibility of
testimony.   If the court admit improper or reject
proper testimony, it is an error of judgment, but it is
an error committed in the direct exercise of their
judicial functions.

The present indictment charges the prisoner with
levying war against the United States, and alleges an
overt act of levying war.   That overt act must be
proved, according to the mandates of the constitution
and of the act of Congress, by two witnesses.   It is not
proved by a single witness.   The presence of the
accused has been stated to be an essential component
part of the overt act in this indictment, unless the
common law principle respecting accessories should
render it unnecessary ; and there is not only no wit-

ness who has proved his actual or legal presence ; but
the fact of his absence is not controverted. The
counsel for the prosecution offer to give in evidence
subsequent transactions, at a different place, and in a
different state, in order to prove what ? The overt
act laid in the indictment ? That the prisoner was
one of those who assembled at Blennerhassett's island ?
No, that is not alleged. It is well known that such
testimony is not competent to establish such a fact.
The constitution and law require that the fact should
be established by two witnesses, not by the establishment of other facts from which the jury might reason
to this fact. The testimony, then, is not relevant. If
it can be introduced, it is only in the character of corroborative or confirmatory testimony, after the overt
act has been proved by two witnesses, in such manner
that the question of fact ought to be left with the
jury. The conclusion that in this state of things no
testimony can be admissible, is so inevitable, that the
counsel for the United States could not resist it. I
do not understand them to deny, that if the overt act
be not proved by two witnesses so as to be submitted
to the jury, that all other testimony must be
* 507   * irrelevant, because no other testimony can
prove the act. Now an assemblage on Blennerhassett's island is proved by the requisite number of witnesses, and the court might submit it to the jury,
whether that assemblage amounted to a levying of
war, but the presence of the accused at that assemblage being nowhere alleged except in the indictment,
the overt act is not proved by a single witness,

and of consequence, all other testimony must be irrelevant.

The only difference between this motion as made, and the motion in the form which the counsel for the United States would admit to be regular, is this. It is now general for the rejection of all testimony. It might be particular with respect to each witness as adduced. But can this be wished, or can it be deemed necessary? If enough is proved to show that the indictment cannot be supported, and that no testimony, unless it be of that description which the attorney for the United States declares himself not to possess, can be relevant, why should a question be taken on each witness?

The opinion of this court on the order of testimony has frequently been adverted to as deciding this question against the motion.

If a contradiction between the two opinions does exist, the court cannot perceive it. It was said that levying war is an act compounded of law and fact, of which the jury, aided by the court, must judge. To that declaration the court still adheres.

It was said that if the overt act was not proved by two witnesses, no testimony in its nature, corroborative or confirmatory, was admissible, or could be relevant.

From that declaration there is certainly no departure. It has been asked, in allusion to the present case, if a general, commanding an army, should detach troops for a distant service, would the men composing that detachment be traitors, and would the commander-in-chief escape punishment.

Let the opinion which has been given answer this
question.   Appearing at the head of an army would,
according to this opinion, be an overt act of levying
war; detaching a military corps from it for military
purposes might also be an overt act of levying war.
It is not pretended that he would not be punishable
for these acts, it is only said that he may be tried and
convicted on his own acts, in the state where those
acts were committed, not on the acts of others in the
state where those others acted.

Much has been said in the course of the argument
on points, on which the court feels no inclination to
comment particularly, but which may, perhaps, not
improperly, receive some notice.

That this court dares not usurp power is most
true.

That this court dares not shrink from its duty is
not less true.

No man is desirous of placing himself in a disagreeable situation.   No man is desirous of becoming the
peculiar subject of calumny.   No man, might he let
the bitter cup pass from him without self-reproach,
would drain it to the bottom.   But if he has no choice
in the case; if there is no alternative presented to
* 508   him but a dereliction of duty, or * the op-
probrium of those who are denominated the
world, he merits the contempt as well as the indignation of his country, who can hesitate which to
embrace.

That, gentlemen, in a case the most interesting, in
the zeal with which they advocate particular opinions,

and under the conviction in some measure produced by that zeal, should on each side press their arguments too far, should be impatient at any deliberation in the court, and should suspect or fear the operation of motives to which alone they can ascribe that deliberation, is a perhaps, frailty incident to human nature; but if any conduct on the part of the court could warrant a sentiment that they would deviate to the one side or the other from the line prescribed by duty and by law, that conduct would be viewed by the judges themselves with an eye of extreme severity, and would long be recollected with deep and serious regret.

The arguments on both sides have been intently and deliberately considered. Those which could not be noticed, since to notice every argument and authority would swell this opinion to a volume, have not been disregarded. The result of the whole is a conviction as complete as the mind of the court is capable of receiving on a complex subject, that the motion must prevail.

No testimony relative to the conduct or declarations of the prisoner elsewhere, and subsequent to the transaction on Blennerhassett's island, can be admitted, because such testimony, being in its nature merely corroborative, and incompetent to prove the overt act in itself, is irrelevant, until there be proof of the overt act by two witnesses.

This opinion does not comprehend the proof by two witnesses that the meeting on Blennerhassett's island was procured by the prisoner. On that point the court, for the present, withholds its opinion for reasons which have been already assigned ; and as it is understood from the statements made on the part of the prosecution, that no such testimony exists, if there be such, let it be offered and the court will decide upon it.

The jury have now heard the opinion of the court on the law of the case.

They will apply that law to the facts, and will find a verdict of guilty or not guilty, as their own consciences may direct.

[*Documents accompanying the President's Message of January 22, 1807.*]

WILKINSON'S FIRST AFFIDAVIT.

I, James Wilkinson, Brigadier-General and Commander in Chief of the army of the United States, to warrant the arrest of Doctor Erick Bollman, on a charge of treason, misprision of treason, or such other offense against the government and laws of the United States as the following facts may legally charge him with, on my honor as a soldier ; and on the Holy Evangelists of Almighty God, do declare and swear, that on the sixth day of November last, when in command at Natchitoches, I received by the hands of a Frenchman, a stranger to me, a letter from Doctor Erick Bollman, of which the following is a correct copy :

"NEW ORLEANS, *September 27*, 1806.

"SIR : I have the honor to forward to your excellency the enclosed letters, which I was charged to deliver to you by our mutual friend : I shall remain for some time at this place, and should be glad to learn where and when I may have the pleasure of an interview with you.　Have the goodness to inform me of it, and please to direct your letter to me, care of , or enclose it under cover to them.

    " I have the honor to be,
     " With great respect, Sir,
   " Your excellency's most obedient servant,
    (Signed)   " ERICK BOLLMAN.
" Gen. Wilkinson."

.Covering a communication in cipher from Colonel Aaron Burr, of which the following is substantially as fair an interpretation as I have heretofore been able to make, the original of which I hold in my possession : " I (Aaron Burr) have obtained funds, and have actually commenced the enterprise.　Detachments from different points, and under different pretences, will rendezvous on the Ohio, 1st November.　Everything internal and external favors views ; protection of England is secured.

 T. [1] is gone to Jamaica to arrange with the admiral of that station, and will meet at the Mississippi—— England——navy of the United States are ready to join, and final orders are given to my friends and followers ; it will be a host of choice spirits.　Wilkinson shall be second to Burr only ; Wilkinson shall dictate the rank and promotion of his officers.　Burr will proceed westward 1st August, never to return ; with him go his daughter ; the husband will follow in

     [1] Truxton.

October with a corps of worthies; send forthwith an
intelligent and confidential friend, with whom Burr
may confer; he shall return immediately with further
interesting details; this is essential to concert and
harmony of movement; send a list of all persons
known to Wilkinson west of the mountains, who could
be useful, with a note delineating their characters.

"By your messenger send me four or five of the
commissions of your officers, which you can borrow
under any pretence you please; they shall be returned faithfully; already are orders to the contractor given to forward six months' provisions to points
Wilkinson may name; this shall not be used until
the last moment, and then under proper injunctions:
the project is brought to the point so long desired;
Burr guarantees the result with his life and honor,
the lives, the honor and fortunes of hundreds, the
best blood of our country; Burr's plan of operations
is to move down rapidly from the falls on the fifteenth
of November, with the first five hundred or one thousand men, in light boats, now constructing for that
purpose; to be at Natchez between the fifth and
fifteenth of December, then to meet Wilkinson; then
to determine whether it will be expedient, in the first
instance, to seize on, or pass by, Baton Rogue; on
receipt of this send Burr an answer; draw on Burr
for all expenses, &c.   The people of the country to
which we are going are prepared to receive us; their
agents now with Burr say that if we will protect their
religion, and will not subject them to a foreign power,
that in three weeks all will be settled.   The Gods

invite to glory and fortune ; it remains to be seen whether we deserve the boon ; the bearer of this goes express to you ; he will hand a formal letter of introduction to you from Burr, a copy of which is hereunto subjoined ; he is a man of inviolable honor and perfect discretion ; formed to execute rather than to project ; capable of relating facts with fidelity, and incapable of relating them otherwise ; he is thoroughly informed of the plans and intentions of   , and will disclose to you as far as you inquire, and no further ; he has imbibed a reverence for your character, and may be embarrassed in your presence ; put him at ease and he will satisfy you ; Doctor Bollman, equally confidential, better informed on the subject, and more intelligent, will hand this duplicate.

" *29th July.*"

The day after my arrival at this city, the 26th of November last, I received another letter from the doctor, of which the following is a correct copy :

" NEW ORLEANS, *November 25th,* 1806.

" SIR : Your letter of the 16th inst. has been duly received ; supposing that you will be much engaged this morning, I defer waiting on your excellency till you will be pleased to inform me of the time when it will be convenient for you to see me.   I remain with great respect,

" Your excellency's most obedient servant,

" ERICK BOLLMAN.

" His Excellency Gen. Wilkinson, Fauxbourg.

"*Marigny, the house between Madame Trevigne and M. Macarty.*"

On the 30th of the same month I waited in person on Doctor E. Bollman, when he informed me that he had not heard from Colonel Burr since his arrival here. That he (the said Doctor E. Bollman) had sent despatches to Colonel Burr by a Lieutenant Spence, of the navy, and that he had been advised of Spence's arrival at Nashville, in the state of Tennessee, and observed that Colonel Burr had proceeded too far to retreat ; that he (Colonel Burr) had numerous and powerful friends in the United States, who stood pledged to support him with their fortunes, and that he must succeed. That he (the said Doctor E. Bollman) had written to Colonel Burr on the subject of provisions, and that he expected a supply would be sent from New York, and also from Norfolk, where Colonel Burr had strong connections. I did not see or hear from the doctor again until the 5th inst., when I called on him the second time. The mail having arrived the day before, I asked him whether he had received any intelligence from Colonel Burr ; he informed me that he had seen a letter from Colonel Burr of the 30th October, in which he (Colonel Burr) gave assurances that he should be at Natchez with 2,000 men on the 20th December, inst., where he should wait until he heard from this place ; that he would be followed by 4,000 men more, and that he, (Colonel Burr,) if he had chosen, could have raised or got 12,000 as easily as 6,000, but that he did not think that number necessary. Confiding fully in this information, I became indifferent about further disguise. I then told the doctor that I should most certainly oppose Colonel Burr if he came this way. He replied that they must come here for equipments and shipping, and observed that he did not know what had passed between Colonel Burr and myself, obliqued at a sham defence, and waived the subject.

From the documents in my possession, and the several communications, verbal as well as written, from the said Doctor Erick Bollman, on this subject, I feel no hesitation in declaring under the solemn obligation of an oath, that he has committed misprision of treason against the government of the United States. (Signed) JAMES WILKINSON.

Signed and sworn to this 14th day of December, 1806, before me, one of the justices of the peace of this county. (Signed) J. CARRICK.

" PHILADELPHIA, *July* 25, 1806.

" DEAR SIR :

" Mr. Swartwout, the brother of Colonel S., of New York, being on his way down the Mississippi, and presuming that he may pass you at some post on the river, has requested of me a letter of introduction, which I give with pleasure, as he is a most amiable young man, and highly respectable from his character and connections. I pray you to afford him any friendly offices which his situation may require, and beg you to pardon the trouble which this may give you. With entire respect,

" Your friend and obedient servant,

" A. BURR.

" His Excellency Gen. Wilkinson."

*Message from the President of the United States to the Senate and
House of Representatives:*

I received from Gen. Wilkinson, on the 23d inst.,
his affidavit, charging Samuel Swartwout, Peter V.
Ogden, and James Alexander, with the crimes described in the affidavit, a copy of which is now communicated to both houses of Congress.

It was announced to me at the same time, that
Swartwout and Bollman, two of the persons apprehended by him, were arrived in this city in custody
each of a military officer.   I immediately delivered to
the attorney of the United States, in this district, the
evidence received against them, with instructions to
lay the same before the judges, and apply for their
process to bring the accused to justice, and I put into
his hands orders to the officers having them in custody,
to deliver them to the marshal on his application.

Th. Jefferson.

January, 26, 1807.

WILKINSON'S SECOND AFFIDAVIT.

I, James Wilkinson, Brigadier General and commander in chief of the army of the United States, to
warrant the arrest of Samuel Swartwout, James Alexander, Esq., and Peter V. Ogden, on a charge of
treason, misprision of treason, or such other offence
against the government and laws of the United States,
as the following facts may legally charge them with, on
the honor of a soldier, and on the Holy Evangelists
of Almighty God, do declare and swear, that in the
beginning of the month of October last, when in

command at Natchitoches, a stranger was introduced to me by Colonel Cushing, by the name of Swartwout, who a few minutes after the colonel retired from the room, slipt into my hand a letter of formal introduction from Colonel Burr, of which the following is a correct copy :

"PHILADELPHIA, 25*th July*, 1806.

" DEAR SIR :

" Mr. Swartwout, the brother of Colonel S., of New York, being on his way down the Mississippi, and presuming that he may pass you at some post on the river, has requested of me a letter of introduction, which I give with pleasure, as he is a most amiable young man, and highly respected from his character and connections. I pray you to afford him any friendly offices which his situation may require, and beg you to pardon the trouble which this may give you.

" With entire respect,
       "Your friend and obedient servant,
   (Signed)   " A. BURR.
" His Excellency General Wilkinson."

Together with a packet, which, he informed me, he was charged by the same person to deliver me in private ; this packet contained a letter in cipher from Colonel Burr, of which the following is substantially as fair an interpretation as I have heretofore been able to make, the original of which I hold in my possession :

" I, Aaron Burr, have obtained funds and have actually commenced the enterprise. Detachments from different points and under different pretences, will rendezvous on the Ohio, 1st November. Everything internal and external favors views; protection of England is secured; T—— is going to Jamaica, to arrange with the admiral on that station; it will meet on the Mississippi——England——Navy of the United States are ready to join, and final orders are given to my friends and followers; it will be a host of choice spirits. Wilkinson shall be second to Burr only; Wilkinson shall dictate the rank and promotion of his officers. Burr will proceed westward 1st August, never to return; with him go his daughter; the husband will follow in October, with a corps of worthies.

"Send forthwith an intelligent and confidential friend with whom Burr may confer; he shall return immediately with further interesting details; this is essential to concert and harmony of movement; send a list of all persons known to Wilkinson, west of the mountains, who may be useful, with a note delineating their characters. By your messenger send me four or five of the commissions of your officers, which you can borrow under any pretence you please; they shall be returned faithfully. Already are orders to the contractor given to forward six months' provisions to points Wilkinson may name; this shall not be used until the last moment, and then under proper injunctions; the project is brought to the point so long desired; Burr guarantees the result with his life and honor; with the lives, the honor and fortunes of hundreds, the best blood of our country. Burr's plan of operations is to move down rapidly from the falls on the 15th November, with the first 500 or 1,000 men, in light boats now constructing for that purpose, to be at Natchez between the 5th and 15th of December; there to meet Wilkinson; there to determine whether it will be expedient, in the first instance, to seize on, or pass by, Baton Rouge; on receipt of this, send an answer; draw on Burr for all expenses, &c. The people of the country to which we are going are prepared to receive us; their agents now with Burr say, that if we will protect their religion, and will not subject them to a foreign power, that in three weeks all will be settled. The Gods invite to glory and fortune; it remains to be seen whether we deserve the boon; the bearer of this goes express to you; he will hand a formal letter of introduction to you from Burr; he is a man of inviolable honor and perfect discretion; formed to execute rather than to project; capable of relating facts with fidelity, and incapable of relating them otherwise; he is thoroughly informed of the plans and intentions of   , and will disclose to you as far as you inquire, and no further; he has imbibed a reverence for your character, and may be embarrassed in your presence; put him at ease and he will satisfy you.

"*29th July.*"

I instantly resolved to avail myself of the reference made to the bearer, and in the course of some days drew from him (the said Swartwout) the following disclosure: "That he had been dispatched by Colonel

Burr from Philadelphia, had passed through the states of Ohio and Kentucky, and proceeded from Louisville for St. Louis, where he expected to find me, but discovering at Kaskaskias that I had descended the river, he procured a skiff, hired hands, and followed me down the Mississippi to Fort Adams, and from thence set out for Natchitoches, in company with Captains Sparks and Hooke, under the pretense of a disposition to take part in the campaign against the Spaniards, then depending.   That Colonel Burr with the support of a powerful association, extending from New York to New Orleans, was levying an armed body of 7,000 men from the state of New York and the western states and territories, with a view to carry an expedition against the Mexican provinces, and that 500 men under Colonel Swartwout and a Colonel or Major Tyler, were to descend the Alleghany, for whose accommodation light boats had been built, and were ready." I inquired what would be their course; he said, "This territory would be revolutionized, where the people were ready to join them, and that there would be some seizing, he supposed, at New Orleans; that they expected to be ready to embark about the first of February, and intended to land at Vera Cruz, and to march from thence to Mexico." I observed that there were several millions of dollars in the bank of this place; to which he replied, "We know it full well;" and on remarking that they certainly did not mean to violate private property, he said they "merely meant to borrow, and would return it; that they must equip themselves in New Orleans;

that they expected naval protection from Great Britain ; that the Capt. ———, and the officers of our navy, were so disgusted with the government that they were ready to join ; that similar disgusts prevailed throughout the western country, where the people were zealous in favor of the enterprise, and that pilot boat built schooners were contracted for along our southern coast for their service ; that he had been accompanied from the falls of Ohio to Kaskaskias, and from thence to Fort Adams, by a Mr. Ogden, who had proceeded on to New Orleans with letters from Colonel Burr to his friends there." Swartwout asked me whether I had heard from Doctor Bollman ; and on my answering in the negative, he expressed great surprise, and observed, " That the doctor and a Mr. Alexander had left Philadelphia before him, with despatches for me, and that they were to proceed by sea to New Orleans, where he said they must have arrived."

Though determined to deceive him if possible, I could not refrain telling Mr. Swartwout it was impossible that I could ever dishonor my commission ; and I believe I duped him by my admiration of the plan, and by observing, " That although I could not join in the expedition, the engagements which the Spaniards had prepared for me in my front, might prevent my opposing it ;" yet I did, the moment I had deciphered the letter, put it into the hands of Colonel Cushing, my adjutant and inspector, making the declaration that I should oppose the lawless enterprise with my utmost force.

Mr. Swartwout informed me he was under engagements to meet Colonel Burr at Nashville the 20th of
November, and requested of me to write him, which
I declined; and on his leaving Natchitoches, about
the 18th of October, I immediately employed Lieutenant T. A. Smith to convey the information, in
substance, to the President, without the commitment
of names; for, from the extraordinary nature of the
project, and the more extraordinary appeal to me, I
could not but doubt its reality, notwithstanding the
testimony before me, and I did not attach solid belief
to Mr. Swartwout's reports respecting their intentions
on this territory and city, until I received confirmatory advice from St. Louis.

After my return from the Sabine, I crossed the
country to Natchez, and on my descent of the Mississippi from that place, I found Swartwout and Peter
V. Ogden at Fort Adams; with the latter I held no
communication, but was informed by Swartwout, that
he (Ogden) had returned so far from New Orleans,
on his route to Tennessee, but had been so much
alarmed by certain reports in circulation that he was
afraid to proceed. I inquired whether he bore letters
with him from New Orleans, and was informed by
Swartwout that he did not, but that a Mr. Spence
had been sent from New Orleans through the country
to Nashville, with letters for Colonel Burr.

I reached this city the 25th ultimo, and on the
next morning James Alexander, Esq., visited me; he
inquired of me aside whether I had seen Doctor Bollman, and on my answering in the negative, he asked

me whether I would suffer him to conduct Bollman to me, which I refused. He appeared desirous to communicate something, but I felt no inclination to inculpate this young man, and he left me. A few days after he paid me a second visit, and seemed desirous to communicate, which I avoided until he had risen to take leave ; I then raised my finger, and observed, " Take care, you are playing a dangerous game." He answered, " It will succeed." I again observed, " Take care ; " and he replied with a strong affirmation, " Burr will be here by the beginning of next month." In addition to these corroborating circumstances against Alexander, I beg leave to refer to the accompanying documents, A. B. From all which I feel no hesitation in declaring, under the solemn obligation of an oath, that I do believe the said Swartwout, Alexander, and Ogden, have been parties to, and have been concerned in, the insurrection formed, or forming, in the states and territories on the Ohio and Mississippi rivers, against the laws and constitution of the United States.

(Signed)   JAMES WILKINSON.

Sworn to, and subscribed before me, this 26th day of December, in the year of our Lord 1806.

(Signed)   GEORGE POLLOCK.

Justice of the Peace, for the County of Orleans.

THE DEPOSITION OF WILLIAM EATON, ESQ.

Early last winter Col. Aaron Burr, late Vice-President of the United States, signified to me, at

this place, that, under the authority of the general
government, he was organizing a secret expedition
against the Spanish provinces on our south-western
borders, which expedition he was to lead, and in
which he was authorized to invite me to take the
command of a division.   I had never before been
made personally acquainted with Col. Burr, and,
having for many years been employed in foreign
service, I knew but little about the estimation this
gentleman now held in the opinion of his countrymen
and his government; the rank and confidence by
which he had so lately been distinguished, left me no
right to suspect his patriotism.   I knew him a soldier.
In case of a war with the Spanish nation, which, from
the tenor of the President's message to both houses
of Congress, seemed probable, I should have thought
it my duty to obey so honorable a call of my country ;
and, under that impression, I did engage to embark
in the expedition.   I had frequent interviews with
Col. Burr in this city, and, for a considerable time,
his object seemed to be to instruct me by maps, and
other information, the feasibility of penetrating to
Mexico ; always carrying forward the idea that the
measure was authorized by government.   At length,
some time in February, he began by degrees to un-
veil himself.   He reproached the government with
want of character, want of gratitude, and want of
justice.   He seemed desirous of irritating resentment
in my breast by dilating on certain injuries he felt I
had suffered from reflections made on the floor of the
house of representatives concerning my operations in

Barbary, and from the delays of government in ad-
justing my claims for disbursements on that coast
during my consular agency at Tunis; and he said he
would point me to an honorable mode of indemnity.
I now began to entertain a suspicion that Mr. Burr
was projecting an unauthorized military expedition,
which, to me, was enveloped in mystery; and, desirous to draw an explanation from him, I suffered
him to suppose me resigned to his counsel.   He now
laid open his project of revolutionizing the western
country; separating it from the union; establishing a
monarchy there, of which he was to be the sovereign,
and New Orleans to be his capital; organizing a
force on the waters of the Mississippi, and extending
conquest to Mexico.   I suggested a number of im-
pediments to his scheme; such as the republican
habits of the citizens of that country, and their affec-
tion towards our present administration of government; the want of funds; the resistance he would
meet from the regular army of the United States on
those frontiers; and the opposition of Miranda, in
case he should succeed to republicanize the Mexicans.

Mr. Burr found no difficulty in removing these
obstacles; he said he had, the preceding season, made
a tour through that country, and had secured the
attachment of the principal citizens of Kentucky,
Tennessee and Louisiana, to his person and his measures; declared he had inexhaustible resources to
funds; assured me the regular army would act with
him, and would be re-inforced by ten or twelve thousand men from the above-mentioned states and terri-

tory, and from other parts of the union ; said he had
powerful agents in the Spanish territory ; and, as for
Miranda, said Mr. Burr, we must hang Miranda.
He now proposed to give me the second command in
his army.   I asked him who should have the chief
command ?   He said, General Wilkinson.   I observed it was singular that he should count on
General Wilkinson ; the elevated rank and high trust
he now held as commander in chief of our army and
governor of a province, he would hardly put at hazard
for any precarious prospects of aggrandizement.   Mr.
Burr said, General Wilkinson, balanced in the confidence of government, was doubtful of retaining
much longer the consideration he now enjoyed, and
was, consequently, prepared to secure to himself a
permanency.   I asked Mr. Burr if he knew General
Wilkinson ?   He answered yes, and echoed the question.   I said I knew him well.   " What do you know
of him ? " said Mr. Burr.   I know, I replied, that
General Wilkinson will act as lieutenant to no man
in existence.   " You are in an error," said Mr. Burr ;
" Wilkinson will act as lieutenant to me."   From the
tenor of repeated conversations with Mr. Burr, I was
induced to believe the plan of separating the union,
which he had contemplated, had been communicated
to, and approved of by, General Wilkinson ; (though
I now suspect it an artful argument of seduction ;)
and he often expressed a full confidence that the
general's influence, the offer of double pay and double
rations, the prospect of plunder, and the ambition of
achievement, would draw the army into his measures.

Mr. Burr talked of the establishment of an independent government west of the Alleghany as a matter of inherent constitutional right of the people, a change which would eventually take place, and for the operation of which the present crisis was peculiarly favorable. There was, said he, no energy in the government to be dreaded, and the divisions of political opinions throughout the union was a circumstance of which we should profit. There were very many enterprising men among us, who aspired to something beyond the dull pursuits of civil life, and who would volunteer in this enterprise, and the vast territory belonging to the United States, which offered to adventurers, and the mines of Mexico, would bring strength to his standard from all quarters. I listened to the exposition of Colonel Burr's views with seeming acquiescence. Every interview convinced me more and more that he had organized a deep-laid plot of treason in the west, in the accomplishment of which he felt fully confident. Till, at length, I discovered that his ambition was not bounded by the waters of the Mississippi and Mexico, but that he meditated overthrowing the present government of our country. He said, if he could gain over the marine corps, and secure the naval commanders, Truxton, Preble, Decatur, and others, he would turn Congress neck and heels out of doors, assassinate the President, seize on the treasury and the navy, and declare himself the protector of an energetic government. The honorable trust of corrupting the marine corps, and of sounding Commodore Preble and Cap-

tain Decatur, Colonel Burr proposed confiding to me.
Shocked at this proposition, I dropped the mask, and
exclaimed against his views.   He talked of the de-
graded situation of our country, and the necessity of
a blow by which its energy and its dignity should be
restored; said, if that blow could be struck here at
this time, he was confident of the support of the best
blood of America.   I told Colonel Burr he deceived
himself in presuming that he, or any other man, could
excite a party in this country who would countenance
him in such a plot of desperation, murder and
treason.   He replied, that he, perhaps, knew better
the dispositions of the influential citizens of this
country than I did.   I told him one solitary word
would destroy him.   He asked what word?   I answered, Usurper!   He smiled at my hesitation, and
quoted some great examples in his favor.   I observed
to him, that I had lately traveled from one extreme
of the union to the other; and though I found a
diversity of political opinion among the people, they
appeared united at the most distant aspect of national
danger.   That, for the section of the union to which
I belonged, I would vouch, that should he succeed in
the first instance here, he would within six weeks
afterwards have his throat cut by Yankee militia.

Though wild and extravagant Mr. Burr's last project, and though fraught with premeditated slaughter,
I felt very easy on the subject, because its defeat he
had deposited in my own hands.   I did not feel so secure concerning that of disjointing the union.   But the
very interesting and embarrassing situation in which

his communications placed me, left me, I confess, at a stand to know how to conduct myself with propriety.   He had committed no overt act of aggression against law.   I could draw nothing from him in writing, nor could I learn that he had exposed his plans to any person near me, by whom my testimony could be supported.   He had mentioned to me no persons who were principally and decidedly engaged with him, except General Wilkinson, a Mr. Alston, who I found was his son-in-law, and a Mr. Ephraim Kibby, late a captain of rangers in General Wayne's army. Satisfied that Mr. Burr was resolute in pushing his project of rebellion in the west of the Alleghany, and apprehensive that it was too well and too extensively organized to be easily suppressed, though I dreaded the weight of his character when laid in the balance against my solitary assertion, I brought myself to the resolution to endeavor to defeat it by getting him removed from among us, or to expose myself to all consequences by a disclosure of his intentions.   Accordingly, I waited on the President of the United States, and after some desultory conversation, in which I aimed to draw his view to the westward, I used the freedom to say to the President I thought Mr. Burr should be sent out of this country, and gave for reason that I believed him dangerous in it.   The President asked where he should be sent?   I mentioned London and Cadiz.   The President thought the trust too important, and seemed to entertain a doubt of Mr. Burr's integrity.   I intimated that no one, perhaps, had stronger grounds to mistrust Mr.

Burr's moral integrity than myself; yet, I believed ambition so much predominated over him, that when placed on an eminence, and put on his honor, respect to himself would insure his fidelity; his talents were unquestionable. I perceived the subject was disagreeable to the President; and to give it the shortest course to the point, declared my concern that if Mr. Burr were not in some way disposed of, we should, within eighteen months, have an insurrection, if not a revolution, on the waters of the Mississippi. The President answered, that he had too much confidence in the information, the integrity, and the attachment to the union, of the citizens of that country, to admit an apprehension of the kind. I am happy that events prove this confidence well placed. As no interrogatories followed my expression of alarm, I thought silence on the subject, at that time and place, became me. But I detailed, about the same time, the whole projects of Mr. Burr to certain members of Congress. They believed Colonel Burr capable of anything, and agreed that the fellow ought to be hanged; but thought his projects too chimerical, and his circumstances too desperate, to give the subject the merit of serious consideration. The total security of feeling in those to whom I had rung the tocsin, induced me to suspect my own apprehensions unseasonable, or at least too deeply admitted; and, of course, I grew indifferent about the subject.

Mr. Burr's visits to me became less frequent, and his conversation less familiar. He appeared to have abandoned the idea of a general revolution, but seemed determined on that of the Mississippi ; and, although I could perceive symptoms of distrust in him towards me, he manifested great solicitude to engage me with him in the enterprise. Weary of his importunity, and at once to convince him of my serious attachments, I gave the following toast to the public : The United States—Palsy to the brain that should plot to dismember, and leprosy to the hand that will not draw to defend, our union !

I doubt whether the sentiment was better understood by any of my acquaintance than Colonel Burr. Our intercourse ended here ; we met but seldom afterwards. I returned to my farm in Massachusetts, and thought no more of Mr. Burr, nor his empire, till some time late in September or beginning of October, when a letter from Maurice Belknap, of Marietta, to Timothy E. Danielson, fell into my hands at Brimfield, which satisfied me that Mr. Burr had actually commenced his preparatory operations on the Ohio. I now spoke publicly of the fact ; transmitted a copy of the letter from Belknap to the department of state, and about the same time forwarded, through the hands of the Postmaster-General, to the President of the United States, a statement in substance of what is here above detailed concerning the Mississippi conspiracy of the said Colonel Aaron Burr, which is said to have been the first formal intelligence received by the executive on the subject of the conspirator being in motion.

I know not whether my country will allow me the merit of correctness of conduct in this affair. The novelty of the duty might, perhaps, have embarrassed stronger minds than mine. The uprightness of my intentions, I hope will not be questioned.

The interviews between Colonel Burr and myself, from which the foregoing statement has resulted, were chiefly in this city, in the months of February and March, last year.

WILLIAM EATON.

Washington City, Jan. 26, 1807.

Sworn to in open court this 26th day of January, 1807.

WILLIAM BRENT, Clerk.

Hope Insurance Company
v.
Boardman,
AND
Bank of the United States
v.
Deveaux.

NOTE.

The case of the *Bank of the United States* v. *Deveaux* arose out of an attempt by the State of Georgia to tax the branch of the Bank of the United States in Savannah. This suit was brought by the Bank in the United States Circuit Court for Georgia to recover certain moneys collected. The defendants objected that the federal court was without jurisdiction, since no federal question was raised, and it was not a controversy "between citizens of different states," and that the jurisdiction of the court under the Constitution was thus limited. The argument of the Bank was that this was a suit brought by certain natural citizens of Pennsylvania, acting in their corporate capacity, and that in such capacity they had a right to resort to the federal court, since they were citizens of a different state from the defendants, and that it was therefore a controversy "between citizens of different states." The case was argued on those lines. The opinion adopted the argument of the Bank and decided that the citizens of Pennsylvania had a right thus to litigate in their corporate capacity,—Marshall refused the narrower interpretation of the Constitution. The case was considered decisive of similar points raised in the Insurance Company case. The jurisdiction over corporations had been constantly exercised by the federal courts before that time and there is no evidence of any general jealousy of that jurisdiction. At that time corporations played a smaller part in business affairs; they were smaller and usually composed of fewer members, in each case probably all citizens of one state, and there was no demand for a still broader construction of the powers of the federal courts as to their jurisdiction over corporations. The point to be noted is that the decision went as far as necessary.

But practical difficulties came of it almost at once. It had not been argued that a corporation as such was a " citizen " of the state of its incorporation for the purposes of that clause of the Constitution. Marshall had said in his opinion: " That invisible, intangible, and artificial being, that mere legal entity, a corporation aggregate, is certainly not a citizen, and, consequently, cannot sue or be sued in the courts of the United States, unless the rights of the members, in this respect, can be exercised in their corporate name." But as a practical matter this rule did not work. As corporate organization became more common and invaded all forms of business, as the corporations grew in size until their members were of many states, it was necessary that the federal courts should stretch their jurisdiction and overrule the words of Marshall and say that a corporation is, for the purposes of that clause, a citizen of the state of its incorporation, but with that curious habit of the legal mind of never casting away an established theory, and of distinguishing rather than overruling, the doctrine was later established that a presumption existed that all the members of a corporation were citizens of the state of its incorporation, and then, that this presumption is conclusive and may not be contradicted. Now no doctrine is better established, and the theory of Marshall, sufficient for his time, is abandoned. The growth of that doctrine is a curious example of the unobtrusive elasticity of the Constitution in the hands of lawyers trained at the English common law.

The Hope Insurance Company of Providence

v.

Boardman *et al.*

[5 Cranch, 57.]

1809.

Mr. Ingersoll for Plaintiffs in Error.
Mr. Adams, contra.

The Court having, in the case of *The Bank of the United States* v. *Deveaux et al.*, decided that the right of a corporation to litigate in the courts of the United States depended upon the character (as to citizenship) of the members which compose the body corporate, and that a body corporate as such cannot be a citizen, within the meaning of the constitution, reversed the judgment, for want of jurisdiction in the court below.[1]

---

[1] A similar question of jurisdiction being involved in the case of *The Bank of the United States* v. *Deveaux et al.*, and the counsel in that case expressing a wish to be heard before this case should be decided, the court agreed to hear both cases at the same time; the further arguments in this case were consequently blended with those in the other.

The Bank of the United States

v.

Deveaux *et al.*

[5 Cranch 61.]

1809.

Mr. Binney for plaintiffs in error.   Mr. Harper with him.

Mr. P. B. Key, contra.

March 15.   *Marshall, Ch. J.*, delivered the opinion of the court as follows :

Two points have been made in this cause.

1. That a corporation, composed of citizens of *one state, may sue a citizen of another state in the federal courts.

*85

2. That a right to sue in those courts is conferred on this bank by the law which incorporates it.

The last point will be first considered.

The judicial power of the United States, as defined in the constitution, is dependent, 1st. On the nature of the case ; and, 2d. On the character of the parties.

By the judicial act, the jurisdiction of the circuit courts is extended to cases where the constitutional

right to plead and be impleaded, in the courts of the
Union, depends on the character of the parties; but
where that right depends on the nature of the case,
the circuit courts derive no jurisdiction from that act,
except in the single case of a controversy between
citizens of the same state, claiming lands under grants
from different states.

Unless, then, jurisdiction over this cause has been
given to the Circuit Court by some other than the
judicial act, the bank of the United States had not a
right to sue in that court, upon the principle that the
case arises under a law of the United States.

The plaintiffs contend that the incorporating act
confers this jurisdiction.

That act creates the corporation, gives it a capacity to make contracts and to acquire property, and
enables it "to sue and be sued, plead and be impleaded, answer and be answered, defend and be defended, in courts of record, or any other place whatsoever."

This power, if not incident to a corporation, is
conferred by every incorporating act, and is not understood to enlarge the jurisdiction of any particular
court, but to give a capacity to the corporation to
*86   * appear, as a corporation, in any court
which would, by law, have cognizance of
the cause, if brought by individuals. If jurisdiction
is given by this clause to the federal courts, it is
equally given to all courts having original jurisdiction, and for all sums however small they may be.

But the 9th article of the 7th section of the act

furnishes a conclusive argument against the construction for which the plaintiffs contend.   That section subjects the president and directors, in their individual capacity, to the suit of any person aggrieved by their putting into circulation more notes than is permitted by law, and expressly authorizes the bringing of that action in the federal or state courts.

This evinces the opinion of Congress, that the right to sue does not imply a right to sue in the courts of the Union unless it be expressed.   This idea is strengthened also by the law respecting patent rights.   That law expressly recognizes the right of the patentee to sue in the circuit courts of the United States.

The court, then, is of opinion, that no right is conferred on the bank, by the act of incorporation, to sue in the federal courts.

2. The other point is one of much more difficulty.

The jurisdiction of this court being limited, so far as respects the character of the parties in this particular case, "to controversies between citizens of different states," both parties must be citizens, to come within the description.

That invisible, intangible, and artificial being, that mere legal entity, a corporation aggregate, is certainly not a citizen ; and, consequently, cannot sue or be sued in the courts of the United States, unless the rights of the members, in this respect, can be exercised in their corporate name.   If the corpora-

*87   tion * be considered as a mere faculty, and not as a company of individuals, who, in transacting their joint concerns, may use a legal name, they must be excluded from the courts of the Union.

The duties of this court, to exercise jurisdiction where it is conferred, and not to usurp it where it is not conferred, are of equal obligation. The constitution, therefore, and the law, are to be expounded, without a leaning the one way or the other, according to those general principles which usually govern in the construction of fundamental or other laws.

A constitution, from its nature, deals in generals, not in detail. Its framers cannot perceive minute distinctions which arise in the progress of the nation, and therefore confine it to the establishment of broad and general principles.

The judicial department was introduced into the American constitution under impressions, and with views, which are too apparent not to be perceived by all. However true the fact may be, that the tribunals of the states will administer justice as impartially as those of the nation, to parties of every description, it is not less true that the constitution itself either entertains apprehensions on this subject, or views with such indulgence the possible fears and apprehensions of suitors, that it has established national tribunals for the decision of controversies between aliens and a citizen, or between citizens of different states. Aliens, or citizens of different states, are not less susceptible of these apprehensions, nor can they be supposed to be less the objects of constitutional provision, because they are allowed to sue by a corporate name. That name, indeed, cannot be an alien or a citizen ; but the persons whom it represents may be the one or the other ; and the controversy is, in fact and in law, between those persons suing in their corporate character, by their corporate name, for a corporate right, and the individual against whom the suit may be instituted.

* 88 Substantially *and essentially, the parties in such a case, where the members of the corporation are aliens, or citizens of a different state from the opposite party, come within the spirit and terms of the jurisdiction conferred by the constitution on the national tribunals.

Such has been the universal understanding on the subject. Repeatedly has this court decided causes between a corporation and an individual without feeling a doubt respecting its jurisdiction. Those decisions are not cited as authority ; for they were made without considering this particular point ; but they have much weight, as they show that this point neither occurred to the bar or the bench ; and that the common understanding of intelligent men is in favor of the right of incorporated aliens, or citizens of a different state from the defendant, to sue in the national courts. It is by a course of acute, metaphysical and abstruse reasoning, which has been most ably employed on this occasion, that this opinion is shaken.

As our ideas of a corporation, its privileges and its disabilities, are derived entirely from the English books, we resort to them for aid, in ascertaining its character. It is defined as a mere creature of the law, invisible, intangible and incorporeal. Yet, when we examine the subject further, we find that corporations have been included within terms of description appropriated to real persons.

The statute of Henry VIII. concerning bridges and highways, enacts, that bridges and highways shall be made and repaired by the "inhabitants of the city, shire, or riding," and that the justices shall have power to tax every "inhabitant of such city," &c., and that the collectors may "distrain every such inhabitant as shall be taxed and refuse payment thereof, in his lands, goods and chattels."

Under this statute those have been construed inhabitants who hold lands within the city where *89   the *bridge to be repaired lies, although they reside elsewhere.

Lord Coke says, "every corporation and body politic residing in any county, riding, city, or town corporate, or having lands or tenements in any shire, *quæ propriis manibus et sumptibus possident et habent*, are said to be inhabitants there, within the purview of this statute."

The tax is not imposed on the person, whether he be a member of the corporation or not, who may happen to reside on the lands ; but is imposed on the corporation itself, and, consequently, this ideal existence is considered as an inhabitant, when the general spirit and purpose of the law requires it.

In the case of the *King* v. *Gardner*, reported by Cowper, a corporation was decided, by the Court of King's bench, to come within the description of

" occupiers or inhabitants." In that case the poor
rates to which the lands of the corporation were
declared to be liable, were not assessed to the actual
occupant, for there was none, but to the corporation.
And the principle established by the case appears
to be, that the poor rates on vacant ground belonging
to a corporation, may be assessed to the corporation,
as being inhabitants or occupiers of that ground. In
this case Lord Mansfield notices and overrules an in-
considerate *dictum* of Justice Yates, that a corporation
could not be an inhabitant or occupier.

These opinions are not precisely in point ; but they
serve to show that, for the general purposes and
objects of a law, this invisible, incorporeal creature
of the law may be considered as having corporeal
qualities.

It is true that as far as these cases go they serve
to show that the corporation itself, in its incorporeal
character, may be considered as an inhabitant or an
occupier; and the argument from them would be
** 90* more strong in favor of considering the corporation *itself as endowed for this special
purpose with the character of a citizen, than to consider the character of the individuals who compose
it as a subject which the court can inspect, when
they use the name of the corporation, for the purpose of asserting their corporate rights. Still the
cases show that this technical definition of a corporation does not uniformly circumscribe its capacities, but that courts for legitimate purposes will
contemplate it more substantially.

There is a case, however, reported in 12 Mod. which is thought precisely in point. The corporation of London brought a suit against Wood, by their corporate name, in the Mayor's Court. The suit was brought by the mayor and commonalty, and was tried before the mayor and aldermen. The judgment rendered in this cause was brought before the Court of King's bench and reversed, because the court was deprived of its jurisdiction by the character of the individuals who were members of the corporation.

In that case the objection, that a corporation was an invisible, intangible thing, a mere incorporeal legal entity, in which the characters of the individuals who composed it were completely merged, was urged and was considered. The judges unanimously declared that they could look beyond the corporate name, and notice the character of the individual. In the opinions, which were delivered *seriatim*, several cases are put which serve to illustrate the principle and fortify the decision.

The case of *The Mayor and Commonalty* v. *Wood*, is the stronger because it is on the point of jurisdiction. It appears to the court to be a full authority for the case now under consideration. It seems not possible to distinguish them from each other.

If, then, the Congress of the United States had, in terms, enacted that incorporated aliens might *91 sue *a citizen, or that the incorporated citizens of one state might sue a citizen of another state, in the federal courts, by its corporate name, this court would not have felt itself justified in declaring that such a law transcended the constitution.

The controversy is substantially between aliens, suing by a corporate name, and a citizen, or between citizens of one state, suing by a corporate name, and those of another state. When these are said to be substantially the parties to the controversy, the court does not mean to liken it to the case of a trustee. A trustee is a real person capable of being a citizen or an alien, who has the whole legal estate in himself. At law, he is the real proprietor, and he represents himself, and sues in his own right. But in this case the corporate name represents persons who are members of the corporation.

If the constitution would authorize Congress to give the courts of the Union jurisdiction in this case, in consequence of the character of the members of the corporation, then the judicial act ought to be construed to give it. For the term citizen ought to be understood as it is used in the constitution, and as it is used in other laws. That is, to describe the real persons who come into court, in this case, under their corporate name.

That corporations composed of citizens are considered by the legislature as citizens, under certain circumstances, is to be strongly inferred from the registering act. It never could be intended that an American registered vessel, abandoned to an insurance company composed of citizens, should lose her character as an American vessel; and yet this would be the consequence of declaring that the members of the corporation were, to every intent and purpose, out of view, and merged in the corporation.

The court feels itself authorized by the case in 12 Mod., on a question of jurisdiction, to look to the *character of the individuals who compose the corporation, and they think that the precedents of this court, though they were not decisions on argument, ought not to be absolutely disregarded.

* *92*

If a corporation may sue in the courts of the Union, the court is of opinion that the averment in this case is sufficient.

Being authorized to sue in their corporate name, they could make the averment, and it must apply to the plaintiffs as individuals, because it could not be true as applied to the corporation.

Judgment reversed; plea in abatement overruled, and cause remanded.

The United States *v.* Peters.

NOTE.

THE case is of interest mainly as it shows the temper of the country toward the federal courts in the first decade of the nineteenth century. The legislature of Pennsylvania, disliking a judgment of the federal court in Pennsylvania, passed an act which was, in substance, a cancellation of that judgment on the ground that the federal court was without jurisdiction. Such an act would be unthinkable to any modern lawyer or in any legislature to-day, but it is an admirable example of the hostility and jealousy existing toward the federal courts for a long period after their inception, until, under the strong hands of Marshall and his successors, they became an integral part of the business system of the country. And the case is alike remarkable as illustrating the need of the federal courts to establish a consistent and just system of admiralty law among the states.

The case arose on an application for a writ of mandamus commanding Judge Richard Peters, judge of the District Court for the Pennsylvania District, to order process to issue to enforce obedience to the judgment in a civil cause between one Olmstead and others, which had seemed obnoxious to the Pennsylvania legislature. This Judge Peters had refused to do because he could not or dared not, for reasons that cogently appear from a note that is attached to the report of the case. That note reads as follows :

"On Saturday, March 5th, 1808, upon the affidavit of Olmstead, a rule was granted that Judge Peters should show cause by the next Saturday, why a *mandamus* should not issue. On Saturday,

March 12th, a letter was received by one of the counsel for Olmstead, from Judge Peters, acknowledging service of the rule ; and stating that an act of the legislature of Pennsylvania had commanded the governor of that state to call out an armed force to prevent the execution of any process to enforce the performance of the sentence. That such being the state of things he should not direct process to issue unless he should be so ordered by this court ; whereupon a *mandamus nisi* was granted, returnable at the next term."

The United States

v.

Judge Peters.

[5 Cranch, 135.]

1809.

The facts appear sufficiently in the opinion. Rodney (Attorney General), Lewis, and F. S. Key of counsel for Olmstead and others submitted the return of the mandamus to the consideration of the court without argument.

February 20. *Marshall, Ch. J.,* delivered the opinion of the court as follows :

With great attention, and with serious concern, the court has considered the return made by the judge for the District of Pennsylvania to the *mandamus* directing him to execute the sentence pronounced by him in the case of *Gideon Olmstead and others* v. *Rittenhouse's Executrixes,* or to show cause for not so doing. The cause shown is an act of the legislature of Pennsylvania, passed subsequent to the rendition of his sentence. This act authorizes and requires the governor to demand, for the use of the state of Pennsylvania, the money which had been decreed to Gideon Olmstead and others; and which was in the hands of the executrixes of David Rittenhouse; and, in default of payment, to direct the Attorney General to institute a suit for the recovery thereof. This act further authorizes and requires the governor to use any further means he * may think necessary for the protection of what it denominates "the just rights of the state," and also to protect the persons and properties of the said executrixes of David Rittenhouse, deceased, against any process whatever, issued out of any federal court in consequence of their obedience to the requisition of the said act.

* *136*

If the legislatures of the several states may, at will, annul the judgment of the courts of the United States, and destroy the rights acquired under those judgments, the constitution itself becomes a solemn mockery, and the nation is deprived of the means of enforcing its laws by the instrumentality of its own tribunals. So fatal a result must be deprecated by all; and the people of Pennsylvania, not less than the citizens of every other state, must feel a deep interest in resisting principles so destructive of the Union, and in averting consequences so fatal to themselves.

The act in question does not, in terms, assert the universal right of the state to interpose in every case whatever; but assigns, as a motive for its interposition in this particular case, that the sentence, the execution of which it prohibits, was rendered in a cause over which the federal courts have no jurisdiction.

If the ultimate right to determine the jurisdiction of the courts of the Union is placed by the constitution in the several state legislatures, then this act concludes the subject ; but if that power necessarily resides in the supreme judicial tribunal of the nation, then the jurisdiction of the District Court of Pennsylvania, over the case in which that jurisdiction was exercised, ought to be most deliberately examined ; and the act of Pennsylvania, with whatever respect it may be considered, cannot be permitted to prejudice the question.

In the early part of the war between the United States and Great Britain, Gideon Olmstead and *others, citizens of Connecticut, who say they had been carried to Jamaica as prisoners, were employed as part of the crew of the sloop *Active*, bound from Jamaica to New York, and laden with a cargo for the use of the British army in that place.   On the voyage they seized the vessel, confined the captain, and sailed for Egg Harbor.   In sight of that place, the *Active* was captured by the *Convention*, an armed ship belonging to the state of Pennsylvania, brought into port, libeled and condemned as prize to the captors.   From this sentence Gideon Olmstead and others, who claimed the vessel and cargo, appealed to the Court of Appeals established by Congress, by which tribunal the sentence of condemnation was reversed, the *Active* and her cargo condemned as prize to the claimants, and process was directed to issue out of the Court of Admiralty, commanding the marshal of that court to sell the

*137

said vessel and cargo, and to pay the net proceeds to the claimants.

The mandate of the appellate court was produced in the inferior court, the judge of which admitted the general jurisdiction of the court established by Congress, as an appellate court, but denied its power to control the verdict of a jury which had been rendered in favor of the captors, the officers and crew of the *Convention ;* and therefore refused obedience to the mandate ; but directed the marshal to make the sale, and, after deducting charges, to bring the residue of the money into court, subject to its future order.

The claimants then applied to the judges of appeals for an injunction to prohibit the marshal from paying the money, arising from the sales, into the Court of Admiralty ; which was awarded, and served upon him: in contempt of which, on the 4th of January, 1778, he paid the money to the judge, who acknowledged the receipt thereof at the foot of the marshal's return.

On the 1st of May, 1779, George Ross, the judge *138 * of the Court of Admiralty, delivered to David Rittenhouse, who was then treasurer of the state of Pennsylvania, the sum of 11,496*l.* 9*s.* 9*d.*, in loan-office certificates ; which was the proportion of the prize money to which that state would have been entitled, had the sentence of the Court of Admiralty remained in force. On the same day, David Rittenhouse executed a bond of indemnity to George Ross, in which, after reciting that the money was paid to him for the use of the state of Pennsylvania, he binds himself to repay the same, should the said George Ross be thereafter compelled, by due course of law, to pay that sum according to the decree of the Court of Appeals.

These loan-office certificates were in the name of Matthew Clarkson, who was marshal of the Court of Admiralty, and were dated the 6th of November, 1778. Indents were issued on them to David Rittenhouse, and the whole principal and interest were afterwards funded by him, in his own name, under the act of Congress making provision for the debt of the United States.

Among the papers of David Rittenhouse was a memorandum, made by himself at the foot of a list of the certificates mentioned above, in these words: "Note. The above certificates will be the property of the state of Pennsylvania, when the state releases me from the bond I gave in 1778, to indemnify George Ross, Esq., judge of the admiralty, for paying the 50 original certificates into the treasury, as the state's share of the prize."

The state did not release David Rittenhouse from the bond mentioned in this memorandum. These certificates remained in the private possession of David Rittenhouse, who drew the interest on them during his life, and after his death they remained in possession of his representatives; against whom the libel in this case was filed, for the purpose of carrying into execution the decree of the Court of Appeals.

*139   * While this suit was depending, the state of Pennsylvania forbore to assert its title, and, in January, 1803, the court decreed in favor of the libellants ; soon after which, the legislature passed the act which has been stated.

It is contended that the federal courts were deprived of jurisdiction, in this cause, by that amendment of the constitution which exempts states from being sued in those courts by individuals. This amendment declares, " that the judicial power of the United States shall not be construed to extend to any suit, in law or equity, commenced or prosecuted against one of the United States by citizens of another state, or by citizens or subjects of any foreign state."

The right of a state to assert, as plaintiff, any interest it may have in a subject, which forms the matter of controversy between individuals, in one of the courts of the United States, is not affected by this amendment ; nor can it be so construed as to oust the court of its jurisdiction, should such claim be suggested. The amendment simply provides, that no suit shall be commenced or prosecuted against a state. The state cannot be made a defendant to a suit brought by an individual ; but it remains the duty of the courts of the United States to decide all cases brought before them by citizens of one state against citizens of a different state, where a state is not necessarily a defendant. In this case, the suit was not instituted against the state or its treasurer, but against the executrixes of David Rittenhouse, for the proceeds of a vessel condemned in the court of admiralty, which were admitted to be in their possession. If these proceeds had been the actual property of Pennsylvania, however wrongfully acquired, the disclosure of that fact would have presented a case on which it is unnecessary to give an opinion ; but it certainly can never be alleged that a mere suggestion of title in a state to property, in possession of an individual, must arrest the proceedings of the court, and prevent

*140 their * looking into the suggestion, and examining the validity of the title.

If the suggestion in this case be examined, it is deemed perfectly clear that no title whatever to the certificates in question was vested in the state of Pennsylvania.

By the highest judicial authority of the nation it has been long since decided, that the Court of Appeals erected by Congress had full authority to revise and correct the sentence of the courts of admiralty of the several states, in prize causes. That question, therefore, is at rest. Consequently, the decision of the Court of Appeals in this case annulled the sentence of the Court of Admiralty, and extinguished the interest of the state of Pennsylvania in the *Active* and her cargo, which was acquired by that sentence. The full right to that property was immediately vested in the claimants, who might rightfully pursue it, into whosesoever hands it might come. These certificates, in the hands, first, of Matthew Clarkson, the marshal, and afterwards of George Ross, the judge of the Court of Admiralty, were the absolute property of the claimants. Nor did they change their character on coming into the possession of David Rittenhouse.

Although Mr. Rittenhouse was treasurer of the

state of Pennsylvania, and the bond of indemnity
which he executed states the money to have been
paid to him for the use of the state of Pennsylvania,
it is apparent that he held them in his own right,
until he should be completely indemnified by the
state. The evidence to this point is conclusive. The
original certificates do not appear to have been deposited in the state treasury, to have been designated
in any manner as the property of the state, or to have
been delivered over to the successor of David Rittenhouse. They remained in his possession. The indents, issued upon them for interest, were drawn by
David Rittenhouse, and preserved with the original
certificates. When funded as * part of the
*141 debt of the United States, they were funded
by David Rittenhouse, and the interest was drawn by
him. The note made by himself at the foot of
the list, which he preserved, as explanatory of the
whole transaction, demonstrates that he held the certificates as security against the bond he had executed
to George Ross; and that bond was obligatory, not
on the state of Pennsylvania, but on David Rittenhouse, in his private capacity.

These circumstances demonstrate, beyond the
possibility of doubt, that the property which represented the *Active* and her cargo, was in possession,
not of the state of Pennsylvania, but of David Rittenhouse as an individual; after whose death it passed,
like other property, to his representatives.

Since, then, the state of Pennsylvania had neither
possession of, nor right to, the property on which the

sentence of the District Court was pronounced, and since the suit was neither commenced nor prosecuted against that state, there remains no pretext for the allegation that the case is within that amendment of the constitution which has been cited ; and, consequently, the state of Pennsylvania can possess no constitutional right to resist the legal process which may be directed in this cause.

It will be readily conceived that the order which this court is enjoined to make by the high obligations of duty and of law, is not made without extreme regret at the necessity which has induced the application.   But it is a solemn duty, and therefore must be performed.   A peremptory *mandamus* must be awarded.

Fletcher *v.* Peck.

NOTE.

THIS is one of Marshall's greatest cases,—first, because it dealt with a political issue that had been a subject of dispute for years; second, because it was the earliest case in which he construed one of those provisions of the Constitution which directly restrict the power of the states under the union. This was the first case in which he decided that the decision of the United States courts could nullify the act of a state legislature. "No heavier or better directed blow was ever struck against States rights when those rights were invoked in order to thwart or cripple the National power."[1]

Fletcher v. *Peck* decided that a state had no power to revoke a grant of land made by it; the decision rested mainly on the ground that such a revocation was an impairment of a contract and so contrary to the Constitution of the United States. That is the exact decision, and for that point the case is constantly cited and undoubted law. The circumstances under which the case arose and the entire failure of the judgment to settle the controversy which it considered seem almost universally forgotten.

The case was an action on certain covenants on a deed made by one Peck to one Fletcher conveying certain lands which, in 1795, had been sold to James Gunn and others, in accordance

---

[1] Hon. Henry Cabot Lodge. Address before the Associated Committees of Illinois, on John Marshall Day, 1901. Reprinted in Dillon's *John Marshall*, vol. ii., pp. 303, 327. The place of *Fletcher* v. *Peck* in Marshall's scheme of constitutional law, its relation to the Dartmouth College case, and its influence on the law are dealt with in the introduction to these volumes.

with the authority of a special act of the legislature of Georgia. The grantor in this deed had covenanted in substance that the sale by the state of Georgia was legal and gave good title. The grounds of the action were, first, that the state had no title; second, that the act of the legislature authorizing it was obtained by fraud and corruption and thus was void; third, that the grant by the state was rescinded by a later act. The real question of the case was in regard to the validity of that act and the power of Georgia to pass it. A secondary objection to the title granted by the state was that it was subject to certain rights of occupancy by the Indians. The case arose on writ of error to the Circuit Court for the district of Massachusetts.

But there were certain other facts, not on the record, which were, humanly speaking, before Marshall and the Supreme Court. The lands in question, which had been granted to James Gunn, were some 15,000 acres, which in 1810 lay in the then territory of Mississippi. They were bounded on the west by the Mississippi, on the east by the Tombigbee. From the close of the revolution for independence until 1800, one of the most bitterly contested political questions, as Marshall said in his opinion, "a momentous question which, at one time, threatened to shake the American confederacy to its foundation," was whether the lands west of the Alleghanies were the property of the separate states or of the United States. The jealousy of the smaller states and the real patriotism of some of the states, like New York, led finally to the gradual cession of these lands to the federal government. One of the earliest phases of this controversy was Georgia's claim to the lands lying between it and the Mississippi which had been obtained from Spain. This region was sparsely settled and had no definite form of government. In 1788, Georgia ceded its claims in this region to the United States, but with such conditions that the grant was refused. In 1789, a great part of the land was sold to certain land companies, but the bargain was never carried out. In 1795, four new companies, commonly known as the Yazoo Companies, secured from the legislature of Georgia a grant of about thirty-five million acres for five hundred thousand dollars. The iniquity of the transaction was amazing. It was a matter of public record that every man, save one, who had voted for the measure obtained rights in the granted land. "No sooner did the true character of the sale become known," says McMaster,[1] "than the State of Georgia, from the mountains to the sea, was aflame. The Grand Juries of every county but two presented the act as a public grievance. The Convention which assembled in May had its table heaped up with petitions, memorials, remonstrances. Hardly a freeman in the State but put his name to some such document. Every member of the Legislature of 1796 came solemnly pledged to the repeal of the act. Accordingly, on the thirteenth of February, 1796, the Legislature pronounced the sale unconstitutional, null, and void." And the title of land included in these acts in 1810 came before the Supreme Court in *Fletcher* v. *Peck*, and it was the righteous repealing act that the court declared unconstitutional. Surely no case ever demanded a decision more contrary to the lay ideas of justice. In 1790, certain of the western lands of Georgia were included by Congress in the territory of Mississippi, and later commissioners were appointed to settle the conflicting claims of the state of Georgia. In 1802, the claims of Georgia to govern the disputed territory were finally yielded. The commissioners appointed went on to deal with the title to the lands. They compromised with the original holders under British title, and with some of the Yazoo titles under the Georgia grant of 1795. The Georgia grants of 1789 were ignored. It was a provision of the compromise with Georgia in 1802 that the Georgia titles should be recognized. In 1803, an act was passed by Congress adopting the settlement provisions of the commissioners as to title to land in the disputed territory. As a matter of fact, that settlement did not recognize the claims of the Yazoo Companies as a whole at all. In every Congress up to 1809 the canny and farseeing New Englanders who had formed the greater part of the members of the Yazoo Companies attempted to get relief from Congress. In 1809 and 1810, *Fletcher* v. *Peck* was brought before the Supreme Court. On the face of it the case bears every evidence of

[1] *History of the United States*, (Appleton, 1897), vol. ii., p. 480.

being a friendly controversy, prepared for the sake of getting Marshall's judgment in favor of the Yazoo claimants. Justice Johnson, in his opinion on the case, which dissented sharply from some points made by Marshall, said: "I have been very unwilling to proceed to the decision of this cause at all. It appears to me to bear strong evidence, upon the face of it, of being a mere feigned case. It is our duty to decide on the rights, but not on the speculations of parties. My confidence, however, in the respectable gentlemen who have been engaged for the parties, has induced me to abandon my scruples, in the belief that they would never consent to impose a mere feigned case upon this court."

Such was the case that the Supreme Court attempted to settle.

Marshall decided that the court had no power to inquire into the alleged fraud in the Georgia legislature which passed the act of 1795. Obviously correct and inevitable as this decision was, it was unpalatable to the public taste, and it is quite clear that any tribunal which tried to settle the Yazoo claims without jurisdiction to inquire into the frauds which were the basis of them labored at a great disadvantage. Then Marshall decided that the repealing act, which, on broad moral grounds, was highly admirable, was unconstitutional. A less great judge, a judge who felt less keenly the necessity for upholding the Constitution for fair weather and foul, might have temporized in such a situation. For there was, it seems, a way out. The Constitution forbade the impairment of "contracts" by the states. The conveyances under the act of 1795 were grants, executed contracts perhaps, but not necessarily contracts. Justice Johnson, in his acute opinion dissenting on this point, said: "Whether the words 'acts impairing the obligation of contracts' can be construed as having the same force as must have been given to the words 'obligation and effect of contracts' is the difficulty in my mind"; and again, "To give it (this clause of the Constitution) the general effect of a restriction on the state powers in favor of private rights, is certainly going very far beyond the obvious and necessary import of the words, and would operate to restrict the states in the exercise of that right which every community must exercise

of possessing itself of the property of the individual, when
necessary for public uses." But the broader construction given
by Marshall has never since been questioned, and is now clear
and unshakable law. It is typical of the mind of Marshall and
of his attitude toward the Constitution that his construction
tended toward a stricter political morality, and likewise toward
the tightening of the restrictions on the powers of the separate
states.

But though these words of Marshall have established the law,
they by no means settled the Yazoo difficulties. It is to be noted
that Marshall's opinion carefully refrained from any comment
on the validity of the settlement act passed by Congress, or in
regard to the political question as to the sovereignty over the
disputed territory. The case simply decided the abstract rights
of the parties, but the Supreme Court possessed no machinery to
settle so complicated a quarrel, and four years later Congress
voted eight million dollars in land scrip to quiet the disgruntled
claimants.[1]

Not a hint of that helplessness, that inability to settle the whole
controversy appears in the opinion; truly Marshall's court sat to
pronounce principles to guide posterity.

One minor point in the case deserves notice, because it shows
clearly how deeply Marshall felt the necessity of restraint on
arbitrary legislative power, a feeling perhaps engendered by the
arbitrary action of the British Parliament before the revolution.
In the course of the opinion he said:

"It may well be doubted whether the nature of society and
of government does not prescribe some limits to the legislative
power, and if any be prescribed, where are they to be found, if
the property of an individual, fairly and honestly acquired, may
be seized without compensation?"

And Justice Johnson said: "I do not hesitate to declare that a
state does not possess the power of revoking its own grants. But
I do it on a general principle, on the reason and nature of things;
a principle which will impose laws even on the Deity."

---

[1] Thirteenth Congress. Second Session, chap. xxxix., Act of March 31,
1814.

Such a view, that some such basic principles of society exist which are within the province of the courts to expound and apply, has often found expression in later opinions that hark back to these phrases, but they are not the law, and, it would seem, wisely, and in no case did Marshall base a decision on such a ground.

Fletcher

v.

Peck.

[6 Cranch, 87.]

1810.

The case was twice argued, first by Luther Martin for the plaintiff in error, and by J. Q. Adams and R. G. Harper for the defendant, and again by Martin for the plaintiff and by Harper and Joseph Story for the defendant.

March 16, 1810. *Marshall, Ch. J.*, delivered the opinion of the court as follows:

The pleadings being now amended, this cause comes on again to be heard on sundry demurrers, and on a special verdict.

The suit was instituted on several covenants contained in a deed made by John Peck, the defendant in error, conveying to Robert Fletcher, the plaintiff in error, certain lands which were part of a large purchase made by James Gunn and others, in the year 1795, from the state of Georgia, the contract for which was made in the form of a bill passed by the legislature of that state.

The first count in the declaration set forth a breach
*in the second covenant contained in the
*128 deed. The covenant is, "that the legisla-
ture of the state of Georgia, at the time of passing
the act of sale aforesaid, had good right to sell and
dispose of the same in the manner pointed out by the
said act." The breach assigned is, that the legislature
had no power to sell.

The plea in bar sets forth the constitution of the
state of Georgia, and avers that the lands sold by the
defendant to the plaintiff, were within that state. It
then sets forth the granting act, and avers the power
of the legislature to sell and dispose of the premises
as pointed out by the act.

To this plea the plaintiff below demurred, and the
defendant joined in demurrer.

That the legislature of Georgia, unless restrained
by its own constitution, possesses the power of dis-
posing of the unappropriated lands within its own
limits, in such manner as its own judgment shall dictate, is a proposition not to be controverted. The
only question, then, presented by this demurrer, for
the consideration of the court, is this, did the then
constitution of the state of Georgia prohibit the legislature to dispose of the lands, which were the subject
of this contract, in the manner stipulated by the
contract?

The question, whether a law be void for its repugnancy to the constitution, is, at all times, a question
of much delicacy, which ought seldom, if ever, to be
decided in the affirmative in a doubtful case. The

court, when impelled by duty to render such a judgment, would be unworthy of its station, could it be
unmindful of the solemn obligations which that station imposes.   But it is not on slight implication and
vague conjecture that the legislature is to be pronounced to have transcended its powers, and its acts
to be considered as void.   The opposition between
the constitution and the law should be such that the
judge feels a clear and strong conviction of their incompatibility with each other.

In this case the court can perceive no such opposition.   In the constitution of Georgia, adopted in the
*129   *year 1789, the court can perceive no re-
striction on the legislative power, which
inhibits the passage of the act of 1795.   The court
cannot say that, in passing that act, the legislature has
transcended its powers and violated the constitution.

In overruling the demurrer, therefore, to the first
plea, the Circuit Court committed no error.

The 3d covenant is, that all the title which the
state of Georgia ever had in the premises had been
legally conveyed to John Peck, the grantor.

The 2d count assigns, in substance, as a breach of
this covenant, that the original grantees from the
state of Georgia promised and assured divers members of the legislature, then sitting in general assembly, that if the said members would assent to,
and vote for, the passing of the act, and if the said
bill should pass, such members should have a share
of, and be interested in, all the lands purchased from
the said state by virtue of such law.   And that divers

of the said members, to whom the said promises were made, were unduly influenced thereby, and, under such influence, did vote for the passing of the said bill; by reason whereof the said law was a nullity, &c., and so the title of the state of Georgia did not pass to the said Peck, &c.

The plea to this count, after protesting that the promises it alleges were not made, avers, that until after the purchase made from the original grantees by James Greenleaf, under whom the said Peck claims, neither the said James Greenleaf, nor the said Peck, nor any of the mesne vendors between the said Greenleaf and Peck, had any notice or knowledge that any such promises or assurances were made by the said original grantees, or either of them, to any of the members of the legislature of the state of Georgia.

To this plea the plaintiff demurred generally, and the defendant joined in the demurrer.

*130   *That corruption should find its way into the governments of our infant republics, and contaminate the very source of legislation, or that impure motives should contribute to the passage of a law, or the formation of a legislative contract, are circumstances most deeply to be deplored. How far a court of justice would, in any case, be competent, on proceedings instituted by the state itself, to vacate a contract thus formed, and to annul rights acquired, under that contract, by third persons having no notice of the improper means by which it was obtained, is a question which the court would approach with much circumspection. It may well be doubted how

far the validity of a law depends upon the motives of
its framers, and how far the particular inducements,
operating on members of the supreme sovereign
power of a state, to the formation of a contract by
that power, are examinable in a court of justice. If
the principle be conceded, that an act of the supreme
sovereign power might be declared null by a court, in
consequence of the means which procured it, still
would there be much difficulty in saying to what extent those means must be applied to produce this effect.
Must it be direct corruption, or would interest or undue
influence of any kind be sufficient? Must the vitiating
cause operate on a majority, or on what number of the
members? Would the act be null, whatever might
be the wish of the nation, or would its obligation or
nullity depend upon the public sentiment?

If the majority of the legislature be corrupted, it
may well be doubted, whether it be within the province of the judiciary to control their conduct, and, if
less than a majority act from impure motives, the principle by which judicial interference would be regulated, is not clearly discerned.

Whatever difficulties this subject might present,
when viewed under aspects of which it may be susceptible, this court can perceive none in the particular
pleadings now under consideration.

This is not a bill brought by the state of Georgia,
to annul the contract, nor does it appear to the court,
*131   by *this count, that the state of Georgia
is dissatisfied with the sale that has been
made. The case, as made out in the pleadings, is

simply this: One individual who holds lands in the state of Georgia, under a deed covenanting that the title of Georgia was in the grantor, brings an action of covenant upon this deed, and assigns, as a breach, that some of the members of the legislature were induced to vote in favor of the law, which constituted the contract, by being promised an interest in it, and that therefore the act is a mere nullity.

This solemn question cannot be brought thus collaterally and incidentally before the court. It would be indecent in the extreme, upon a private contract between two individuals, to enter into an inquiry respecting the corruption of the sovereign power of a state. If the title be plainly deduced from a legislative act, which the legislature might constitutionally pass, if the act be clothed with all the requisite forms of a law, a court, sitting as a court of law, cannot sustain a suit brought by one individual against another founded on the allegation that the act is a nullity, in consequence of the impure motives which influenced certain members of the legislature which passed the law.

The Circuit Court, therefore, did right in overruling this demurrer.

The 4th covenant in the deed is, that the title to the premises has been in no way, constitutionally or legally, impaired by virtue of any subsequent act of any subsequent legislature of the state of Georgia.

The third count recites the undue means practiced on certain members of the legislature, as stated in the second count, and then alleges that, in consequence

of these practices, and of other causes, a subsequent
legislature passed an act annulling and rescinding
the law under which the conveyance to the original
grantees was made, declaring that conveyance void,
and asserting the title of the state to the lands it
*132   contained. The *count proceeds to recite
at large, this rescinding act, and concludes
with averring that, by reason of this act the title of
the said Peck in the premises was constitutionally and
legally impaired, and rendered null and void.

After protesting, as before, that no such promises
were made as stated in this count, the defendant again
pleads that himself and the first purchaser under the
original grantees, and all intermediate holders of the
property, were purchasers without notice.

To this plea there is a demurrer and joinder.

The importance and the difficulty of the questions,
presented by these pleadings, are deeply felt by the
court.

The lands in controversy vested absolutely in James
Gunn and others, the original grantees, by the conveyance of the governor, made in pursuance of an act
of assembly to which the legislature was fully competent. Being thus in full possession of the legal
estate, they, for a valuable consideration, conveyed
portions of the land to those who were willing to
purchase. If the original transaction was infected
with fraud, these purchasers did not participate
in it, and had no notice of it. They were innocent.
Yet the legislature of Georgia has involved them
in the fate of the first parties to the transaction,

and, if the act be valid, has annihilated their rights also.

The legislature of Georgia was a party to this transaction; and for a party to pronounce its own deed invalid, whatever cause may be assigned for its invalidity, must be considered as a mere act of power which must find its vindication in a train of reasoning not often heard in courts of justice.

But the real party, it is said, are the people, and when their agents are unfaithful, the acts of those agents cease to be obligatory.

It is, however, to be recollected that the people can
*133   * act only by these agents, and that, while within the powers conferred on them, their acts must be considered as the acts of the people. If the agents be corrupt, others may be chosen, and, if their contracts be examinable, the common sentiment, as well as common usage of mankind, points out a mode by which this examination may be made, and their validity determined.

If the legislature of Georgia was not bound to submit its pretensions to those tribunals which are established for the security of property, and to decide on human rights, if it might claim to itself the power of judging in its own case, yet there are certain great principles of justice, whose authority is universally acknowledged, that ought not to be entirely disregarded.

If the legislature be its own judge in its own case, it would seem equitable that its decision should be regulated by those rules which would have regulated the decision of a judicial tribunal. The question was, in its nature, a question of title, and the tribunal which decided it was either acting in the character of a court of justice, and performing a duty usually assigned to a court, or it was exerting a mere act of power in which it was controlled only by its own will.

If a suit be brought to set aside a conveyance obtained by fraud, and the fraud be clearly proved, the conveyance will be set aside, as between the parties; but the rights of third persons, who are purchasers without notice, for a valuable consideration, cannot be disregarded. Titles which, according to every legal test, are perfect, are acquired with that confidence which is inspired by the opinion that the purchaser is safe. If there be any concealed defect, arising from the conduct of those who had held the property long before he acquired it, of which he had no notice, that concealed defect cannot be set up against him. He has paid his money for a title good at law, he is innocent, whatever may be the guilt of others, and equity will not subject him to the penalties attached to that guilt. All titles would be insecure, and the intercourse *between man and *134* man would be very seriously obstructed, if this principle be overturned.

A court of chancery, therefore, had a bill been brought to set aside the conveyance made to James Gunn and others, as being obtained by improper practices with the legislature, whatever might have been its decision as respected the original grantees, would have been bound, by its own rules, and by the clearest principles of equity, to leave unmolested those who were purchasers, without notice, for a valuable consideration.

If the legislature felt itself absolved from those rules of property which are common to all the citizens of the United States, and from those principles of equity which are acknowledged in all our courts, its act is to be supported by its power alone, and the same power may devest any other individual of his lands, if it shall be the will of the legislature so to exert it.

It is not intended to speak with disrespect of the legislature of Georgia, or of its acts. Far from it. The question is a general question, and is treated as one. For although such powerful objections to a legislative grant, as are alleged against this, may not again exist, yet the principle, on which alone this rescinding act is to be supported, may be applied to every case to which it shall be the will of any legislature to apply it. The principle is this: that a legislature may, by its own act, divest the vested estate of any man whatever, for reasons which shall, by itself, be deemed sufficient.

In this case the legislature may have had ample proof that the original grant was obtained by practices which can never be too much reprobated, and which would have justified its abrogation so far as respected those to whom crime was imputable. But the grant, when issued, conveyed an estate in fee-simple to the grantee, clothed with all the solemnities which law can bestow. This estate was transferable;

and those who purchased parts of it were not stained

*135   by that * guilt which infected the original

transaction. Their case is not distinguishable from the ordinary case of purchasers of a legal
estate without knowledge of any secret fraud which
might have led to the emanation of the original grant.
According to the well known course of equity, their
rights could not be affected by such fraud. Their
situation was the same, their title was the same, with
that of every other member of the community who
holds land by regular conveyances from the original
patentee.

Is the power of the legislature competent to the
annihilation of such title, and to a resumption of the
property thus held ?

The principle asserted is, that one legislature is
competent to repeal any act which a former legislature was competent to pass; and that one legislature cannot abridge the powers of a succeeding
legislature.

The correctness of this principle, so far as respects
general legislation, can never be controverted. But,
if an act be done under a law, a succeeding legislature
cannot undo it. The past cannot be recalled by the
most absolute power. Conveyances have been made ;
those conveyances have vested legal estates, and, if
those estates may be seized by the sovereign authority, still, that they originally vested is a fact, and cannot cease to be a fact.

When, then, a law is in its nature a contract, when
absolute rights have vested under that contract, a

repeal of the law cannot devest those rights ; and the
act of annulling them, if legitimate, is rendered so by
a power applicable to the case of every individual in
the community.

It may well be doubted whether the nature of
society and of government does not prescribe some
limits to the legislative power ; and, if any be prescribed, where are they to be found, if the property
of an individual, fairly and honestly acquired, may be
seized without compensation ?

*136   *To the legislature all legislative power is
granted ; but the question, whether the act
of transferring the property of an individual to the
public, be in the nature of the legislative power, is
well worthy of serious reflection.

It is the peculiar province of the legislature to prescribe general rules for the government of society ;
the application of those rules to individuals in society
would seem to be the duty of other departments.
How far the power of giving the law may involve
every other power, in cases where the constitution is
silent, never has been, and perhaps never can be,
definitely stated.

The validity of this rescinding act, then, might well
be doubted, were Georgia a single sovereign power.
But Georgia cannot be viewed as a single, unconnected, sovereign power, on whose legislature no
other restrictions are imposed than may be found in
its own constitution. She is a part of a large empire ;
she is a member of the American Union ; and that
Union has a constitution the supremacy of which all

acknowledge, and which imposes limits to the legislatures of the several states, which none claim a right to pass. The constitution of the United States declares that no state shall pass any bill of attainder, *ex post facto* law, or law impairing the obligation of contracts.

Does the case now under consideration come within this prohibitory section of the constitution?

In considering this very interesting question, we immediately ask ourselves what is a contract? Is a grant a contract?

A contract is a compact between two or more parties, and is either executory or executed. An executory contract is one in which a party binds himself to do, or not to do, a particular thing; such was the law under which the conveyance was made by the governor. A contract executed is one in which the object * of contract is performed; and this, says Blackstone, differs in nothing from a grant. The contract between Georgia and the purchasers was executed by the grant. A contract executed, as well as one which is executory, contains obligations binding on the parties. A grant, in its own nature, amounts to an extinguishment of the right of the grantor, and implies a contract not to re-assert that right. A party is, therefore, always estopped by his own grant.

*137

Since, then, in fact, a grant is a contract executed, the obligation of which still continues, and since the constitution uses the general term contract, without distinguishing between those which are executory

and those which are executed, it must be construed
to comprehend the latter as well as the former.   A
law annulling conveyances between individuals, and
declaring that the grantors should stand seized of
their former estates, notwithstanding those grants,
would be as repugnant to the constitution as a law
discharging the vendors of property from the obligation of executing their contracts by conveyances.   It
would be strange if a contract to convey was secured
by the constitution, while an absolute conveyance
remained unprotected.

If, under a fair construction of the constitution,
grants are comprehended under the term contracts, is
a grant from the state excluded from the operation of
the provision?   Is the clause to be considered as in-
hibiting the state from impairing the obligation of
contracts between two individuals, but as excluding
from that inhibition contracts made with itself?

The words themselves contain no such distinction.
They are general, and are applicable to contracts of
every description.   If contracts made with the state
are to be exempted from their operation, the exception must arise from the character of the contracting
party, not from the words which are employed.

Whatever respect might have been felt for the
state sovereignties, it is not to be disguised that the
framers of the constitution viewed, with some appre-
*138   hension, * the violent acts which might grow
          out of the feelings of the moment; and that
the people of the United States, in adopting that
instrument, have manifested a determination to shield

themselves and their property from the effects of
those sudden and strong passions to which men are
exposed.   The restrictions on the legislative power
of the states are obviously founded in this sentiment; and the constitution of the United States contains what may be deemed a bill of rights for the
people of each state.

No state shall pass any bill of attainder, *ex post
faɛto* law, or law impairing the obligation of contracts.

A bill of attainder may affect the life of an individual, or may confiscate his property, or may do
both.

In this form the power of the legislature over the
lives and fortunes of individuals is expressly restrained.   What motive, then, for implying, in words
which import a general prohibition to impair the
obligation of contracts, an exception in favor of the
right to impair the obligation of those contracts into
which the state may enter?

The state legislatures can pass no *ex post facto* law.
An *ex post facto* law is one which renders an act punishable in a manner in which it was not punishable
when it was committed.   Such a law may inflict
penalties on the person, or may inflict pecuniary
penalties which swell the public treasury.   The legislature is then prohibited from passing a law by which
a man's estate, or any part of it, shall be seized for a
crime which was not declared, by some previous law,
to render him liable to that punishment.   Why, then,
should violence be done to the natural meaning of
words for the purpose of leaving to the legislature

the power of seizing, for public use, the estate of an individual in the form of a law annulling the title by which he holds that estate? The court can perceive no sufficient grounds for making this distinction. This rescinding act would have the effect of an *ex post facto* law. It forfeits the estate of Fletcher for a crime not committed by himself, but by those from

*139 whom he purchased. * This cannot be effected in the form of an *ex post facto* law, or bill of attainder; why, then, is it allowable in the form of a law annulling the original grant?

The argument in favor of presuming an intention to except a case, not excepted by the words of the constitution, is susceptible of some illustration from a principle originally ingrafted in that instrument, though no longer a part of it. The constitution, as passed, gave the courts of the United States jurisdiction in suits brought against individual states. A state, then, which violated its own contract was suable in the courts of the United States for that violation. Would it have been a defense in such a suit to say that the state had passed a law absolving itself from the contract? It is scarcely to be conceived that such a defense could be set up. And yet, if a state is neither restrained by the general principles of our political institutions, nor by the words of the constitution, from impairing the obligation of its own contracts, such a defense would be a valid one. This feature is no longer found in the constitution; but it aids in the construction of those clauses with which it was originally associated.

It is, then, the unanimous opinion of the court, that, in this case, the estate having passed into the hands of a purchaser for a valuable consideration, without notice, the state of Georgia was restrained, either by general principles, which are common to our free institutions, or by the particular provisions of the constitution of the United States, from passing a law whereby the estate of the plaintiff in the premises so purchased could be constitutionally and legally impaired and rendered null and void.

In overruling the demurrer to the 3d plea, therefore, there is no error.

The first covenant in the deed is, that the state of Georgia, at the time of the act of the legislature thereof, entitled as aforesaid, was legally seized in fee of the soil thereof subject only to the extinguishment of part of the Indian title thereon.

*140   *The 4th count assigns, as a breach of this covenant, that the right to the soil was in the United States, and not in Georgia.

To this count the defendant pleads, that the state of Georgia was seized; and tenders an issue on the fact in which the plaintiff joins.   On this issue a special verdict is found.

The jury find the grant of Carolina by Charles second to the Earl of Clarendon and others, comprehending the whole country from 36 deg. 30 min. north lat. to 29 deg. north lat., and from the Atlantic to the South Sea.

They find that the northern part of this territory was afterwards erected into a separate colony, and that the most northern part of the 35 deg. of north lat. was the boundary line between North and South Carolina.

That seven of the eight proprietors of the Carolinas surrendered to George second in the year 1729, who appointed a governor of South Carolina.

That, in 1732, George the second granted, to the Lord Viscount Percival and others, seven-eighths of the territory between the Savannah and the Alatamaha, and extending west to the South Sea, and that the remaining eighth part, which was still the property of the heir of Lord Carteret, one of the original grantees of Carolina, was afterwards conveyed to them. This territory was constituted a colony and called Georgia.

That the governor of South Carolina continued to exercise jurisdiction south of Georgia.

That, in 1752, the grantees surrendered to the crown.

That, in 1754, a governor was appointed by the crown, with a commission describing the boundaries of the colony.

That a treaty of peace was concluded between Great *Britain and Spain, in 1763, in which the latter ceded to the former Florida, with fort St. Augustine and the bay of Pensacola.

141

That, in October, 1763, the King of Great Britain issued a proclamation, creating four new colonies, Quebec, East Florida, West Florida, and Grenada; and prescribing the bounds of each, and further declaring that all the lands between the Alatamaha

and St. Mary's should be annexed to Georgia.   The
same proclamation contained a clause reserving, under the dominion and protection of the crown, for
the use of the Indians, all the lands on the western
waters, and forbidding a settlement on them, or a
purchase of them from the Indians.   The lands conveyed to the plaintiff lie on the western waters.

That, in November, 1763, a commission was issued
to the governor of Georgia, in which the boundaries of
that province are described as extending westward to
the Mississippi.   A commission, describing boundaries
of the same extent, was afterwards granted in 1764.

That a war broke out between Great Britain and
her colonies, which terminated in a treaty of peace
acknowledging them as sovereign and independent
states.

That in April, 1787, a convention was entered into
between the states of South Carolina and Georgia
settling the boundary line between them.

The jury afterwards describe the situation of the
lands mentioned in the plaintiff's declaration, in such
manner that their lying within the limits of Georgia,
as defined in the proclamation of 1763, in the treaty
of peace, and in the convention between that state
and South Carolina, has not been questioned.

The counsel for the plaintiff rest their argument
on a single proposition.   They contend that the
reservation for the use of the Indians, contained in
*142   the proclamation *of 1763, excepts the
lands on the western waters from the colonies within whose bounds they would otherwise have

been, and that they were acquired by the revolutionary war. All acquisitions during the war, it is contended, were made by the joint arms, for the joint
benefit of the United States, and not for the benefit
of any particular state.

The court does not understand the proclamation
as it is understood by the counsel for the plaintiff.
The reservation for the use of the Indians appears to
be a temporary arrangement suspending, for a time,
the settlement of the country reserved, and the
powers of the royal governor within the territory
reserved, but is not conceived to amount to an
alteration of the boundaries of the colony. If the
language of the proclamation be, in itself, doubtful,
the commissions subsequent thereto, which were
given to the governors of Georgia, entirely remove
the doubt.

The question, whether the vacant lands within the
United States became a joint property, or belonged
to the separate states, was a momentous question
which, at one time, threatened to shake the American confederacy to its foundation. This important
and dangerous contest has been compromised, and
the compromise is not now to be disturbed.

It is the opinion of the court, that the particular
land stated in the declaration appears, from this
special verdict, to lie within the state of Georgia,
and that the state of Georgia had power to grant
it.

Some difficulty was produced by the language of
the covenant, and of the pleadings. It was doubted

whether a state can be seized in fee of lands, subject to the Indian title, and whether a decision that they were seized in fee, might not be construed to amount to a decision that their grantee might maintain an ejectment for them, notwithstanding that title.

The majority of the court is of opinion that the nature of the Indian title, which is certainly to be respected *by all courts, until it be legiti-
*143 mately extinguished, is not such as to be absolutely repugnant to seizin in fee on the part of the state.

Judgment affirmed with costs.

New Jersey *v.* Wilson.

NOTE.

THE case decides, briefly, that the repeal by the legislature of New Jersey of a contract of tax exemption previously granted by it was void, as a bill passed by a state "impairing the obligation of contracts." It appeared that the state of New Jersey, in 1858, pursuant to agreement with certain Indian tribes, passed an act authorizing the purchase of certain lands for the Indians and providing "that the lands to be purchased for the Indians aforesaid shall not hereafter be subject to any tax." That act was repealed and the plaintiff in this case, a purchaser from the Indians, was taxed on account of some of the same lands bought for the Indians. Marshall decided shortly, under *Fletcher* v. *Peck* (*supra*, p. 228) that the repeal impaired the obligation of a contract entered into by the Indians and the state, and that, in the absence of any express words, the privilege of exemption attached to the lands after they had been sold by the Indians.

The case is the second of Marshall's great cases on the question of impairment of contracts, the least considered of them, and it would seem now, the most unfortunate of them.

It is, it seems, a sound enough governmental policy to exempt from taxation all state institutions. Such a policy is almost universal in the United States, and the exemption of Indian lands by the state of New Jersey is a sufficiently sound policy so long as the Indians are wards of the state and possessed of those lands. But when the land has passed out of the hands of the Indians the exemption seems absolutely unnecessary and unwise. True, it is of vital importance that legislative contracts made by a state, even when unwise, should not be impaired by later legislation, but as an original question it seems most doubtful whether any legislature has the right to deprive subsequent legislatures of the very bone and sinew of governmental power, the natural incident of sovereignty, the right to tax. In later decisions (*Fertilizing Co.* v. *Hyde Park*, 97 U. S., 659, 666, and in many other cases) the Supreme Court has laid down the doctrine that one legislature cannot contract away the right of a subsequent legislature to protect the public health, safety, and morals,—it is not easy to see how the right to tax differs from these other attributes of sovereignty. But the law has always been regarded as settled according to Marshall's decision, though not without a constantly recurring rumbling of judicial protest against this visiting of the follies of the fathers upon later generations, that found its strongest expression in the dissenting opinion of Catron, J., in *Bank of Ohio* v. *Knoop*, 18 How. (U. S.), 369, 392.

As a matter of construction it would, it seems, have been easy for Marshall to have construed the tax exemption granted by the state of New Jersey to the Indians merely as a revocable license of exemption. Such a construction was adopted in the case of *Grand Lodge, etc.* v. *City of New Orleans*, 166 U. S., 143, and is now generally adopted when exemptions are granted under later laws. *Salt Co.* v. *East Saginaw*, 13 Wall, 373. And this construction would have been perfectly possible in view of the doctrine soon after enunciated in the Charles River Bridge case and the Providence Bank case, that a grant of public right is to be construed most strongly against the grantee, cf. *Pearsall* v. *Great Northern Railway Co.*, 161 U. S., 647.

Again, the exemption could have easily been construed to be a purely personal right lost by the transfer of it, cf. *Yazoo and Mississippi V. Ry. Co.* v. *Adams*, 180 U. S., 1, 23. The Supreme Court to-day is, as they said in the Yazoo case, "astute to seize upon evidence tending to show either that such exemptions were not originally intended, or that they have become inoperative by changes in the original constitution of the companies." See also the case of *Gulf and Ship Island Rd. Co.* v. *Hewes*, 183 U. S., 66.

But the temper of the courts to this case is perhaps best shown in *Given* v. *Wright*, 117 U. S., 648.   The very same exemption in question in *New Jersey* v. *Wilson* came before the Supreme Court.   It appeared that the land had passed out of the hands of the Indians, the original grantees, and the early decision in some way forgotten or overlooked, so that for seventy years this land had been regularly taxed.   This the court held a waiver of the right of exemption.   In that opinion Mr. Justice Bradley said at page 655 : " We do not feel disposed to question the decision in *New Jersey* v. *Wilson*.   It has been referred to and relied on in so many cases from the day of its rendition down to the present time that it would cause a shock to our constitutional jurisprudence to disturb it now.   If the question were a new one we might regard the reasoning of the New Jersey judges as of great weight, especially since the emphatic declarations made by this court in *Providence Bank* v. *Billings*."

The case then is still law, but hampered and limited in every way, almost overruled—standing largely by virtue of Marshall's name.   The main objection to it is that it renders irrevocable exemptions and bounties given in new communities to encourage manufactures and capital which, as communities prosper, become purely arbitrary and monopolistic discriminations which excite violent and just public opposition.   It is hardly to be thought that the clause as to the obligation of contracts was ever intended so far to hamper the repealing of short-sighted laws.   It is simply a case where Marshall construed the restriction against the states more closely than subsequent political experience has warranted.   Later decisions have almost whittled away his doctrine.   The exact questions presented in *New Jersey* v. *Wilson* arise less and less often because of the almost universal provisions in the constitutions or general laws of the various states, reserving the healthful power of amendment and repeal of all corporate charters granted.

The State of New Jersey

v.

Wilson.

[7 Cranch, 164.]

1812.

This case was submitted to this court, upon a statement of facts, without argument.

March 3d. All the Judges being present, *Marshall, Ch. J.*, delivered the opinion of the court as follows :

This is a writ of error to a judgment rendered in the court of last resort in the state of New Jersey, by which the plaintiffs allege they are deprived of a right secured to them by the constitution of the United States.

*165 * The case appears to be this :

The remnant of the tribe of Delaware Indians, previous to the 20th February, 1758, had claims to a considerable portion of lands in New Jersey, to extinguish which became an object with the government and proprietors under the conveyance from King Charles 2d, to the Duke of York. For this purpose a convention was held in February,

258

1758, between the Indians and commissioners appointed by the government of New Jersey; at which
the Indians agreed to specify particularly the lands
which they claimed, release their claim to all others,
and to appoint certain chiefs to treat with commissioners on the part of the government for the final
extinguishment of their whole claim.

On the 9th of August, 1758, the Indian deputies
met the commissioners and delivered to them a proposition reduced to writing—the basis of which was,
that the government should purchase a tract of land
on which they might reside—in consideration of
which they would release their claim to all other
lands in New Jersey south of the river Raritan.

This proposition appears to have been assented to
by the commissioners; and the legislature on the 12th
of August, 1758, passed an act to give effect to this
agreement.

This act, among other provisions, authorizes the
purchase of lands for the Indians, restrains them from
granting leases or making sales, and enacts "that
the lands to be purchased for the Indians aforesaid
shall not hereafter be subject to any tax, any law,
usage or custom to the contrary thereof, in any wise
notwithstanding."

In virtue of this act, the convention with the Indians was executed. Lands were purchased and
conveyed to trustees for their use, and the Indians
released their claim to the south part of New Jersey.

The Indians continued in peaceable possession of
the lands thus conveyed to them until some time in

the year 1801, when, having become desirous of mi-
grating from * the state of New Jersey, and
*166   of joining their brethren at Stockbridge, in
the state of New York, they applied for, and obtained
an act of the legislature of New Jersey, authorizing
a sale of their land in that state.

This act contains no expression in any manner
respecting the privilege of exemption from taxation
which was annexed to those lands by the act under
which they were purchased and settled on the Indians.

In 1803, the commissioners under the last recited
act sold and conveyed the lands to the plaintiffs,
George Painter and others.

In October, 1804, the legislature passed an act repealing that section of the act of August, 1758, which
exempts the lands therein mentioned from taxes.
The lands were then assessed, and the taxes demanded.   The plaintiffs, thinking themselves injured
by this assessment, brought the case before the courts
in the manner prescribed by the laws of New Jersey,
and in the highest court of the state the validity of
the repealing act was affirmed and the land declared
liable to taxation.   The cause is brought into this
court by writ of error, and the question here to be
decided is, does the act of 1804 violate the constitution
of the United States?

The constitution of the United States declares that
no state shall "pass any bill of attainder, *ex post facto*
law, or law impairing the obligation of contracts."

In the case of *Fletcher* v. *Peck*, it was decided in
this court on solemn argument and much delibera-

tion, and this provision of the constitution extends
to contracts to which a state is a party, as well as to
contracts between individuals.   The question, then,
is narrowed to the inquiry whether in the case stated,
a contract existed, and whether that contract is violated by the act of 1804.

Every requisite to the formation of a contract is
found in the proceedings between the then colony
of New Jersey and the Indians.   The subject was a
purchase on the part of the government of extensive
claims of the Indians, the extinguishment of which
would quiet the title to a large portion of the province.   A proposition to this effect is made, the terms
*167   stipulated, the * consideration agreed upon,
which is a tract of land with the privilege of
exemption from taxation ; and then, in consideration
of the arrangement previously made, one of which
this act of assembly is stated to be, the Indians execute their deed of cession.   This is certainly a contract clothed in forms of unusual solemnity.   The
privilege, though for the benefit of the Indians, is
annexed, by the terms which create it, to the land
itself, not to their persons.   It is for their advantage
that it should be annexed to the land, because, in the
event of a sale on which alone the question could
become material, the value would be enhanced by it.

It is not doubted but that the state of New Jersey
might have insisted on a surrender of this privilege
as the sole condition on which a sale of the property
should be allowed.   But this condition has not been
insisted on.   The land has been sold, with the assent

of the state, with all its privileges and immunities. The purchaser succeeds, with the assent of the state, to all the rights of the Indians.   He stands, with respect to this land, in their place, and claims the benefit of their contract.   This contract is certainly impaired by a law which would annul this essential part of it.

New Orleans *v.* Winter.

NOTE.

THE case arose on error from the District Court for the District of Louisiana. The suit was brought by a citizen of Kentucky and by one Winter, who stated himself to be a citizen of the territory of Mississippi, to recover possession of certain lands in New Orleans.

Judgment was given for the plaintiffs, and on appeal from that judgment the question arose whether a citizen of a territory had a right to maintain a suit in the federal court.

The decision was inevitable after the case of *Hepburn & Dundas* v. *Ellzey*, 2 Cranch, 445, *supra*.

The Corporation of New Orleans

v.

Winter *et al.*

[1 Wheaton, 91.]

1816.

Winder and Harper for Plaintiffs in Error.
Key contra.

Marshall, Ch. J., delivered the opinion of the court, and, after stating the facts, proceeded as follows :

The proceedings of the court, therefore, is arrested *in limine*, by a question respecting its jurisdiction. In the case of *Hepburn & Dundas* v. *Ellzey*, this court determined, on mature consideration, that a citizen of the District of Columbia could not maintain a suit in the Circuit Court of the United States. That opinion is still retained.

It has been attempted to distinguish a territory from the District of Columbia ; but the court is of opinion that this distinction cannot be maintained. They may differ in many respects, but neither of them is a state, in the sense in which that term is used in the constitution. Every reason assigned for

264

the opinion of the court, that a citizen of Columbia
was not capable of sueing in the courts of the United
States, under the judiciary act, is equally applicable
to a citizen of a territory.   Gabriel Winter then,
*95   * being a citizen of the Mississippi territory,
was incapable of maintaining a suit alone in
the Circuit Court of Louisiana.   Is his case mended
by being associated with others who are capable of
sueing in that court ?   In the case of *Strawbridge
et al.* v. *Curtis et al.* it was decided that where a
joint interest is prosecuted, the jurisdiction cannot be
sustained, unless each individual be entitled to claim
that jurisdiction.   In this case it has been doubted
whether the parties might elect to sue jointly or sev-
erally.   However this may be, having elected to sue
jointly, the court is incapable of distinguishing their
case, so far as respects jurisdiction, from one in which
they were compelled to unite.   The Circuit Court of
Louisiana, therefore, had no jurisdiction of the cause,
and their judgment must, on that account, be reversed, and the petition dismissed.

Judgment reversed.

Slocum *v.* Mayberry.

NOTE.

THIS case arose on error on a judgment rendered by the Supreme Court for the state of Rhode Island.

John Slocum, the defendant, was surveyor of the customs for the port of Newport, in Rhode Island, and under the directions of the collector had seized the *Venus,* lying in that port with a cargo ostensibly bound to some other port in the United States. The owners of the cargo brought their writ of replevin in the state court of Rhode Island for the restoration of the property. The defendant pleaded that the *Venus* was laden in the night, not under the inspection of the proper revenue officers; and that the collector of the port, suspecting an intention to violate the embargo laws, had directed him to seize and detain her till the opinion of the President should be known on the case, and concluded to the jurisdiction of the court. The owners in the state court demurred, and the defendants joined in demurrer. Judgment was rendered in favor of the plaintiff in the state court, and the cause was removed into the Supreme Court by writ of error.

On these facts the question arose whether, since the judiciary act gave the federal courts exclusive cognizance of all seizures, the Rhode Island court had not trespassed on the federal jurisdiction. The opinion is notable for the firmness with which the federal jurisdiction is confined by the exact language of the acts creating it, while its supremacy within those limits is emphatically asserted. The case is a good example in little of how Marshall built up the federal jurisdiction and the national government, not by a straining to enlarge the field of that jurisdiction and of that government, but by constant and unvarying declaration of its absolute and efficient power within its prescribed limits.

Slocum *v.* Mayberry *et al.*

[2 Wheaton 1.]

1817.

The Attorney-General for the Plaintiff in Error.
Mr. Hunter, contra.

Marshall, Ch. J., delivered the opinion of the court, and, after stating the facts, proceeded as follows:

In considering this case, the first question which presents itself is this; Has the constitution, or any law of the United States, been violated or misconstrued by the court of Rhode Island in exercising its jurisdiction in this cause?

The judiciary act gives to the federal courts exclusive cognizance of all seizures made on land or water. Any intervention of a state authority which, by taking the thing seized out of the possession of the officer of the United States, might obstruct the exercise of this jurisdiction, would unquestionably be a violation of the act; and the federal court having cognizance of the seizure, might enforce a redelivery of the thing by attachment or other summary process against the parties who should devest such a possession. The party supposing himself aggrieved by a seizure cannot, because he considers it tortious, replevy the property out of the custody of the seizing officer, or of the court having cognizance of the cause. If the officer has a right, under the laws of the United States, to seize for a supposed forfeiture, the question, whether that forfeiture has been actually incurred, belongs ex-

*10   clusively to the * federal courts, and cannot be drawn to another forum ; and it depends upon the final decree of such courts whether such seizure is to be deemed rightful or tortious. If the seizing officer should refuse to institute proceedings to ascertain the forfeiture, the District Court may, upon the application of the aggrieved party, compel the officer to proceed to adjudication, or to abandon the seizure. And if the seizure be finally adjudged wrongful, and without reasonable cause, he may proceed, at his election, by a suit at common law, or in the admiralty for damages for the illegal act. Yet, even in that case, any remedy which the law may afford to the party supposing himself to be aggrieved, other than such as might be obtained in a court of admiralty, could be prosecuted only in the state court. The common law tribunals of the United States are closed against such applications, were the party disposed to make them. Congress has refused to the courts of the Union the power of deciding on the conduct of their officers in the execution of their laws, in suits at common law, until the case shall have passed through the state courts, and have received the form which may there be given it. This, however, being an action which takes the thing itself out of the possession of the officer, could certainly

not be maintained in a state court, if, by the act of
Congress, it was seized for the purpose of being proceeded against in the federal court.

A very brief examination of the act of Congress
will be sufficient for the inquiry whether this cargo
*11   was so seized.   The second section of the
act, * pleaded by the defendant in the original action, only withholds a clearance from a vessel
which has committed the offense described in that
section.   This seizure was made under the 11th section, which enacts, "that the collectors of the customs
be, and they are hereby respectively authorized to
detain any vessel ostensibly bound with a cargo to
some other port of the United States, whenever, in
their opinion, the intention is to violate or evade any
of the provisions of the acts laying an embargo, until
the decision of the President of the United States be
had thereupon."

The authority given respects the vessel only.   The
cargo is in no manner the object of the act.   It is
arrested in its course to any other port, by the detention of the vehicle in which it was to be carried;
but no right is given to seize it specifically, or to detain it if separated from that vehicle.   It remains in
custody of the officer, simply because it is placed in
a vessel which is in his custody; but no law forbids
it to be taken out of that vessel, if such be the will
of the owner.   The cargoes thus arrested and detained were generally of a perishable nature, and
it would have been wanton oppression to expose
them to loss by unlimited detention, in a case where

the owner was willing to remove all danger of ex-
portation.

This being the true construction of the act of Congress, the owner has the same right to his cargo that
he has to any other property, and may exercise over
it every act of ownership not prohibited by law.   He
may, consequently, demand it from the offi-
*12   cer * in whose possession it is, that officer
having no legal right to withhold it from him ; and if
it be withheld, he has a consequent right to appeal
to the laws of his country for relief.

To what court can this appeal be made?   The
common law courts of the United States have no
jurisdiction in the case.   They can afford him no
relief.   The party might, indeed, institute a suit for
redress in the District Court acting as an admiralty
and revenue court ; and such court might award resti-
tution of the property unlawfully detained.   But the
act of Congress neither expressly nor by implication
forbids the state courts to take cognizance of suits
instituted for property in possession of an officer of
the United States not detained under some law of
the United States ; consequently, their jurisdiction
remains.   Had this action been brought for the vessel instead of the cargo, the case would have been
essentially different.   The detention would have been
by virtue of an act of Congress, and the jurisdiction
of a state court could not have been sustained.   But
the action having been brought for the cargo, to detain which the law gave no authority, it was triable in
the state court.

The same course of reasoning which sustains the jurisdiction of the court of Rhode Island sustains also its judgment on the plea in bar.   The two pleas contain the same matter ; the one concluding to the jurisdiction of the court, and the other in bar of the action. In examining the plea to the jurisdiction, it has been shown that the officer had no legal right to detain the property ; consequently, his plea was * no sufficient defense, and the court misconstrued no act of Congress, nor committed any error in sustaining the demurrer.

*13

Judgment affirmed with costs.

The United States *v.* Bevans.

NOTE.

THE case presents only a rather technical question of the extent of the federal admiralty jurisdiction under the Constitution and the construction of the acts giving jurisdiction under it to the federal courts. No substantial or disputed question of constitutional law was presented, and the only human interest of the case is the spectacle of a murderer escaping conviction because of an ambiguity of a statute. The facts of the case, which are necessary to a comprehension of it, are stated by the reporter as follows:

"The defendant, William Bevans, was indicted for murder in the Circuit Court for the District of Massachusetts. The indictment was founded on the 8th section of the act of Congress of the 30th of April, 1790, ch. 9, and was tried upon the plea of 'not guilty.' At the trial, it appeared in evidence that the offense charged in the indictment was committed by the prisoner on the sixth day of November, 1816, on board the United States ship of war, *Independence*, rated a ship of the line of seventy-four guns, then in commission, and in the actual service of the United States, under the command of Commodore Bainbridge. At the same time, William Bevans was a marine, duly enlisted, and in the service of the United States, and was acting as sentry regularly posted on board of said ship, and Peter Leinstrum (the deceased, named in the indictment) was at the same time duly enlisted and in the service of the United States as cook's mate on board of said ship. The said ship was at the same time lying at anchor in the main channel of Boston harbor in waters of a sufficient depth at all times of tide for ships of the largest class

and burthen, and to which there is at all times a free and unob-
structed passage to the open sea or ocean.   The nearest land at
low water-mark to the position where the said ship then lay, on
various sides is as follows, viz.: The end of the long wharf so
called in the town of Boston, bearing south-west by south, half
south at the distance of half a mile; the western point of Wil-
liams's Island, bearing north by west, at the distance between
one-quarter and one-third of a mile; the navy yard of the United
States at Charlestown, bearing north-west half-west, at the distance
of three-quarters of a mile, and Dorchester Point so called, bearing south south-east, at the distance of two miles and one-quarter,
and the nearest point of Governor's Island so called (ceded to
the United States), bearing south-east half-east, at the distance
of one mile and three-quarters.   To and beyond the position or
place thus described, the civil and criminal processes of the courts
of the state of Massachusetts have hitherto constantly been
served and obeyed.   The prisoner was first apprehended for the
offense in the District of Massachusetts.

"The jury found a verdict that the prisoner, William Bevans,
was guilty of the offense as charged in the indictment.

"Upon the foregoing statement of facts, which was stated and
made under the direction of the court, the prisoner, by his counsel, after verdict, moved for a new trial, upon which motion two
questions occurred, which also occurred at the trial of the prisoner.   1. Whether upon the foregoing statement of facts, the
offense charged in the indictment, and committed on board the
said ship as aforesaid, was within the jurisdiction of the state of
Massachusetts, or of any court thereof.   2. Whether the offense
charged in the indictment, and committed on board the said
ship as aforesaid, was within the jurisdiction or cognizance of
the Circuit Court of the United States for the District of Massachusetts.   Upon which questions the judges of the said Circuit
Court were at the trial, and upon the motion for a new trial,
opposed in opinion; and thereupon, upon the request of the
district-attorney of the United States, the same questions were
ordered by the said court to be certified under the seal of the
court to the Supreme Court, to be finally decided."

The United States

v.

Bevans.

1818.

[3 Wheaton, 337.]

Mr. Webster for the defendant,
Mr. Wheaton for the United States, the Attorney-General, Mr. Wirt, on the same side.

Marshall, Ch. J., delivered the opinion of the court : The question proposed by the Circuit Court, which will be first considered, is,

Whether the offense charged in this indictment was, according to the statement of facts which accompanies the question, "within the jurisdiction or cognizance of the Circuit Court of the United States for the District of Massachusetts."

The indictment appears to be founded on the 8th sec. of the "act for the punishment of certain crimes against the United States." That section gives the courts of the Union cognizance of certain offenses committed on the high seas, or in any river, haven, basin, or bay, out of the jurisdiction of any particular state.

Whatever may be the constitutional power of Congress it is clear that this power has not been so exercised, in this section of the act, as to confer on its courts jurisdiction over any offense committed in a river, haven, basin or bay ; which river, haven, basin or bay, is within the jurisdiction of any particular state.

What, then, is the extent of jurisdiction which a state possesses ?

We answer, without hesitation, the jurisdiction of *387   * a state is co-extensive with its territory ; co-extensive with its legislative power.

The place described is unquestionably within the original territory of Massachusetts. It is then within the jurisdiction of Massachusetts, unless that jurisdiction has been ceded to the United States.

It is contended to have been ceded by that article in the constitution which declares that "the judicial power shall extend to all cases of admiralty and maritime jurisdiction." The argument is, that the power thus granted is exclusive ; and that the murder committed by the prisoner is a case of admiralty and maritime jurisdiction.

Let this be admitted. It proves the power of Congress to legislate in the case ; not that Congress has exercised that power. It has been argued, and the argument in favor of, as well as that against the proposition, deserves great consideration, that courts of common law have concurrent jurisdiction with courts of admiralty, over murder committed in bays, which are inclosed parts of the sea ; and that for this reason the offense is within the jurisdiction of Massachusetts.   But in construing the act of Congress, the court believes it to be unnecessary to pursue the investigation which has been so well made at the bar respecting the jurisdiction of these rival courts.

To bring the offense within the jurisdiction of the courts of the Union, it must have been committed in a river, &c., out of the jurisdiction of any state. It is not the offense committed, but the bay in which it is committed, which must be out of the jurisdiction *of the state.   If, then, it should be true *388   that Massachusetts can take no cognizance of the offense; yet, unless the place itself be out of her jurisdiction, Congress has not given cognizance of that offense to its courts.   If there be a common jurisdiction, the crime cannot be punished in the courts of the Union.

Can the cession of all cases of admiralty and maritime jurisdiction be construed into a cession of the waters on which those cases may arise?

This is a question on which the court is incapable of feeling a doubt.   The article which describes the judicial power of the United States is not intended for the cession of territory or of general jurisdiction, It is obviously designed for other purposes.   It is in the 8th section of the 2d article we are to look for cessions of territory and of exclusive jurisdiction. Congress has power to exercise exclusive jurisdiction over this district, and over all places purchased by the consent of the legislature of the state in which the same shall be, for the erection of forts, magazines, arsenals, dock-yards, and other needful buildings.

It is observable that the power of exclusive legislation (which is jurisdiction) is united with cession of territory, which is to be the free act of the states. It is difficult to compare the two sections together, without feeling a conviction, not to be strengthened by any commentary on them, that, in describing the judicial power, the framers of our constitution had not in view any cession of territory; or, which is essentially the same, of general jurisdiction.

It is not questioned, that whatever may be necessary to the full and unlimited exercise of admiralty *389 *and maritime jurisdiction, is in the government of the Union. Congress may pass all laws which are necessary and proper for giving the most complete effect to this power. Still, the general jurisdiction over the place, subject to this grant of power, adheres to the territory, as a portion of sovereignty not yet given away. The residuary powers of legislation are still in Massachusetts. Suppose, for example, the power of regulating trade had not been given to the general government. Would this extension of the judicial power to all cases of admiralty and maritime jurisdiction, have devested Massachusetts of the power to regulate the trade of her bay? As the powers of the respective governments now stand, if two citizens of Massachusetts step into shallow water when the tide flows, and fight a duel, are they not within the jurisdiction, and punishable by the laws of Massachusetts? If these questions

must be answered in the affirmative — and we believe they must — then the bay in which this murder
was committed is not out of the jurisdiction of a
state, and the Circuit Court of Massachusetts is not
authorized, by the section under consideration, to take
cognizance of the murder which has been committed.

It may be deemed within the scope of the question
certified to this court to inquire whether any other
part of the act has given cognizance of this murder
to the Circuit Court of Massachusetts.

The third section enacts, "that if any person or
persons shall, within any fort, arsenal, dock-yard,
magazine, or in any other place, or district of country,
under the sole and exclusive jurisdiction of the
*390   * United States, commit the crime of willful
murder, such person or persons, on being
thereof convicted, shall suffer death."

Although the bay on which this murder was committed might not be out of the jurisdiction of Massachusetts, the ship of war on the deck of which it was
committed is, it has been said, "a place within the sole
and exclusive jurisdiction of the United States,"
whose courts may consequently take cognizance of
the offense.

That a government which possesses the broad power
of war ; which "may provide and maintain a navy " ;
which "may make rules for the government and
regulation of the land and naval forces," has power
to punish an offense committed by a marine on board
a ship of war, wherever that ship may lie, is a proposition never to be questioned in this court. On this

section, as on the 8th, the inquiry respects, not the extent of the power of Congress, but the extent to which that power has been exercised.

The objects with which the word "place" is associated, are all, in their nature, fixed and territorial. A fort, an arsenal, a dock-yard, a magazine, are all of this character. When the sentence proceeds with the words, "or in any other place or district of country under the sole and exclusive jurisdiction of the United States," the construction seems irresistible that, by the words "other place," was intended another place of a similar character with those previously enumerated, and with that which follows. Congress might have omitted, in its enumeration, some similar place within its exclusive jurisdiction, *391 * which was not comprehended by any of the terms employed, to which some other name might be given; and, therefore, the words "other place," or "district of country," were added; but the context shows the mind of the legislature to have been fixed on territorial objects of a similar character.

This construction is strengthened by the fact that at the time of passing this law the United States did not possess a single ship of war. It may, therefore, be reasonably supposed, that a provision for the punishment of crimes in the navy might be postponed until some provision for a navy should be made. While taking this view of the subject, it is not entirely unworthy of remark, that afterwards, when a navy was created, and Congress did proceed to make rules for its regulation and government, no jurisdiction is given to the courts of the United States, of any crime committed in a ship of war, wherever it may be stationed. Upon these reasons the court is of opinion, that a murder committed on board a ship of war, lying within the harbor of Boston, is not cognizable in the Circuit Court for the District of Massachusetts; which opinion is to be certified to that court.

The opinion of the court, on this point, is believed to render it unnecessary to decide the question respecting the jurisdiction of the State Court in the case.

Sturges *v.* Crowninshield.

NOTE.

THIS case, with the following ones of *M'Millan* v. *M'Neill* and *Ogden* v. *Saunders*, 12 Wheat., 213, are considered more fully in the note, *infra*, accompanying the case of *Ogden* v. *Saunders*. They can hardly be separately discussed.

This case arose in an action of assumpsit brought in the Circuit Court of Massachusetts on two promissory notes dated in New York. The defendant pleaded his discharge under a New York statute passed subsequent to the making of the notes, for the relief of insolvent debtors. The plaintiff demurred to this plea, and the questions involved were certified to the Supreme Court.

Sturges

v.

Crowninshield.

[4 Wheaton, 122.]

1819.

Mr. Daggett for the plaintiff. Mr. Hopkinson with him.
Mr. Hunter, contra, Mr. D. B. Ogden on the same side.

Marshall, Ch. J., delivered the opinion of the court: This case is adjourned from the court of the United States, for the first circuit and the district of Massachusetts, on several points on which the judges of that court were divided, which are stated **192* * in the record for the opinion of this court. The first is,

Whether, since the adoption of the constitution of the United States, any state has authority to pass a bankrupt law, or whether the power is exclusively vested in the Congress of the United States.

This question depends on the following clause, in the 8th section of the 1st article of the constitution of the United States:

"The Congress shall have power," &c., to establish a uniform rule of naturalization, and "uniform laws

282

on the subject of bankruptcies throughout the United States."

The counsel for the plaintiff contend that the grant of this power to Congress, without limitation, takes it entirely from the several states.

In support of this proposition they argue that every power given to Congress is necessarily supreme; and if, from its nature, or from the words of grant, it is apparently intended to be exclusive, it is as much so as if the states were expressly forbidden to exercise it.

These propositions have been enforced and illustrated by many arguments, drawn from different parts of the constitution. That the power is both unlimited, and supreme is not questioned. That it is exclusive, is denied by the counsel for the defendant.

In considering this question, it must be recollected that, previous to the formation of the new constitution, we were divided into independent states, united for some purposes, but, in most respects, sovereign. These states could exercise almost every legislative power, and, among others, that of passing bankrupt laws.

*193   *When the American people created a national legislature, with certain enumerated powers, it was neither necessary nor proper to define the powers retained by the states. These powers proceed, not from the people of America, but from the people of the several states; and remain, after the adoption of the constitution, what they were before, except so far as they may be abridged by that instrument. In some instances, as in making treaties, we find an express prohibition; and this shows the sense of the convention to have been, that the mere grant of a power to Congress did not imply a prohibition on the states to exercise the same power. But it has never been supposed that this concurrent power of legislation extended to every possible case in which its exercise by the states has not been expressly prohibited. The confusion resulting from such a practice would be endless. The principle laid down by the counsel for the plaintiff, in this respect, is undoubtedly correct. Whenever the terms in which a power is granted to Congress, or the nature of the power, required that it should be exercised exclusively by Congress, the subject is as completely taken from the state legislatures as if they had been expressly forbidden to act on it.

Is the power to establish uniform laws on the subject of bankruptcies, throughout the United States, of this description?

The peculiar terms of the grant certainly deserve notice. Congress is not authorized merely to pass laws, the operation of which shall be uniform, but to establish uniform laws on the subject throughout the *United States. This establishment of uniformity is, perhaps, incompatible with state legislation, on that part of the subject to which the acts of Congress may extend. But the subject is divisible in its nature into bankrupt and insolvent laws; though the line of partition between them is not so distinctly marked as to enable any person to

*194

say, with positive precision, what belongs exclusively to the one, and not to the other class of laws. It is said, for example, that laws which merely liberate the person are insolvent laws, and those which discharge the contract are bankrupt laws. But if an act of Congress should discharge the person of the bankrupt, and leave his future acquisitions liable to his creditors, we should feel much hesitation in saying that this was an insolvent, not a bankrupt act; and, therefore, unconstitutional. Another distinction has been stated, and has been uniformly observed. Insolvent laws operate at the instance of an imprisoned debtor; bankrupt laws at the instance of a creditor. But should an act of Congress authorize a commission of bankruptcy to issue on the application of a debtor, a court would scarcely be warranted in saying that the law was unconstitutional, and the commission a nullity.

When laws of each description may be passed by the same legislature, it is unnecessary to draw a precise line between them. The difficulty can arise only in our complex system, where the legislature of the Union possesses the power of enacting bankrupt laws; and those of the states, the power of enacting insolvent laws. If it be determined that they are not laws of the same character, but are as distinct as bankrupt laws and laws which regulate the course of descents, *a distinct line of separation must
*195   be drawn, and the power of each government marked with precision. But all perceive that this line must be in a great degree arbitrary. Al-

though the two systems have existed apart from each other, there is such a connection between them as to render it difficult to say how far they may be blended together.   The bankrupt law is said to grow out of the exigencies of commerce, and to be applicable solely to traders ; but it is not easy to say who must be excluded from, or may be included within, this description.   It is, like every other part of the subject, one on which the legislature may exercise an extensive discretion.

This difficulty of discriminating with any accuracy between insolvent and bankrupt laws, would lead to the opinion that a bankrupt law may contain those regulations which are generally found in insolvent laws ; and that an insolvent law may contain those which are common to a bankrupt law.   If this be correct, it is obvious that much inconvenience would result from that construction of the constitution, which should deny to the state legislatures the power of acting on this subject, in consequence of the grant to Congress.   It may be thought more convenient that much of it should be regulated by state legislation, and Congress may purposely omit to provide for many cases to which their power extends.   It does not appear to be a violent construction of the constitution, and is certainly a convenient one, to consider the power of the states as existing over such cases as the laws of the Union may not reach. But be this as it may, the power granted to Congress

*196   may be exercised * or declined, as the wisdom of that body shall decide.   If, in the opinion of Congress, uniform laws concerning bankruptcies ought not to be established, it does not follow that partial laws may not exist, or that state legislation on the subject must cease. It is not the mere existence of the power, but its exercise, which is incompatible with the exercise of the same power by the states. It is not the right to establish these uniform laws, but their actual establishment, which is inconsistent with the partial acts of the states.

It has been said that Congress has exercised this power, and, by doing so, has extinguished the power of the states, which cannot be revived by repealing the law of Congress.

We do not think so. If the right of the states to pass a bankrupt law is not taken away by the mere grant of that power to Congress, it cannot be extinguished; it can only be suspended, by the enactment of a general bankrupt law. The repeal of that law cannot, it is true, confer the power on the states; but it removes a disability to its exercise, which was created by the act of Congress.

Without entering farther into the delicate inquiry respecting the precise limitations which the several grants of power to Congress, contained in the constitution, may impose on the state legislatures, than is necessary for the decision of the question before the court, it is sufficient to say, that until the power to pass uniform laws on the subject of bankruptcies be exercised by Congress, the states are not forbidden

* *197*   to pass a bankrupt law, provided it contain no principle * which violates the 10th

section of the first article of the constitution of the United States.

This opinion renders it totally unnecessary to consider the question whether the law of New York is, or is not, a bankrupt law.

We proceed to the great question on which the cause must depend. Does the law of New York, which is pleaded in this case, impair the obligation of contracts, within the meaning of the constitution of the United States?

This act liberates the person of the debtor, and discharges him from all liability for any debt previously contracted, on his surrendering his property in the manner it prescribes.

In discussing the question whether a state is prohibited from passing such a law as this, our first inquiry is into the meaning of words in common use. What is the obligation of a contract? and what will impair it?

It would seem difficult to substitute words which are more intelligible, or less liable to misconstruction, than those which are to be explained. A contract is an agreement in which a party undertakes to do, or not to do, a particular thing. The law binds him to perform his undertaking, and this is, of course, the obligation of his contract. In the case at bar, the defendant has given his promissory note to pay the plaintiff a sum of money on or before a certain day. The contract binds him to pay that sum on that day; and this is its obligation. Any law which releases a part of this obligation, must, in the literal

*198

sense of the word, impair it.   Much more must a * law impair it which makes it totally invalid, and entirely discharges it.

The words of the constitution, then, are express and incapable of being misunderstood.   They admit of no variety of construction, and are acknowledged to apply to that species of contract, an engagement between man and man for the payment of money, which has been entered into by these parties.   Yet the opinion that this law is not within the prohibition of the constitution, has been entertained by those who are entitled to great respect, and has been supported by arguments which deserve to be seriously considered.

It has been contended, that as a contract can only bind a man to pay to the full extent of his property, it is an implied condition that he may be discharged on surrendering the whole of it.

But it is not true that the parties have in view only the property in possession when the contract is formed, or that its obligation does not extend to future acquisitions.   Industry, talents and integrity, constitute a fund which is as confidently trusted as property itself.   Future acquisitions are, therefore, liable for contracts; and to release them from this liability impairs their obligation.

It has been argued that the states are not prohibited from passing bankrupt laws, and that the essential principle of such laws is to discharge the bankrupt from all past obligations; that the states have been in the constant practice of passing insolv-

ent laws, such as that of New York, and if the
framers of the constitution had intended to
deprive them of this * power, insolvent laws
199

would have been mentioned in the prohibition ; that
the prevailing evil of the times, which produced this
clause in the constitution, was the practice of emitting paper money, of making property which was
useless to the creditor a discharge of his debt, and
of changing the time of payment by authorizing
distant installments. Laws of this description, not
insolvent laws, constituted, it is said, the mischief to
be remedied ; and laws of this description, not insolvent laws, are within the true spirit of the
prohibition.

The constitution does not grant to the states the
power of passing bankrupt laws, or any other power ;
but finds them in possession of it, and may either
prohibit its future exercise entirely, or restrain it so
far as national policy may require. It has so far
restrained it as to prohibit the passage of any law
impairing the obligation of contracts. Although,
then, the states may, until that power shall be exercised by Congress, pass laws concerning bankrupts ;
yet they cannot constitutionally introduce into such
laws a clause which discharges the obligations the
bankrupt has entered into. It is not admitted that,
without this principle, an act cannot be a bankrupt
law ; and if it were, that admission would not change
the constitution, nor exempt such acts from its
prohibitions.

The argument drawn from the omission in the

constitution to prohibit the states from passing insolvent laws, admits of several satisfactory answers.
It was not necessary, nor would it have been safe,
had it even been the intention of the framers of the
constitution to * prohibit the passage of all
insolvent laws, to enumerate particular subjects to which the principle they intended to establish
should apply. The principle was the inviolability
of contracts. This principle was to be protected in
whatsoever form it might be assailed. To what
purpose enumerate the particular modes of violation
which should be forbidden, when it was intended to
forbid all ? Had an enumeration of all the laws
which might violate contracts been attempted, the
provision must have been less complete, and involved
in more perplexity than it now is. The plain and
simple declaration, that no state shall pass any law
impairing the obligation of contracts, includes insolvent laws and all other laws, so far as they infringe
the principle the convention intended to hold sacred,
and no farther.

But a still more satisfactory answer to this argument is, that the convention did not intend to prohibit the passage of all insolvent laws. To punish
honest insolvency by imprisonment for life, and to
make this a constitutional principle, would be an
excess of inhumanity which will not readily be imputed to the illustrious patriots who framed our constitution, nor to the people who adopted it. The
distinction between the obligation of a contract,
and the remedy given by the legislature to enforce

* 200

that obligation, has been taken at the bar, and exists
in the nature of things. Without impairing the
obligation of the contract, the remedy may certainly
be modified as the wisdom of the nation shall direct.
Confinement of the debtor may be a punishment for
* *201*   not performing his * contract, or may be
        allowed as a means of inducing him to per-
form it. But the state may refuse to inflict this
punishment, or may withhold this means and leave
the contract in full force. Imprisonment is no part
of the contract, and simply to release the prisoner
does not impair its obligation. No argument can be
fairly drawn from the 61st section of the act for
establishing a uniform system of bankruptcy, which
militates against this reasoning. That section declares that the act shall not be construed to repeal
or annul the laws of any state then in force for the
relief of insolvent debtors, except so far as may
respect persons and cases clearly within its purview ;
and in such cases it affords its sanction to the
relief given by the insolvent laws of the state, if
the creditor of the prisoner shall not, within three
months, proceed against him as a bankrupt.

The insertion of this section indicates an opinion
in Congress that insolvent laws might be considered
as a branch of the bankrupt system, to be repealed
or annulled by an act for establishing that system,
although not within its purview. It was for that
reason only that a provision against this construction could be necessary. The last member of the
section adopts the provisions of the state laws so

far as they apply to cases within the purview of the act.

This section certainly attempts no construction of the constitution, nor does it suppose any provision in the insolvent laws impairing the obligation of contracts. It leaves them to operate, so far as constitutionally they may, unaffected by the act of Congress, * except where that act may apply to individual cases.

* *202*

The argument which has been pressed most earnestly at the bar, is, that although all legislative acts which discharge the obligation of a contract without performance are within the very words of the constitution, yet an insolvent act, containing this principle, is not within its spirit, because such acts have been passed by colonial and state legislatures from the first settlement of the country, and because we know from the history of the times that the mind of the convention was directed to other laws which were fraudulent in their character, which enabled the debtor to escape from his obligation, and yet hold his property, not to this, which is beneficial in its operation.

Before discussing this argument, it may not be improper to premise that, although the spirit of an instrument, especially of a constitution, is to be respected not less than its letter, yet the spirit is to be collected chiefly from its words. It would be dangerous in the extreme to infer from extrinsic circumstances, that a case for which the words of an instrument expressly provide, shall be exempted from its operation. Where words conflict with each other, where the different clauses of an instrument bear upon each other, and would be inconsistent unless the natural and common import of words be varied, construction becomes necessary, and a departure from the obvious meaning of words is justifiable. But if, in any case, the plain meaning of a provision, not contradicted by any other provision * 203 in the same instrument, * is to be disregarded, because we believe the framers of that instrument could not intend what they say, it must be one in which the absurdity and injustice of applying the provision to the case would be so monstrous that all mankind would, without hesitation, unite in rejecting the application.

This is certainly not such a case. It is said the colonial and state legislatures have been in the habit of passing laws of this description for more than a century; that they have never been the subject of complaint, and, consequently, could not be within the view of the general convention.

The fact is too broadly stated. The insolvent laws of many, indeed, of by far the greater number of the states, do not contain this principle. They discharge the person of the debtor, but leave his obligation to pay in full force. To this the constitution is not opposed.

But, were it even true that this principle had been introduced generally into those laws, it would not justify our varying the construction of the section. Every state in the Union, both while a colony and

after becoming independent, had been in the practice
of issuing paper money; yet this practice is in terms
prohibited. If the long exercise of the power to
emit bills of credit did not restrain the convention
from prohibiting its future exercise, neither can it be
said that the long exercise of the power to impair
the obligation of contracts, should prevent a similar
prohibition. It is not admitted that the prohibition
is more express in the one case than in the other.

*204   It does not indeed extend to insolvent laws
        by name, * because it is not a law by name,
but a principle which is to be forbidden; and this
principle is described in as appropriate terms as our
language affords.

Neither, as we conceive, will any admissible rule
of construction justify us in limiting the prohibition
under consideration, to the particular laws which
have been described at the bar, and which furnished
such cause for general alarm. What were those
laws?

We are told they were such as grew out of the
general distress following the war in which our independence was established. To relieve this distress,
paper money was issued, worthless lands, and other
property of no use to the creditor, were made a
tender in payment of debts; and the time of payment, stipulated in the contract, was extended by
law. These were the peculiar evils of the day. So
much mischief was done, and so much more was
apprehended, that general distrust prevailed, and all
confidence between man and man was destroyed.

To laws of this description therefore, it is said, the prohibition to pass laws impairing the obligation of contracts ought to be confined.

Let this argument be tried by the words of the section under consideration.

Was this general prohibition intended to prevent paper money? We are not allowed to say so, because it is expressly provided that no state shall "emit bills of credit"; neither could these words be intended to restrain the states from enabling debtors to discharge their debts by the tender of property of no real value to the creditor, because for that subject also particular provision is made. Nothing but

* *205* * gold and silver coin can be made a tender in payment of debts.

It remains to inquire, whether the prohibition under consideration could be intended for the single case of a law directing that judgments should be carried into execution by installments.

This question will scarcely admit of discussion. If this was the only remaining mischief against which the constitution intended to provide, it would undoubtedly have been, like paper money and tender laws, expressly forbidden. At any rate, terms more directly applicable to the subject, more appropriately expressing the intention of the convention, would have been used. It seems scarcely possible to suppose that the framers of the constitution, if intending to prohibit only laws authorizing the payment of debts by installment, would have expressed that intention by saying "no state shall pass any law

impairing the obligation of contracts." No men would
so express such an intention. No men would use
terms embracing a whole class of laws, for the purpose of designating a single individual of that class.
No court can be justified in restricting such comprehensive words to a particular mischief to which no
allusion is made.

The fair, and, we think, the necessary construction
of the sentence, requires, that we should give these
words their full and obvious meaning. A general
dissatisfaction with that lax system of legislation
which followed the war of our revolution undoubtedly directed the mind of the convention to this
subject. It is probable that laws such as those which
* 206   * have been stated in argument, produced
the loudest complaints, were most immediately felt. The attention of the convention, therefore, was particularly directed to paper money, and
to acts which enabled the debtor to discharge his
debt otherwise than was stipulated in the contract.
Had nothing more been intended, nothing more
would have been expressed. But, in the opinion of
the convention, much more remained to be done.
The same mischief might be effected by other means.
To restore public confidence completely, it was necessary not only to prohibit the use of particular means
by which it might be effected, but to prohibit the use
of any means by which the same mischief might be
produced. The convention appears to have intended
to establish a great principle, that contracts should be
inviolable. The constitution therefore declares, that

no state shall pass "any law impairing the obligation of contracts."

If, as we think, it must be admitted that this intention might actuate the convention; that it is not only consistent with, but is apparently manifested by, all that part of the section which respects this subject; that the words used are well adapted to the expression of it; that violence would be done to their plain meaning by understanding them in a more limited sense; those rules of construction, which have been consecrated by the wisdom of ages, compel us to say that these words prohibit the passage of any law discharging a contract without performance.

By way of analogy, the statute of limitations, and against usury, have been referred to in argument; * and it has been supposed that the construction of the constitution, which this opinion maintains, would apply to them also, and must therefore be too extensive to be correct.

* *207*

We do not think so. Statutes of limitations relate to the remedies which are furnished in the courts. They rather establish, that certain circumstances shall amount to evidence that a contract has been performed, than dispense with its performance. If, in a state where six years may be pleaded in bar to an action of *assumpsit*, a law should pass declaring that contracts already in existence, not barred by the statute, should be construed to be within it, there could be little doubt of its unconstitutionality.

So with respect to the laws against usury. If the law be, that no person shall take more than six per centum per annum for the use of money, and that, if more be reserved, the contract shall be void, a contract made thereafter, reserving seven per cent., would have no obligation in its commencement; but if a law should declare that contracts already entered into, and reserving the legal interest, should be usurious and void, either in the whole or in part, it would impair the obligation of the contract, and would be clearly unconstitutional.

This opinion is confined to the case actually under consideration. It is confined to a case in which a creditor sues in a court, the proceedings of which the legislature, whose act is pleaded, had not a right to control, and to a case where the creditor had not proceeded to execution against the body of his debtor, within the state whose law attempts to absolve a * confined insolvent debtor from
* 208   this obligation. When such a case arises, it will be considered.

It is the opinion of the court that the act of the state of New York, which is pleaded by the defendant in this cause, so far as it attempts to discharge this defendant from the debt in the declaration mentioned, is contrary to the constitution of the United States, and that the plea is no bar to the action.

M'Millan *v.* M'Neill.

NOTE.

THIS case was argued at the same time as *Sturges* v. *Crownin-shield* and to Marshall and the court seemed not to be distin-guished from it. The case arose on a claim for money paid by M'Neil for M'Millan's use in South Carolina in 1813. M'Millan removed to New Orleans and took advantage of the Louisiana law (passed in 1808) to obtain a discharge from his debts, and also obtained a discharge under the English bankrupt law prior to the beginning of this suit in the District Court of Louisiana in 1815. From that court the case came on writ of error to the Supreme Court. It was clearly argued that the case differed from *Sturges* v. *Crowninshield* in that there the law granting the discharge was passed after the creation of the contract sued on, while in this case the law was passed after it. (See note to the case of *Ogden* v. *Saunders, infra.*)

M'Millan

v.

M'Neill.

[4 Wheat, 209.]

1819.

C. J. Ingersoll for defendant in error.

Marshall, Ch. J., delivered the opinion of the court, that this case was not distinguishable in principle from the preceding case of *Sturges* v. *Crowninshield*. That the circumstances of the state law, under which the debt was attempted to be discharged, having been passed before the debt was contracted, made no difference in the application of * the principle. And that as to the certificate under the English bankrupt laws, it had frequently been determined, and was well settled, that a discharge under a foreign law was no bar to an action on the contract made in this country.

* 213

McCulloch *v.* Maryland.

NOTE.

MARSHALL'S opinion in the case of *McCulloch* v. *Maryland* is, it seems, the greatest of his opinions, great because of the importance of the subject, great because luminous and powerful in expression, and great, most of all, because it first declared and established the broad powers of the national government of the United States.

The case arose on an attempt by the state of Maryland to tax the operations of the branch of the Bank of the United States in the city of Baltimore. The state of Maryland in 1818 passed an act requiring all notes issued by banks not operating by authority of the state to be issued upon stamped paper; the rate of taxation varied with the denomination of the notes. The case arose on an agreed statement of facts, presenting the question whether this act was constitutional as applied to the branch Bank of the United States, against which it was obviously aimed. The case came on appeal to the Supreme Court of the United States in 1819.

The political controversy that raged around the Bank of the United States is familiar history. In 1811 the Bank of the United States had failed to be rechartered by Congress and ceased business, just at the beginning of the war with England. It was then hated as a surviving monument of federalism, hated out of patriotism because of its English stockholders, hated out of jealousy by the unsuccessful who did not receive its dividends, and most of all by the state banks, because it was the government depositary and because it forced them to constant redemption of their circulating paper. Judged fairly, it seems its operations had been conservative, successful, and for the public good. Surely it was a policy of rashness to destroy it at that moment.

By 1816 the country found itself in a deplorable situation. The nation was flooded with a debased paper currency, issued from hundreds of banks, which were under no restraint, and irresponsible, or worse. Commerce and manufacture were dormant and the nation was still prostrated from the war. In 1816, with little opposition, a United States Bank was incorporated, to accomplish the resumption of specie payments and to furnish a stable paper currency. But the economic distress of the country lay deeper than that. Specie payments were resumed and the volume of irresponsible currency lessened, but the Bank was hated as badly as ever and was charged as responsible for the increasing depression and " hard times." The attempt to reorganize the financial system at such a time and while land speculation was still hysterical, created in the South and West a condition akin to universal bankruptcy. An effort was made to repeal the Bank's charter, and the state legislatures began to try to tax it out of existence. In such a controversy was born the case of *McCulloch* v. *Maryland.* In North Carolina, Maryland, Ohio, Tennessee, and Kentucky heavy taxes were laid on the branch banks, with the avowed object of destroying them. The Maryland act took the form of requiring the issue of notes on stamped paper. The directors of the Bank refused to obey the act. McCulloch, the cashier, was sued in debt for the tax, and the case came before the Supreme Court.

The questions raised in the case were substantially two: Has Congress constitutional power to incorporate a bank? Has the state constitutional power to tax the bank? Thus there came before the Supreme Court to decide the first great question of the extent of the national power. The previous decisions of the Court restraining and limiting the powers of the several states, explaining and expounding the wording of the Constitution, were in the exercise of a different function; here they sat to decide the boundaries of the central power. The opinion that they gave is marvellous alike for its foresight and its statesmanship and for the dignity and calm with which it is delivered. In the opening paragraph of the opinion Marshall said, "No tribunal can approach such a question without a deep sense of its importance and of the awful responsibility involved in its decision." And in that same spirit, with a complete comprehension of the function of the federal judiciary which the Supreme Court has since upheld, Marshall laid down the doctrines of the implication of the broad powers of a national government to the United States. He said: "But we think the sound construction of the Constitution must allow to the national legislature that discretion, with respect to the means by which the powers it confers are to be carried into execution, which will enable that body to perform the high duties assigned to it, in the manner most beneficial to the people. Let the end be legitimate, let it be within the scope of the Constitution, and all means which are appropriate, which are plainly adapted to that end, which are not prohibited, but consist with the letter and spirit of the Constitution, are constitutional." No written words have done more to mould the nation than those. They are the judicial warrant for the powers of the North in the Rebellion and in the Reconstruction time, for the power of our Presidents in grasping and establishing colonial empires. It is impossible to estimate or appreciate that opinion—its luminousness and its grandeur. Never was a greater doctrine of government more appropriately expressed.

Of that part of the opinion dealing with the right of the state of Maryland to tax the branch bank one is not so far convinced. The phrase, "The power to tax involves the power to destroy," is hardly satisfying. As an original question there would seem great force in the argument that the Constitution shows no more intent to limit the right of the states to tax the property of the national government than to limit the converse right of the national government to tax the property of the various states. The case might perhaps better have rested on the narrower ground that the tax in question was a tax on the actual operation of a governmental function. It would have saved the Court the embarrassment of some later decisions, but the case still stands unquestioned.

But the place of the case in our constitutional law to-day is curiously different from its immediate effect. A few years back the Supreme Court decided in effect that the United States had power under the Constitution to govern colonial dependencies. That settled that question; that decision was entirely and implicitly accepted by the people at large as if a judgment of the Supreme Court possessed some mysterious, intrinsic force. But the opinion of the Supreme Court in *McCulloch* v. *Maryland*, on March 6, 1819, so far from being implicitly accepted as legal gospel, was immediately disregarded and defied. A few weeks before the decision the legislature of Ohio had passed an act taxing the branch bank of the United States in Cincinnati. In September, 1819, Ralph Osborn, the auditor of Ohio, acting under the Ohio statute, attempted to collect the tax, and, on September 17th, one Harper, under his command, made a levy on funds of a new branch bank at Chillicothe. In the face of a writ of injunction the money seized was paid over to the state treasurer. Osborn and his deputy were both sued in trespass in the Circuit Court of the United States in Ohio. This suit and another failed on technical points, and, in 1820, an attempt was made to punish Osborn for contempt of court in paying over the moneys to the state treasurer. Before that proceeding was heard, the legislature of Ohio met. A special committee of the legislature reviewed at length the claims of the Supreme Court as the final arbiter of the constitutionality of laws. They pointed out how the action of Kentucky and Virginia, in 1800, had established the doctrine of states rights, how Marshall's decision in *Marbury* v. *Madison* had been fruitless, and how Marbury had never received his commission, how the decision in *Fletcher* v. *Peck* had never been enforced by the Yazoo claimants. The legislature upheld its committee, and, in 1821, passed a statute withdrawing the protection of the laws of Ohio from the Bank of the United States in certain cases, so that the Bank was practically an outlaw. It was not until 1824 that Osborn's case reached the Supreme Court of the United States, and the rights of the Bank were enforced. Further, the Ohio legislature declared at length an elaborate doctrine of states rights. In

Kentucky a similar tax was laid, though not enforced. Then the controversy took another phase. In Kentucky, financial conditions became so bad that specie payments were suspended and stay laws passed. In Missouri the state created a paper currency. The whole country, particularly the West, was plunged into a terrible state of financial and business depression. The agitation for the protective tariff to remedy these evil days was just commenced, and gradually conditions were readjusted, but neither *McCulloch* v. *Maryland* nor any other decision of the Supreme Court had the power to decide for the people of its own time what it decided for posterity. But in Marshall's opinion there is not a hint of this. In that moment, almost at the low tide of the Republic, Marshall was still looking forward, nation-building, with an almost prophetic confidence and foresight.

McCulloch

v.

The State of Maryland *et al.*

[4 Wheaton 316.]

1819.

Mr. Webster, the Attorney-General (Mr. Wirt), and Mr. Pinkney for the plaintiff in error.
Mr. Hopkinson and Mr. Jones for the defendants in error.

Marshall, Ch. J., delivered the opinion of the court :

In the case now to be determined, the defendant, a sovereign state, denies the obligation of a law enacted by the legislature of the Union, and the plaintiff, on his part, contests the validity of an act which has been passed by the legislature of that state. The constitution of our country, in its most interesting and vital parts, is to be considered ; the conflicting powers of the government of the Union and of its members, as marked in that constitution, are to be discussed ; and an opinion given, which may essentially influence the great operations of the government. No tribunal can approach such a question without a deep sense of its importance, and of the awful responsibility involved in its decision. But it must be decided peacefully, or

* *401*   remain a source of * hostile legislation, perhaps of hostility of a still more serious nature ; and if it is to be so decided, by this tribunal alone can the decision be made. On the Supreme Court of the United States has the constitution of our country devolved this important duty.

The first question made in the cause is, has Congress power to incorporate a bank ?

It has been truly said that this can scarcely be considered as an open question, entirely unprejudiced by the former proceedings of the nation respecting it. The principle now contested was introduced at a very early period of our history, has been recognized by many successive legislatures, and has been acted upon by the judicial department, in cases of peculiar delicacy, as a law of undoubted obligation.

It will not be denied that a bold and daring usurpation might be resisted, after an acquiescence still longer and more complete than this. But it is conceived that a doubtful question, one on which human reason may pause, and the human judgment be suspended, in the decision of which the great principles of liberty are not concerned, but the respective powers of those who are equally the representatives of the people, are to be adjusted ; if not put at rest by the practice of the government, ought to receive a considerable impression from that practice. An exposition of the constitution, deliberately established by legislative acts, on the faith of which an immense property has been advanced, ought not to be lightly disregarded.

The power now contested was exercised by the first Congress elected under the present constitution. *402   *The bill for incorporating the bank of the United States did not steal upon an unsuspecting legislature, and pass unobserved. Its principle was completely understood, and was opposed with equal zeal and ability. After being resisted, first in the fair and open field of debate, and afterwards in the executive cabinet, with as much persevering talent as any measure has ever experienced, and being supported by arguments which convinced minds as pure and as intelligent as this country can boast, it became a law. The original act was permitted to expire; but a short experience of the embarrassments to which the refusal to revive it exposed the government, convinced those who were most prejudiced against the measure of its necessity and induced the passage of the present law. It would require no ordinary share of intrepidity to assert that a measure adopted under these circumstances was a bold and plain usurpation, to which the constitution gave no countenance.

These observations belong to the cause; but they are not made under the impression that, were the question entirely new, the law would be found irreconcilable with the constitution.

In discussing this question, the counsel for the state of Maryland have deemed it of some importance in the construction of the constitution, to consider that instrument not as emanating from the people, but as the act of sovereign and independent states. The powers of the general government, it has been said, are delegated by the states, who alone are truly sovereign ; and must be exercised in subordination to the states, who alone possess supreme dominion.

*403   * It would be difficult to sustain this proposition.   The convention which framed the constitution was indeed elected by the state legislatures.   But the instrument, when it came from their hands, was a mere proposal, without obligation, or pretensions to it.   It was reported to the then existing Congress of the United States, with a request that it might " be submitted to a convention of delegates, chosen in each state by the people thereof, under the recommendation of its legislature, for their assent and ratification."   This mode of proceeding was adopted ; and by the convention, by Congress, and by the state legislatures, the instrument was submitted to the people.   They acted upon it in the only manner in which they can act safely, effectively, and wisely, on such a subject, by assembling in convention.   It is true, they assembled in their several states—and where else should they have assembled ? No political dreamer was ever wild enough to think of breaking down the lines which separate the states, and of compounding the American people into one common mass.   Of consequence, when they act, they act in their states.   But the measures they adopt do not, on that account, cease to be the measures of the people themselves, or become the measures of the state governments.

From these conventions the constitution derives its whole authority. The government proceeds directly from the people ; is " ordained and established" in the name of the people ; and is declared to be ordained, " in order to form a more perfect union, establish justice, insure domestic tranquillity, and secure *404 *the blessings of liberty to themselves and to their posterity." The assent of the states, in their sovereign capacity, is implied in calling a convention, and thus submitting that instrument to the people. But the people were at perfect liberty to accept or reject it ; and their act was final. It required not the affirmance, and could not be negatived, by the state governments. The constitution, when thus adopted, was of complete obligation, and bound the state sovereignties.

It has been said that the people had already surrendered all their powers to the state sovereignties, and had nothing more to give. But, surely, the question whether they may resume and modify the powers granted to government does not remain to be settled in this country. Much more might the legitimacy of the general government be doubted, had it been created by the states. The powers delegated to the state sovereignties were to be exercised by themselves, not by a distinct and independent sovereignty, created by themselves. To the formation of a league, such as was the confederation, the state sovereignties were certainly competent. But when, " in order to form a more perfect union," it was deemed necessary to change this alliance into an effective government, possessing great and sovereign powers, and acting directly on the people, the necessity of referring it to the people, and of deriving its powers directly from them, was felt and acknowledged by all.

The government of the Union, then (whatever may be the influence of this fact on the case), is, *405   * emphatically, and truly, a government of the people. In form and in substance it emanates from them. Its powers are granted by them, and are to be exercised directly on them, and for their benefit.

This government is acknowledged by all to be one of enumerated powers. The principle, that it can exercise only the powers granted to it, would seem too apparent to have required to be enforced by all those arguments which its enlightened friends, while it was depending before the people, found it necessary to urge. That principle is now universally admitted. But the question respecting the extent of the powers actually granted, is perpetually arising, and will probably continue to arise, as long as our system shall exist.

In discussing these questions, the conflicting powers of the general and state governments must be brought into view, and the supremacy of their respective laws, when they are in opposition, must be settled.

If any one proposition could command the universal assent of mankind, we might expect it would be this—that the government of the Union, though limited in its powers, is supreme within its sphere of action. This would seem to result necessarily from its nature. It is the government of all; its powers are delegated by all; it represents all, and acts for all. Though any one state may be willing to control its operations, no state is willing to allow others to control them. The nation, on those subjects on which it can act, must necessarily bind its component parts. But this question is not left to mere reason; the people have, in express terms, decided it by saying, *406 * "this constitution, and the laws of the United States, which shall be made in pursuance thereof," "shall be the supreme law of the land," and by requiring that the members of the state legislatures, and the officers of the executive and judicial departments of the states shall take the oath of fidelity to it.

The government of the United States, then, though limited in its powers, is supreme; and its laws, when made in pursuance of the constitution, form the supreme law of the land, "anything in the constitution or laws of any state to the contrary notwithstanding."

Among the enumerated powers, we do not find that of establishing a bank or creating a corporation. But there is no phrase in the instrument which, like the articles of confederation, excludes incidental or implied powers; and which requires that everything granted shall be expressly and minutely described. Even the 10th amendment, which was framed for the purpose of quieting the excessive jealousies which had been excited, omits the word " expressly," and declares only that the powers " not delegated to the United States, nor prohibited to the states, are reserved to the states or to the people;" thus leaving the question, whether the particular power which may become the subject of contest has been delegated to the one government, or prohibited to the other, to depend on a fair construction of the whole instrument. The men who drew and adopted this amendment had experienced the embarrassments resulting from the insertion of this word in the

*407   articles * of confederation, and probably omitted it to avoid those embarrassments. A constitution, to contain an accurate detail of all the subdivisions of which its great powers will admit, and of all the means by which they may be carried into execution, would partake of a prolixity of a legal code, and could scarcely be embraced by the human mind. It would probably never be understood by the public. Its nature, therefore, requires, that only its great outlines should be marked, its important objects designated, and the minor ingredients which compose those objects be deduced from the nature of the objects themselves. That this idea was entertained by the framers of the American constitution, is not only to be inferred from the nature of the instrument, but from the language. Why else were some of the limitations, found in the ninth section of the 1st article, introduced? It is also, in some degree, warranted by their having omitted to use any restrictive term which might prevent its receiving a fair and just interpretation. In considering this question, then, we must never forget that it is a constitution we are expounding.

Although, among the enumerated powers of government, we do not find the word "bank" or "incorporation," we find the great powers to lay and collect taxes ; to borrow money ; to regulate commerce ; to declare and conduct a war ; and to raise and support armies and navies.   The sword and the purse, all the external relations, and no inconsiderable portion of the industry of the nation, are entrusted to its government.   It can never be pretended *that *408   these vast powers draw after them others of inferior importance, merely because they are inferior. Such an idea can never be advanced.   But it may with great reason be contended, that a government, entrusted with such ample powers, on the due execution of which the happiness and prosperity of the nation so vitally depends, must also be entrusted with ample means for their execution.   The power being given, it is the interest of the nation to facilitate its execution.   It can never be their interest, and cannot be presumed to have been their intention, to clog and embarrass its execution by withholding the most appropriate means.   Throughout this vast republic, from the St. Croix to the Gulf of Mexico, from the Atlantic to the Pacific, revenue is to be collected and expended, armies are to be marched and supported. The exigencies of the nation may require that the treasure raised in the north should be transported to the south, that raised in the east conveyed to the west, or that this order should be reversed.   Is that construction of the constitution to be preferred which would render these operations difficult, hazardous,

and expensive ? Can we adopt that construction (unless the words imperiously require it) which would impute to the framers of that instrument, when granting these powers for the public good, the intention of impeding their exercise by withholding a choice of means ? If, indeed, such be the mandate of the constitution, we have only to obey ; but that instrument does not profess to enumerate the means by which the powers it confers may be executed ; nor does it prohibit the creation of a corporation, * if the
*409
existence of such a being be essential to the beneficial exercise of those powers. It is, then, the subject of fair inquiry, how far such means may be employed. It is not denied that the powers given to the government imply the ordinary means of execution. That, for example of raising revenue, and applying it to national purposes, is admitted to imply the power of conveying money from place to place, as the exigencies of the nation may require, and of employing the usual means of conveyance. But it is denied that the government has its choice of means ; or, that it may employ the most convenient means, if, to employ them, it be necessary to erect a corporation.

On what foundation does this argument rest ? On this alone : The power of creating a corporation, is one appertaining to sovereignty, and is not expressly conferred on Congress. This is true. But all legislative powers appertain to sovereignty. The original power of giving the law on any subject whatever, is a sovereign power ; and if the government of the Union is restrained from creating a corporation, as a means

for performing its functions, on the single reason that
the creation of a corporation is an act of sovereignty ;
if the sufficiency of this reason be acknowledged,
there would be some difficulty in sustaining the
authority of Congress to pass other laws for the
accomplishment of the same objects.

The government which has a right to do an act,
and has imposed on it the duty of performing that
act, must, according to the dictates of reason, be allowed * to select the means ; and those who
*410   contend that it may not select any appropri-
ate means, that one particular mode of effecting the
object is excepted, take upon themselves the burden
of establishing that exception.

The creation of a corporation, it is said, appertains
to sovereignty.   This is admitted.   But to what portion of sovereignty does it appertain ?   Does it belong to one more than to another ?   In America, the
powers of sovereignty are divided between the government of the Union, and those of the States.
They are each sovereign, with respect to the objects
committed to it, and neither sovereign with respect
to the objects committed to the other.   We cannot
comprehend that train of reasoning which would
maintain that the extent of power granted by the
people is to be ascertained, not by the nature and
terms of the grant, but by its date.   Some state constitutions were formed before, some since that of
the United States.   We cannot believe that their
relation to each other is in any degree dependent
upon this circumstance.   Their respective powers

must, we think, be precisely the same as if they had been formed at the same time. Had they been formed at the same time, and had the people conferred on the general government the power contained in the constitution, and on the states the whole residuum of power, would it have been asserted that the government of the Union was not sovereign with respect to those objects which were entrusted to it, in relation to which its laws were declared to be supreme? If this could not have been asserted, we cannot well comprehend the process of reasoning *411 which * maintains that a power appertaining to sovereignty cannot be connected with that vast portion of it which is granted to the general government, so far as it is calculated to subserve the legitimate objects of that government. The power of creating a corporation, though appertaining to sovereignty, is not, like the power of making war, or levying taxes, or of regulating commerce, a great substantive and independent power, which cannot be implied as incidental to other powers, or used as a means of executing them. It is never the end for which other powers are exercised, but a means by which other objects are accomplished. No contributions are made to charity for the sake of an incorporation, but a corporation is created to administer the charity; no seminary of learning is instituted in order to be incorporated, but the corporate character is conferred to subserve the purposes of education. No city was ever built with the sole object of being incorporated, but is incorporated as affording the best

means of being well governed. The power of creating a corporation is never used for its own sake,
but for the purpose of effecting something else. No
sufficient reason is, therefore, perceived, why it may
not pass as incidental to those powers which are expressly given, if it be a direct mode of executing them.

But the constitution of the United States has not
left the right of Congress to employ the necessary
means for the execution of the powers conferred on
the government to general reasoning. To its enumeration of powers is added that of making "all
*412   * laws which shall be necessary and proper,
             for carrying into execution the foregoing
powers, and all other powers vested by this constitution, in the government of the United States, or in
any department thereof."

The counsel for the State of Maryland have urged
various arguments, to prove that this clause, though
in terms a grant of power, is not so in effect; but is
really restrictive of the general right, which might
otherwise be implied, of selecting means for executing the enumerated powers.

In support of this proposition, they have found it
necessary to contend, that this clause was inserted
for the purpose of conferring on Congress the power
of making laws. That, without it, doubts might be
entertained whether Congress could exercise its powers in the form of legislation.

But could this be the object for which it was inserted? A government is created by the people,
having legislative, executive, and judicial powers.

Its legislative powers are vested in a Congress, which is to consist of a senate and house of representatives. Each house may determine the rule of its proceedings ; and it is declared that every bill which shall have passed both houses, shall, before it becomes a law, be presented to the President of the United States.   The 7th section describes the course of proceedings, by which a bill shall become a law ; and, then, the 8th section enumerates the powers of Congress.   Could it be necessary to say that a legislature should exercise legislative powers in the shape of legislation ?   After allowing each house to prescribe
*413   * its own course of proceeding, after describing the manner in which a bill should become a law, would it have entered into the mind of a single member of the convention that an express power to make laws was necessary to enable the legislature to make them ?   That a legislature, endowed with legislative powers, can legislate, is a proposition too self-evident to have been questioned.

But the argument on which most reliance is placed, is drawn from the peculiar language of this clause. Congress is not empowered by it to make all laws, which may have relation to the powers conferred on the government, but such only as may be " necessary and proper" for carrying them into execution.   The word " necessary" is considered as controlling the whole sentence, and as limiting the right to pass laws for the execution of the granted powers, to such as are indispensable, and without which the power would be nugatory.   That it excludes the choice of means, and leaves to Congress, in each case, that only which is most direct and simple.

Is it true that this is the sense in which the word " necessary" is always used? Does it always import an absolute physical necessity, so strong that one thing, to which another may be termed necessary, cannot exist without that other? We think it does not. If reference be had to its use, in the common affairs of the world, or in approved authors, we find that it frequently imports no more than that one thing is convenient, or useful, or essential to another. To employ the means necessary to an end, is generally understood as employing any means calculated to *414   * produce the end, and not as being confined to those single means, without which the end would be entirely unattainable. Such is the character of human language, that no word conveys to the mind, in all situations, one single definite idea; and nothing is more common than to use words in a figurative sense. Almost all compositions contain words, which, taken in their rigorous sense, would convey a meaning different from that which is obviously intended. It is essential to just construction, that many words which import something excessive should be understood in a more mitigated sense—in that sense which common usage justifies. The word " necessary" is of this description. It has not a fixed character peculiar to itself. It admits of all degrees of comparison ; and is often connected with other words, which increase or diminish the impression the mind receives of the urgency it imports. A thing

may be necessary, very necessary, absolutely or indispensably necessary. To no mind would the same idea be conveyed by these several phrases. This comment on the word is well illustrated by the passage cited at the bar, from the 10th section of the 1st article of the constitution. It is, we think, impossible to compare the sentence which prohibits a state from laying "imposts or duties on imports or exports, except what may be absolutely necessary for executing its inspection laws," with that which authorizes Congress "to make all laws which shall be necessary and proper for carrying into execution" the powers of the general government, without feeling a conviction that the convention understood itself to change materially * the meaning of the word "necessary," by prefixing the word "absolutely."
*415
This word, then, like others, is used in various senses; and, in its construction, the subject, the context, the intention of the person using them, are all to be taken into view.

Let this be done in the case under consideration. The subject is the execution of those great powers on which the welfare of a nation essentially depends. It must have been the intention of those who gave these powers, to insure, as far as human prudence could insure, their beneficial execution. This could not be done by confining the choice of means to such narrow limits as not to leave it in the power of Congress to adopt any which might be appropriate, and which were conducive to the end. This provision is made in a constitution intended to endure for ages to

come, and, consequently, to be adapted to the various crises of human affairs. To have prescribed the
means by which government should, in all future
time, execute its powers, would have been to change,
entirely, the character of the instrument, and give it
the properties of a legal code. It would have been
an unwise attempt to provide, by immutable rules,
for exigencies which, if foreseen at all, must have
been seen dimly, and which can be best provided for
as they occur. To have declared that the best means
shall not be used, but those alone without which the
power given would be nugatory, would have been to
deprive the legislature of the capacity to avail itself of
experience, to exercise its reason, and to accommo-
date its legislation to circumstances.   * If
*416   we apply this principle of construction to any
of the powers of the government, we shall find it so
pernicious in its operation that we shall be compelled
to discard it. The powers vested in Congress may
certainly be carried into execution, without prescribing an oath of office. The power to exact this
security for the faithful performance of duty, is not
given, nor is it indispensably necessary. The different departments may be established; taxes may be
imposed and collected; armies and navies may be
raised and maintained; and money may be borrowed,
without requiring an oath of office. It might be
argued, with as much plausibility as other incidental
powers have been assailed, that the convention was
not unmindful of this subject. The oath which might
be exacted—that of fidelity to the constitution—is

prescribed, and no other can be required. Yet, he would be charged with insanity who should contend that the legislature might not superadd, to the oath directed by the constitution, such other oath of office as its wisdom might suggest.

So, with respect to the whole penal code of the United States : whence arises the power to punish in cases not prescribed by the constitution ? All admit that the government may, legitimately, punish any violation of its laws ; and yet, this is not among the enumerated powers of Congress. The right to enforce the observance of law, by punishing its infraction, might be denied with the more plausibility because it is expressly given in some cases. Congress is empowered " to provide for the punishment *417 * of counterfeiting the securities and current coin of the United States," and " to define and punish piracies and felonies committed on the high seas, and offences against the law of nations." The several powers of Congress may exist, in a very imperfect state, to be sure, but they may exist and be carried into execution, although no punishment should be inflicted in cases where the right to punish is not expressly given.

Take, for example, the power " to establish post-offices and post-roads." This power is executed by the single act of making the establishment. But, from this has been inferred the power and duty of carrying the mail along the post-road, from one post-office to another. And, from this implied power, has again been inferred the right to punish those who steal

letters from the post-office, or rob the mail.   It may
be said, with some plausibility, that the right to carry
the mail, and to punish those who rob it, is not indispensably necessary to the establishment of a post-
office and post-road.   This right is indeed essential to
the beneficial exercise of the power, but not indispensably necessary to its existence.   So, of the punishment of the crimes of stealing or falsifying a record
or process of a court of the United States, or of perjury in such court.   To punish these offenses is certainly conducive to the due administration of justice.
But courts may exist, and may decide the causes
brought before them, though such crimes escape
punishment.

The baneful influence of this narrow construction
on all the operations of the government, and the
absolute *impracticability of maintaining it
without rendering the government incompetent to its great objects, might be illustrated by
numerous examples drawn from the constitution, and
from our laws.   The good sense of the public has
pronounced, without hesitation, that the power of
punishment appertains to sovereignty, and may be
exercised whenever the sovereign has a right to act,
as incidental to his constitutional powers.   It is a
means for carrying into execution all sovereign powers, and may be used, although not indispensably
necessary.   It is a right incidental to the power, and
conducive to its beneficial exercise.

If this limited construction of the word "necessary"
must be abandoned in order to punish, whence is de-

*418

rived the rule which would re-instate it, when the government would carry its powers into execution by means not vindictive in their nature ? If the word " necessary" means " needful," " requisite," " essential," " conducive to," in order to let in the power of punishment for the infraction of law ; why is it not equally comprehensive when required to authorize the use of means which facilitate the execution of the powers of government without the infliction of punishment ?

In ascertaining the sense in which the word " necessary" is used in this clause of the constitution, we may derive some aid from that with which it is associated. Congress shall have power " to make all laws which shall be necessary and proper to carry into execution" the powers of the government. If the word " necessary" was used in that strict and rigorous sense for which the counsel for the state of *Maryland contend, it would be an extraordinary departure from the usual course of the human mind, as exhibited in composition, to add a word, the only possible effect of which is to qualify that strict and rigorous meaning ; to present to the mind the idea of some choice of means of legislation not straightened and compressed within the narrow limits for which gentlemen contend.

*419

But the argument which most conclusively demonstrates the error of the construction contended for by the counsel for the state of Maryland, is founded on the intention of the convention, as manifested in the whole clause. To waste time and argument in proving that without it Congress might carry its powers into execution, would be not much less idle than to hold a lighted taper to the sun.   As little can it be required to prove, that in the absence of this clause, Congress would have some choice of means.   That it might employ those which, in its judgment, would most advantageously effect the object to be accomplished.   That any means adapted to the end, any means which tended directly to the execution of the constitutional powers of the government, were in themselves constitutional.   This clause, as construed by the state of Maryland, would abridge, and almost annihilate this useful and necessary right of the legislature to select its means.   That this could not be intended, is, we should think, had it not been already controverted, too apparent for controversy.   We think so for the following reasons :

1st.   The clause is placed among the powers of Congress, not among the limitations on those powers.

*420

*2d. Its terms purport to enlarge, not to diminish the powers vested in the government.   It purports to be an additional power, not a restriction on those already granted.   No reason has been, or can be assigned for thus concealing an intention to narrow the discretion of the national legislature under words which purport to enlarge it.   The framers of the constitution wished its adoption, and well knew that it would be endangered by its strength, not by its weakness.   Had they been capable of using language which would convey to the eye one idea, and, after deep reflection, impress on the mind another, they would rather have disguised the grant of power than its limitation. If, then, their intention had been, by this clause, to restrain the free use of means which might otherwise have been implied, that intention would have been inserted in another place, and would have been expressed in terms resembling these. "In carrying into execution the foregoing powers, and all others," &c., "no laws shall be passed but such as are necessary and proper." Had the intention been to make this clause restrictive, it would unquestionably have been so in form as well as in effect.

The result of the most careful and attentive consideration bestowed upon this clause is, that if it does not enlarge, it cannot be construed to restrain the powers of Congress, or to impair the right of the legislature to exercise its best judgment in the selection of measures to carry into execution the constitutional powers of the government. If no other motive for its insertion can be suggested, a sufficient one is found in the desire to remove all doubts respecting *the right to legislate on that vast mass of

*421   incidental powers which must be involved in the constitution, if that instrument be not a splendid bauble.

We admit, as all must admit, that the powers of the government are limited, and that its limits are not to be transcended. But we think the sound construction of the constitution must allow to the national legislature that discretion, with respect to the means by which the powers it confers are to be carried into execution, which will enable that body to perform the high duties assigned to it, in the manner most beneficial to the people. Let the end be legitimate, let it be within the scope of the constitution, and all means which are appropriate, which are plainly adapted to that end, which are not prohibited, but consist with the letter and spirit of the constitution, are constitutional.

That a corporation must be considered as a means not less usual, not of higher dignity, not more requiring a particular specification than other means, has been sufficiently proved. If we look to the origin of corporations, to the manner in which they have been framed in that government from which we have derived most of our legal principles and ideas, or to the uses to which they have been applied, we find no reason to suppose that a constitution, omitting, and wisely omitting, to enumerate all the means for carrying into execution the great powers vested in government, ought to have specified this. Had it been intended to grant this power as one which should be distinct and independent, to be exercised in any case whatever, it * would have found a place among the enumerated powers of the government. But being considered merely as a means, to be employed only for the purpose of carrying into execution the given powers, there could be no motive for particularly mentioning it.

*422

The propriety of this remark would seem to be generally acknowledged by the universal acquiescence in the construction which has been uniformly put on the 3d section of the 4th article of the constitution. The power to "make all needful rules and regulations respecting the territory or other property belonging to the United States," is not more comprehensive, than the power "to make all laws which shall be necessary and proper for carrying into execution" the powers of the government. Yet all admit the constitutionality of a territorial government, which is a corporate body.

If a corporation may be employed indiscriminately with other means to carry into execution the powers of the government, no particular reason can be assigned for excluding the use of a bank, if required for its fiscal operations. To use one, must be within the discretion of Congress, if it be an appropriate mode of executing the powers of government. That it is a convenient, a useful, and essential instrument in the prosecution of its fiscal operations, is not now a subject of controversy. All those who have been concerned in the administration of our finances, have concurred in representing the importance and necessity; and so strongly have they been felt, that statesmen of the first class, whose previous opinions *against it had been confirmed by every *423   circumstance which can fix the human judgment, have yielded those opinions to the exigencies of the nation. Under the confederation, Congress, justifying the measure by its necessity, transcended perhaps its powers to obtain the advantage of a bank; and our own legislation attests the universal conviction of the utility of this measure. The time has passed away when it can be necessary to enter into any discussion in order to prove the importance of this instrument, as a means to effect the legitimate objects of the government.

But, were its necessity less apparent, none can deny its being an appropriate measure ; and if it is, the degree of its necessity, as has been very justly observed, is to be discussed in another place. Should Congress, in the execution of its powers, adopt measures which are prohibited by the constitution ; or should Congress, under the pretext of executing its powers pass laws for the accomplishment of objects not intrusted to the government, it would become the painful duty of this tribunal, should a case requiring such a decision come before it, to say that such an act was not the law of the land. But where the law is not prohibited, and is really calculated to effect any of the objects entrusted to the government, to undertake here to inquire into the degree of its necessity, would be to pass the line which circumscribes the judicial department, and to tread on legislative ground. This court disclaims all pretensions to such a power.

*424   * After this declaration, it can scarcely be necessary to say that the existence of state banks can have no possible influence on the question. No trace is to be found in the constitution of an intention to create a dependence of the government of the Union on those of the States, for the execution of the great powers assigned to it. Its means are adequate to its ends ; and on those means alone was it expected to rely for the accomplishment of its ends.   To impose on it the necessity of resorting to means which it cannot control, which another government may furnish or withhold, would render its course precarious ; the result of its measures uncertain, and create a dependence on other governments, which might disappoint its most important designs, and is incompatible with the language of the constitution.   But were it otherwise, the choice of means implies a right to choose a national bank in preference to state banks, and Congress alone can make the election.

After the most deliberate consideration, it is the unanimous and decided opinion of this court that the act to incorporate the bank of the United States is a law made in pursuance of the constitution, and is a part of the supreme law of the land.

The branches, proceeding from the same stock, and being conducive to the complete accomplishment of the object, are equally constitutional.   It would have been unwise to locate them in the charter, and it would be unnecessarily inconvenient to employ the legislative power in making those subordinate arrangements.   The great duties of the bank are prescribed ; those duties require branches ; and the bank itself *425 *may, we think, be safely trusted with the selection of places where those branches shall be fixed ; reserving always to the government the right to require that a branch shall be located where it may be deemed necessary.

It being the opinion of the court that the act incorporating the bank is constitutional, and that the power of establishing a branch in the state of Maryland might be properly exercised by the bank itself, we proceed to inquire :

2. Whether the state of Maryland may, without violating the constitution, tax that branch ?

That the power of taxation is one of vital importance ; that it is retained by the states ; that it is not abridged by the grant of a similar power to the government of the Union ; that it is to be concurrently exercised by the two governments : are truths which have never been denied. But, such is the paramount character of the constitution that its capacity to withdraw any subject from the action of even this power, is admitted. The states are expressly forbidden to lay any duties on imports or exports, except what may be absolutely necessary for executing their inspection laws. If the obligation of this prohibition must be conceded—if it may restrain a state from the exercise of its taxing power on imports and exports—the same paramount character would seem to restrain, as it certainly may restrain, a state from such other exercise of this power, as is in its nature incompatible with, and repugnant to, the constitutional laws of the Union. A law, absolutely repugnant to another, as entirely *repeals that other as if express terms of repeal were used.

*426

On this ground the counsel for the bank place its claim to be exempted from the power of a state to tax its operations. There is no express provision for the case, but the claim has been sustained on a principle which so entirely pervades the constitution, is so intermixed with the materials which compose it, so interwoven with its web, so blended with its texture, as to be incapable of being separated from it without rending it into shreds.

This great principle is, that the constitution and the laws made in pursuance thereof are supreme; that they control the constitution and laws of the respective states, and cannot be controlled by them. From this, which may be almost termed an axiom, other propositions are deduced as corollaries, on the truth or error of which, and on their application to this case, the cause has been supposed to depend. These are, 1st. That a power to create implies a power to preserve. 2d. That a power to destroy if wielded by a different hand, is hostile to, and incompatible with these powers to create and to preserve. 3d. That where this repugnancy exists, that authority which is supreme must control, not yield to that over which it is supreme.

These propositions as abstract truths, would, perhaps, never be controverted. Their application to this case, however, has been denied; and, both in maintaining the affirmative and the negative, a splendor of eloquence, and strength of argument seldom, if ever, surpassed, have been displayed.

*427   * The power of Congress to create, and of course to continue, the bank, was the subject of the preceding part of this opinion; and is no longer to be considered as questionable.

That the power of taxing it by the states may be exercised so as to destroy it, is too obvious to be

denied. But taxation is said to be an absolute power,
which acknowledges no other limits than those expressly prescribed in the constitution, and like sovereign power of every other description, is trusted to the
discretion of those who use it.   But the very terms
of this argument admit that the sovereignty of the
state, in the article of taxation itself, is subordinate
to, and may be controlled by the constitution of the
United States.   How far it has been controlled by
that instrument must be a question of construction.
In making this construction, no principle not declared
can be admissible, which would defeat the legitimate
operations of a supreme government.   It is of the
very essence of supremacy to remove all obstacles to
its action within its own sphere, and so to modify
every power vested in subordinate governments as to
exempt its own operations from their own influence.
This effect need not be stated in terms.   It is so
involved in the declaration of supremacy, so necessarily implied in it, that the expression of it could not
make it more certain.   We must, therefore, keep it
in view while construing the constitution.

The argument on the part of the state of Maryland is, not that the states may directly resist a
law of Congress, but that they may exercise their
*428   * acknowledged powers upon it, and that
the constitution leaves them this right in
the confidence that they will not abuse it.

Before we proceed to examine this argument, and
to subject it to the test of the constitution, we must
be permitted to bestow a few considerations on the

nature and extent of this original right of taxation, which is acknowledged to remain with the states. It is admitted that the power of taxing the people and their property is essential to the very existence of government, and may be legitimately exercised on the objects to which it is applicable, to the utmost extent to which the government may chose to carry it. The only security against the abuse of this power is found in the structure of the government itself. In imposing a tax the legislature acts upon its constituents. This is in general a sufficient security against erroneous and oppressive taxation.

The people of a state, therefore, give to their government a right of taxing themselves and their property, and as the exigencies of government cannot be limited, they prescribe no limits to the exercise of this right, resting confidently on the interest of the legislator, and on the influence of the constituents over their representative, to guard them against its abuse. But the means employed by the government of the Union have no such security, nor is the right of a state to tax them sustained by the same theory. Those means are not given by the people of a particular state, not given by the constituents of the legislature, which claim the right to tax them, but by the people of all the states. They are given *429 by all, * for the benefit of all—and upon theory, should be subjected to that government only which belongs to all.

It may be objected to this definition, that the power of taxation is not confined to the people and property of a state. It may be exercised upon every object brought within its jurisdiction.

This is true. But to what source do we trace this right? It is obvious that it is an incident of sovereignty, and is co-extensive with that to which it is an incident. All subjects over which the sovereign power of a state extends, are objects of taxation; but those over which it does not extend, are, upon the soundest principles, exempt from taxation. This proposition may almost be pronounced self-evident.

The sovereignty of a state extends to everything which exists by its own authority, or is introduced by its permission; but does it extend to those means which are employed by Congress to carry into execution—powers conferred on that body by the people of the United States? We think it demonstrable that it does not. Those powers are not given by the people of a single state. They are given by the people of the United States, to a government whose laws, made in pursuance of the constitution, are declared to be supreme. Consequently, the people of a single state cannot confer a sovereignty which will extend over them.

If we measure the power of taxation residing in a state, by the extent of sovereignty which the people of a single state possess, and can confer on its government, we have an intelligible standard, applicable *to every case to which the power may be applied. We have a principle which leaves the power of taxing the people and property of a state unimpaired; which leaves to a state the com-

*430

mand of all its resources, and which places beyond its reach, all those powers which are conferred by the people of the United States on the government of the Union, and all those means which are given for the purpose of carrying those powers into execution. We have a principle which is safe for the states, and safe for the Union. We are relieved, as we ought to be, from clashing sovereignty; from interfering powers; from a repugnancy between a right in one government to pull down what there is an acknowledged right in another to build up; from the incompatibility of a right in one government to destroy what there is a right in another to preserve. We are not driven to the perplexing inquiry, so unfit for the judicial department, what degree of taxation is the legitimate use, and what degree may amount to the abuse of the power. The attempt to use it on the means employed by the government of the Union, in pursuance of the constitution, is itself an abuse, because it is the usurpation of a power which the people of a single state cannot give.

We find, then, on just theory, a total failure of this original right to tax the means employed by the government of the Union, for the execution of its powers. The right never existed, and the question whether it has been surrendered, cannot arise.

But, waiving this theory for the present, let us resume the inquiry, whether this power can be exercised * by the respective states, consistently

* *431*

with a fair construction of the constitution.

That the power to tax involves the power to

destroy ; that the power to destroy may defeat and render useless the power to create ; that there is a plain repugnance, in conferring on one government a power to control the constitutional measures of another, which other, with respect to those very measures, is declared to be supreme over that which exerts the control, are propositions not to be denied. But all inconsistencies are to be reconciled by the magic of the word CONFIDENCE. Taxation, it is said, does not necessarily and unavoidably destroy. To carry to the excess of destruction would be an abuse, to presume which, would banish that confidence which is essential to all government.

But is this a case of confidence ? Would the people of any one state trust those of another with a power to control the most insignificant operations of their state government ? We know they would not. Why, then, should we suppose that the people of any one state should be willing to trust those of another with a power to control the operations of a government to which they have confided the most important and most valuable interests ? In the legislature of the Union alone, are all represented. The legislature of the Union alone, therefore, can be trusted by the people with the power of controlling measures which concern all, in the confidence that it will not be abused. This, then, is not a case of confidence, and we must consider it as it really is.

*432   * If we apply the principle for which the state of Maryland contends, to the constitution generally, we shall find it capable of changing totally the character of that instrument. We shall find it capable of arresting all the measures of the government, and ·of prostrating it at the foot of the states. The American people have declared their constitution, and the laws made in pursuance thereof, to be supreme ; but this principle would transfer the supremacy, in fact, to the states.

If the states may tax one instrument, employed by the government in the execution of its powers, they may tax any and every other instrument. They may tax the mail ; they may tax the mint ; they may tax patent-rights ; they may tax the papers of the custom-house ; they may tax judicial process; they may tax all the means employed by the government, to an excess which would defeat all the ends of government. This was not intended by the American people. They did not design to make their government dependent on the states.

Gentlemen say they do not claim the right to extend state taxation to these objects. They limit their pretensions to property. But on what principle is this distinction made ? Those who make it have furnished no reason for it, and the principle for which they contend denies it. They contend that the power of taxation has no other limit than is found in the 10th section of the 1st article of the constitution ; that, with respect to everything else, the power of the states is supreme, and admits of no control. If this be true, the distinction between prop-*433 erty and * other subjects to which the power of taxation is applicable, is merely arbitrary, and can never be sustained. This is not all. If the controlling power of the states be established ; if their supremacy as to taxation be acknowledged ; what is to restrain their exercising this control in any shape they may please to give it ? Their sovereignty is not confined to taxation. That is not the only mode in which it might be displayed. The question is, in truth, a question of supremacy ; and if the right of the states to tax the means employed by the general government be conceded, the declaration that the constitution, and the laws made in pursuance thereof, shall be the supreme law of the land, is empty and unmeaning declamation.

In the course of the argument, *The Federalist* has been quoted ; and the opinions expressed by the authors of that work have been justly supposed to be entitled to great respect in expounding the constitution. No tribute can be paid to them which exceeds their merit; but in applying their opinions to the cases which may arise in the progress of our government, a right to judge of their correctness must be retained ; and, to understand the argument, we must examine the proposition it maintains, and the objections against which it is directed. The subject of those numbers, from which passages have been cited, is the unlimited power of taxation which is vested in the general government. The objection to this unlimited power, which the argument seeks to remove, is stated with fullness and clearness. It is, " that an indefinite power of taxation in the latter (the government * of the Union) might, and probably

* *434* would, in time, deprive the former (the gov-

ernment of the states) of the means of providing for
their own necessities; and would subject them entirely to the mercy of the national legislature.   As
the laws of the Union are to become the supreme
law of the land; as it is to have power to pass all laws
that may be necessary for the carrying into execution
the authorities with which it is proposed to vest it;
the national government might at any time abolish the
taxes imposed for state objects, upon the pretense of
an interference with its own.   It might allege a necessity for doing this, in order to give efficacy to the
national revenues; and thus all the resources of taxation might, by degrees, become the subjects of federal
monopoly, to the entire exclusion and destruction of
the state governments."

The objections to the constitution which are noticed in these numbers, were to the undefined power
of the government to tax, not to the incidental privilege of exempting its own measures from state
taxation.   The consequences apprehended from this
undefined power were, that it would absorb all the
objects of taxation, " to the exclusion and destruction
of the state governments."   The arguments of *The
Federalist* are intended to prove the fallacy of these
apprehensions; not to prove that the government
was incapable of executing any of its powers, without exposing the means it employed to the embarrassments of state taxation.   Arguments urged
against these objections, and these apprehensions,
are to be understood as relating to the points
*435   they * mean to prove.   Had the authors of

those excellent essays been asked, whether they contended for that construction of the constitution, which would place within the reach of the states those measures which the government might adopt for the execution of its powers; no man, who has read their instructive pages, will hesitate to admit that their answer must have been in the negative.

It has also been insisted, that, as the power of taxation in the general and state governments is acknowledged to be concurrent, every argument which would sustain the right of the general government to tax banks chartered by the states, will equally sustain the right of the states to tax banks chartered by the general government.

But the two cases are not on the same reason. The people of all the states have created the general government, and have conferred upon it the general power of taxation. The people of all the states, and the states themselves, are represented in Congress, and, by their representatives, exercise this power. When they tax the chartered institutions of the states, they tax their constituents; and these taxes must be uniform. But, when a state taxes the operations of the government of the United States, it acts upon institutions created, not by their own constituents, but by people over whom they claim no control. It acts upon the measures of a government created by others as well as themselves, for the benefit of others in common with themselves. The difference is that *436 which always exists, and always must exist, between the action of the whole on a * part, and the action of a part on the whole—between the laws of a government declared to be supreme, and those of a government which, when in opposition to those laws, is not supreme.

But if the full application of this argument could be admitted, it might bring into question the right of Congress to tax the state banks, and could not prove the right of the states to tax the Bank of the United States.

The court has bestowed on this subject its most deliberate consideration. The result is a conviction that the states have no power, by taxation or otherwise, to retard, impede, burden, or in any manner control the operations of the constitutional laws enacted by Congress to carry into execution the powers vested in the general government. This is, we think, the unavoidable consequence of that supremacy which the constitution has declared.

We are unanimously of opinion that the law passed by the legislature of Maryland, imposing a tax on the Bank of the United States, is unconstitutional and void.

This opinion does not deprive the states of any resources which they originally possessed. It does not extend to a tax paid by the real property of the bank, in common with the other real property within the state, nor to a tax imposed on the interest which the citizens of Maryland may hold in this institution, in common with other property of the same description throughout the state. But this is a tax on the operations of the bank, and is, consequently, a tax on

the operation of an instrument employed by the
government * of the Union to carry its pow-
*437   ers into execution.   Such a tax must be
unconstitutional.

Trustees of Dartmouth College *v.* Woodward.

NOTE.

No case of Marshall's has been productive of so much discussion and comment as the Dartmouth College case. It has been thrashed over again and again, lauded and analyzed. Surely, in its results, it was one of the greatest of his judgments. The case arose from a controversy as to the administration of Dartmouth College that finally took on a political aspect, and in 1816 resulted in an act of the New Hampshire legislature that practically put in a new management of the College and placed it directly in the control of the dominant political faction in the state. The case was bitterly fought below and finally came to the Supreme Court on the question whether it was in the power of the state to so alter the corporate charter of the College.

No more picturesque case ever came before the Supreme Court ; on one side against the College were Holmes and Wirt, on the other Hopkinson and Webster.

"Holmes," says Shirley in the *Dartmouth College Causes* (St. Louis, 1879), p. 231, "was a scheming, busy, restless, rollicking politician . . . he was as much out of place before Judge Marshall's court and pitted against such a man as Webster as it was possible to be . . . he had neither taste, time, inclination, nor the mental qualities to grasp, prepare, and argue a cause like this." With him was Wirt, Attorney-General, a man overburdened with work, known as an ardent Jeffersonian and Jefferson's personal adviser, an orator and a declaimer, rather than a great lawyer.

Against these two men came Hopkinson and Webster, the first a trained and able lawyer, the second just reaching the zenith of his legal career. Webster's speech in his argument in this court, as we have it reported, making all allowances, occupied an hour longer than it would take to read it (Shirley, p. 237). The inference is unavoidable that in that hour he argued, and the Court listened, outside the record. There can be little question that, by the influence of counsel, by some subtle influence of politics or friendships, there seems to have crept into the consideration of the Dartmouth College case, a distinct bias in favor of the College. It is not easy to support such an assertion; but it is the inference from Marshall's opinion. It is characteristic of Marshall's opinions to be argumentative, combative, to state logically, cogently, but one rises from this opinion dissatisfied. There is bias in the statement of facts, a bias in the statement of premises; and surely, what seems now to us the main issue of the case, the assumption that the charter of the College was a "contract," as that term is used in the Constitution, is too hasty and too barely supported.

The Dartmouth College case is one of the greatest of Marshall's cases, great in its daring, great in its results. The bare legal proposition for which it stands, that a corporate franchise is a contract, and so inviolate, and beyond the control of the state, has woven itself into the tissue of our law as has, perhaps, no other paper-made doctrine of constitutional law.

True it has been greatly limited. First, there is a long series of cases that lay down the important limitation that, in spite of any grant in a corporate charter, a legislature may still legislate in the interests of the public safety, health, and morals, so far as to impair the obligation, nay ruin, a corporate charter, that no legislature, sovereign as it may be, has the power to grant away the rights of succeeding legislatures and succeeding peoples to regulate health, morals, and public safety. It is not easy to define so broad a limitation. In the case of *The Beer Co.* v. *Massachusetts* (97 U. S., 25), it appeared that a corporation had been chartered with the right to manufacture and sell beer. Succeeding state legislation impaired that right. But the Court then held that, in spite of their contract, the legislature might still so legislate, saying that a police power extending at least "to the protection of the lives, health, and property of the citizens, and to the preservation of good order and public morals," was a residuum lying beyond the constitutional protection. Mr. Justice Miller said : "The legislature cannot by any contract divest itself of the power to provide for these objects. They belong emphatically to that class of objects which demand the application of the maxim, *Salus populi suprema lex*, and they are to be attained and provided for by such appropriate means as the legislative discretion may devise. That discretion can no more be bargained away than the power itself." The same rule has been applied to charters granting the right to conduct lotteries (*Stone v. Mississippi*, 101 U. S., 814), to a charter granting the right to convert dead animal matter of slaughter houses by chemical processes into fertilizer (*Fertilizing Co.* v. *Hyde Park*, 97 U. S., 659), and to a charter granting the right to conduct slaughter houses (*Butchers' Union Co.* v. *Crescent City Co.*, 111 U. S., 746). The exact limits of this modification have never been assigned—the courts expressly refuse to assign limits; it is a doctrine capable of almost indefinite extension or of great contraction to suit the popular opinion—I use the word broadly,—but from the purely legal point of view it cuts deeply into the doctrine of the Dartmouth College case.

There is another limitation of the doctrine far earlier, perhaps more sweeping, more generally applicable. In the Charles River Bridge case Judge Story suggested that any legislature might, in granting any corporate charter or franchise, reserve to itself the power to alter, amend, or repeal it, and that suggestion has been followed, almost without exception, either by constitutional provision or by general law, in nearly every state in the Union, so that almost every corporate charter is now subject to that limitation. Again, the doctrine of construction laid down in the Charles River Bridge case that a franchise granting public rights is to be construed most strongly in favor of the state, has, as a practical matter, gone far toward curbing monopolistic powers of corporations which have secured valuable franchise grants.

Still another limitation of the Dartmouth College case is the development of the broad power of the states laid down in *Munn v. Illinois* (94 U. S., 113), and the other so-called Granger cases, to restrict and control the operations of corporations engaged in public or quasi-public callings. Perhaps these cases are consonant with the doctrine of the Dartmouth College case, but they are far removed from the temper of it.

It is such limitations as these that led that most acute writer on American constitutional law, Judge Hare, to observe: "The state was stripped under this interpretation [the Dartmouth College case and the cases following it] of prerogatives that are commonly regarded as inseparable from sovereignty, and might have stood, like Lear, destitute before her offspring, had not the police power been dexterously declared paramount, and used as a means of rescinding improvident grants" (I. Hare, *American Constitutional Law*, 607).

But these cases and modifications, much as they have pared down the Dartmouth College case, have been very far from destroying it. The rise of the limitations of the Dartmouth College case has been slow and gradual, to meet varying economic and political conditions of the country. The courts have clung tenaciously to the idea of the sacredness of corporate charters—even in times of public excitement and the modern feeling against the power of great aggregations of capital. In cases like *People v. O'Brien* (111 N. Y., 1), they have carefully conserved the corporate interests and in the main the opinion of the people at large has been with them. That is the great effect, the great point of the case,—that it fixed the popular as well as the legal mind in favor of the stability of corporate enterprise and securities.[1] Its

---

[1] Maine's statement of this aspect of the doctrine is most suggestive. He said: "I have seen the rule which denies to the several States the power to make any laws impairing the obligation of contracts criticised as if it were a mere politico-economical flourish; but in point of fact there is no more important provision in the whole Constitution. Its principle was much extended by a decision of the Supreme Court, which ought now to interest a large number of Englishmen, since it is the basis of the credit of many of the great American railway incorporations. But it is this prohibition which has in reality secured

doctrine became a legal watchword—a maxim. It fixed the point of view toward corporations. That stability that the British company found in the conservatism of its parliaments Marshall gave to the United States in its written Constitution. The influence of the case cannot, of course, be measured or conceived of with any exactness, but it seems a sound statement to say that the business world, and its methods of industry, have never been so far moulded and affected by any other American judicial decision. No decision save *McCullough* v. *Maryland* shows more clearly the administrative and political function of the American constitutional judge.

full play to the economical forces by which the achievement of cultivating the soil of the North American continent has been performed; it is the bulwark of American individualism against democratic impatience and socialistic fantasy." —Maine, *Popular Government* (Essay IV.), p. 247.

The Trustees of Dartmouth College

v.

Woodward.

[4 Wheat, 518.]

1819.

Mr. Webster and Mr. Hopkinson for the plaintiffs in error.
Mr. Holmes and Wirt, Attorney-General, contra.

The opinion of the court was delivered by *Marshall, Ch. J.:*

This is an action of trover, brought by the trustees of Dartmouth College against William H. Woodward, in the State Court of New Hampshire, for the book of records, corporate seal, and other corporate property, to which the plaintiffs allege themselves to be entitled.

A special verdict, after setting out the rights of the parties, finds for the defendant, if certain acts of the legislature of New Hampshire, passed on the 27th of June, and on the 18th of December, 1816, be valid, and binding on the trustees without their assent, and not repugnant to the constitution of the United States; otherwise, it finds for the plaintiffs.

351

* *625*   * The Superior Court of Judicature of New Hampshire rendered a judgment upon this verdict for the defendant, which judgment has been brought before this court by writ of error. The single question now to be considered is, do the acts to which the verdict refers violate the constitution of the United States?

This court can be insensible neither to the magnitude nor delicacy of this question. The validity of a legislative act is to be examined; and the opinion of the highest law tribunal of a state is to be revised: an opinion which carries with it intrinsic evidence of the diligence, of the ability, and the integrity, with which it was formed. On more than one occasion this court has expressed the cautious circumspection with which it approaches the consideration of such questions; and has declared that, in no doubtful case would it pronounce a legislative act to be contrary to the constitution. But the American people have said, in the constitution of the United States, that "no state shall pass any bill of attainder, *ex post facto* law, or law impairing the obligation of contracts." In the same instrument they have also said, "that the judicial power shall extend to all cases in law and equity arising under the constitution." On the judges of this court, then, is imposed the high and solemn duty of protecting, from even legislative violation, those contracts which the constitution of our country has placed beyond legislative control; and, however irksome the task may be, this is a duty from which we dare not shrink.

* *626*   * The title of the plaintiffs originates in a charter dated the 13th day of December, in the year 1769, incorporating twelve persons therein mentioned, by the name of " The Trustees of Dartmouth College," granting to them and their successors the usual corporate privileges and powers, and authorizing the trustees, who are to govern the college, to fill up all vacancies which may be created in their own body.

The defendant claims under three acts of the legislature of New Hampshire, the most material of which was passed on the 27th of June, 1816, and is entitled, " an act to amend the charter, and enlarge and improve the corporation of Dartmouth College." Among other alterations in the charter, this act increases the number of trustees to twenty-one, gives the appointment of the additional members to the executive of the state, and creates a board of overseers, with power to inspect and control the most important acts of the trustees. This board consists of twenty-five persons. The president of the senate, the speaker of the house of representatives, of New Hampshire, and the Governor and Lieutenant-Governor of Vermont, for the time being, are to be members *ex officio*. The board is to be completed by the Governor and council of New Hampshire, who are also empowered to fill all vacancies which may occur. The acts of the 18th and 26th of December are supplemental to that of the 27th of June, and are principally intended to carry that act into effect.

The majority of the trustees of the college have

refused to accept this amended charter, and have
* brought this suit for the corporate property,
*627   which is in possession of a person holding
by virtue of the acts which have been stated.

It can require no argument to prove that the circumstances of this case constitute a contract. An
application is made to the crown for a charter to incorporate a religious and literary institution. In the
application, it is stated that large contributions have
been made for the object, which will be conferred on
the corporation as soon as it shall be created. The
charter is granted, and on its faith the property is
conveyed. Surely in this transaction every ingredient
of a complete and legitimate contract is to be found.

The points for consideration are :

1. Is this contract protected by the constitution
of the United States ?

2. Is it impaired by the acts under which the defendant holds ?

1. On the first point it has been argued, that the
word "contract," in its broadest sense, would comprehend the political relations between the government and its citizens, would extend to offices held
within a state for state purposes, and to many of
those laws concerning civil institutions, which must
change with circumstances, and be modified by ordinary legislation; which deeply concern the public,
and which, to preserve good government, the public
judgment must control. That even marriage is a
contract, and its obligations are affected by the
laws respecting divorces. That the clause in the

constitution, if construed in its greatest latitude,

* 628 *would prohibit these laws. Taken in its broad unlimited sense, the clause would be an unprofitable and vexatious interference with the internal concerns of a state, would unnecessarily and unwisely embarrass its legislation, and render immutable those civil institutions which are established for purposes of internal government, and which, to subserve those purposes, ought to vary with varying circumstances. That as the framers of the constitution could never have intended to insert in that instrument a provision so unnecessary, so mischievous, and so repugnant to its general spirit, the term " contract " must be understood in a more limited sense. That it must be understood as intended to guard against a power of at least doubtful utility, the abuse of which had been extensively felt; and to restrain the legislature in future from violating the right to property. That anterior to the formation of the constitution, a course of legislation had prevailed in many, if not in all, of the states, which weakened the confidence of man in man, and embarrassed all transactions between individuals, by dispensing with a faithful performance of engagements. To correct this mischief, by restraining the power which produced it, the state legislatures were forbidden " to pass any law impairing the obligation of contracts," that is, of contracts respecting property, under which some individual could claim a right to something beneficial to himself ; and that since the clause in the constitution must in construction receive some limitation, it may be confined,

* *629*   and ought to be confined, to cases of this *description ; to cases within the mischief it
was intended to remedy.

The general correctness of these observations cannot be controverted.   That the framers of the constitution did not intend to restrain the states in the
regulation of their civil institutions, adopted for internal government, and that the instrument they have
given us is not to be so construed, may be admitted.
The provision of the constitution never has been understood to embrace other contracts than those which
respect property, or some object of value, and confer
rights which may be asserted in a court of justice.   It
never has been understood to restrict the general
right of the legislature to legislate on the subject of
divorces.   Those acts enable some tribunal, not to
impair a marriage contract, but to liberate one of the
parties because it has been broken by the other.
When any state legislature shall pass an act annulling
all marriage contracts, or allowing either party to annul it without the consent of the other, it will be time
enough to inquire whether such an act be constitutional.

The parties in this case differ less on general principles, less on the true construction of the constitution in the abstract, than on the application of those
principles to this case, and on the true construction of
the charter of 1769.   This is the point on which the
cause essentially depends.   If the act of incorporation be a grant of political power, if it create a civil
institution to be employed in the administration of
the government, or if the funds of the college be

*630   *public property, or if the state of New Hampshire, as a government, be alone interested in its transactions, the subject is one in which the legislature of the state may act according to its own judgment, unrestrained by any limitation of its power imposed by the constitution of the United States.

But if this be a private eleemosynary institution, endowed with a capacity to take property for objects unconnected with government, whose funds are bestowed by individuals on the faith of the charter; if the donors have stipulated for the future disposition and management of those funds in the manner prescribed by themselves, there may be more difficulty in the case, although neither the persons who have made these stipulations nor those for whose benefit they were made, should be parties to the cause. Those who are no longer interested in the property, may yet retain such an interest in the preservation of their own arrangements as to have a right to insist that those arrangements shall be held sacred. Or, if they have themselves disappeared, it becomes a subject of serious and anxious inquiry, whether those whom they have legally empowered to represent them forever may not assert all the rights which they possessed, while in being; whether, if they be without personal representatives who may feel injured by a violation of the compact, the trustees be not so completely their representatives, in the eye of the law, as to stand in their place, not only as respects the government of the college, but also as respects the maintenance of the college charter.

It becomes, then, the duty of the court most
*seriously to examine this charter, and to
ascertain its true character.

*631

From the instrument itself, it appears that about
the year 1754, the Rev. Eleazar Wheelock established
at his own expense, and on his own estate, a charity
school for the instruction of Indians in the Christian
religion. The success of this institution inspired him
with the design of soliciting contributions in England
for carrying on, and extending, his undertaking. In
this pious work he employed the Rev. Nathaniel
Whitaker, who, by virtue of a power of attorney from
Dr. Wheelock, appointed the Earl of Dartmouth and
others, trustees of the money which had been, and
should be, contributed; which appointment Dr.
Wheelock confirmed by a deed of trust authorizing
the trustees to fix on a site for the college. They
determined to establish the school on Connecticut
River, in the western part of New Hampshire; that
situation being supposed favorable for carrying on
the original design among the Indians, and also for
promoting learning among the English; and the
proprietors in the neighborhood having made large
offers of land, on condition that the college should
there be placed. Dr. Wheelock then applied to the
crown for an act of incorporation, and represented
the expediency of appointing those whom he had, by
his last will, named as trustees in America, to be
members of the proposed corporation. " In consideration of the premises," "for the education and instruction of the youth of the Indian tribes," &c., "and

also of English youth, and any others," the charter was granted, and the trustees of Dartmouth college

*632 were by that name created a body *corporate, with power, for the use of the said college, to acquire real and personal property, and to pay the president, tutors, and other officers of the college, such salaries as they shall allow.

The charter proceeds to appoint Eleazar Wheelock, "the founder of said college," president thereof, with power by his last will to appoint a successor, who is to continue in office until disapproved by the trustees. In case of vacancy, the trustees may appoint a president, and in case of the ceasing of a president, the senior professor or tutor, being one of the trustees, shall exercise the office, until an appointment shall be made. The trustees have power to appoint and displace professors, tutors, and other officers, and to supply any vacancies which may be created in their own body, by death, resignation, removal, or disability ; and also to make orders, ordinances, and laws, for the government of the college, the same not being repugnant to the laws of Great Britain, or of New Hampshire, and not excluding any person on account of his speculative sentiments in religion, or his being of a religious profession different from that of the trustees.

This charter was accepted, and the property, both real and personal, which had been contributed for the benefit of the college, was conveyed to, and vested in, the corporate body.

From this brief review of the most essential parts

of the charter, it is apparent that the funds of the college consisted entirely of private donations. It is, perhaps, not very important who were the donors. The probability is, that the Earl of Dartmouth, and the other trustees in England, were, in fact, the largest *contributors. Yet the legal conclusion, from the facts recited in the charter, would probably be, that Dr. Wheelock was the founder of the college.

*633

The origin of the institution was, undoubtedly, the Indian charity-school, established by Dr. Wheelock, at his own expense. It was at his instance, and to enlarge this school, that contributions were solicited in England. The person soliciting these contributions was his agent; and the trustees, who received the money, were appointed by, and acted under, his authority. It is not too much to say that the funds were obtained by him, in trust, to be applied by him to the purposes of his enlarged school. The charter of incorporation was granted at his instance. The persons named by him in his last will, as the trustees of his charity-school, compose a part of the corporation, and he is declared to be the founder of the college, and its president for life. Were the inquiry material, we should feel some hesitation in saying that Dr. Wheelock was not, in law, to be considered as the founder[1] of this institution, and as possessing all the rights appertaining to that character. But be this as it may, Dartmouth College is really endowed by private individuals, who have bestowed their funds

---

[1] 1 Bl. Com. 481.

for the propagation of the Christian religion among the Indians, and for the promotion of piety and learning generally. From these funds the salaries of the tutors are drawn; and these salaries lessen the expense of education to the students. It *is,

*634

then, an eleemosynary,[1] and, as far as respects its funds, a private corporation.

Do its objects stamp on it a different character? Are the trustees and professors public officers, invested with any portion of political power, partaking in any degree in the administration of civil government, and performing duties which flow from the sovereign authority?

That education is an object of national concern, and a proper subject of legislation, all admit. That there may be an institution founded by government, and placed entirely under its immediate control, the officers of which would be public officers, amenable exclusively to government, none will deny. But is Dartmouth College such an institution? Is education altogether in the hands of government? Does every teacher of youth become a public officer, and do donations for the purpose of education necessarily become public property, so far that the will of the legislature, not the will of the donor, becomes the law of the donation? These questions are of serious moment to society, and deserve to be well considered.

Doctor Wheelock, as the keeper of his charity-school, instructing the Indians in the art of reading, and in our holy religion; sustaining them at his own

---

[1] 1 Bl. Com. 471.

expense, and on the voluntary contributions of the charitable, could scarcely be considered as a public officer, exercising any portion of those duties which belong to government ; nor could the legislature have

*635   *supposed that his private funds, or those given by others, were subject to legislative management, because they were applied to the purposes of education. When, afterwards, his school was enlarged, and the liberal contributions made in England, and in America, enabled him to extend his cares to the education of the youth of his own country, no change was wrought in his own character, or in the nature of his duties. Had he employed assistant tutors with the funds contributed by others, or had the trustees in England established a school with Dr. Wheelock at its head, and paid salaries to him and his assistants, they would still have been private tutors ; and the fact that they were employed in the education of youth could not have converted them into public officers, concerned in the administration of public duties, or have given the legislature a right to interfere in the management of the fund. The trustees, in whose care that fund was placed by the contributors, would have been permitted to execute their trust uncontrolled by legislative authority.

Whence, then, can be derived the idea that Dartmouth College has become a public institution, and its trustees public officers, exercising powers conferred by the public for public objects ? Not from the source whence its funds were drawn ; for its foundation is purely private and eleemosynary. Not from the plication of those funds ; for money may be given for education, and the persons receiving it do not, by being employed in the education of youth, become members of the civil government.   Is it from * *636*   * the act of incorporation ?   Let this subject be considered.

A corporation is an artificial being, invisible, intangible, and existing only in contemplation of law. Being the mere creature of law, it possesses only those properties which the charter of its creation confers upon it, either expressly or as incidental to its very existence.   These are such as are supposed best calculated to effect the object for which it was created. Among the most important are immortality, and, if the expression may be allowed, individuality ; properties by which a perpetual succession of many persons are considered as the same, and may act as a single individual.   They enable a corporation to manage its own affairs, and to hold property without the perplexing intricacies, the hazardous and endless necessity, of perpetual conveyances for the purpose of transmitting it from hand to hand.   It is chiefly for the purpose of clothing bodies of men, in succession, with these qualities and capacities, that corporations were invented, and are in use.   By these means, a perpetual succession of individuals are capable of acting for the promotion of the particular object, like one immortal being.   But this being does not share in the civil government of the country, unless that be the purpose for which it was created.   Its immortality no more confers on it political power, or a political character, than immortality would confer such power or character on a natural person. It is no more a state instrument than a natural person exercising the same powers would be. If, then, a natural person, employed * *637* *by individuals in the education of youth, or for the government of a seminary in which youth is educated, would not become a public officer, or be considered as a member of the civil government, how is it that this artificial being, created by law, for the purpose of being employed by the same individuals for the same purposes, should become a part of the civil government of the country ? Is it because its existence, its capacities, its powers, are given by law ?   Because the government has given it the power to take and to hold property in a particular form, and for particular purposes, has the government a consequent right substantially to change that form, or to vary the purposes to which the property is to be applied ?   This principle has never been asserted or recognized, and is supported by no authority.   Can it derive aid from reason ?

The objects for which a corporation is created are universally such as the government wishes to promote. They are deemed beneficial to the country ; and this benefit constitutes the consideration, and, in most cases, the sole consideration of the grant.   In most eleemosynary institutions, the object would be difficult, perhaps unattainable, without the aid of a charter of incorporation.   Charitable, or public-spirited individuals, desirous of making permanent appropriations for charitable or other useful purposes, find it impossible to effect their design securely, and certainly, without an incorporating act.   They apply to the government, state their beneficent object, and offer to advance the money necessary for its accom-

*638
plishment, * provided the government will confer on the instrument which is to execute their designs the capacity to execute them.   The proposition is considered and approved.   The benefit to the public is considered as an ample compensation for the faculty it confers, and the corporation is created. If the advantages to the public constitute a full compensation for the faculty it gives, there can be no reason for exacting a further compensation, by claiming a right to exercise over this artificial being a power which changes its nature, and touches the fund, for the security and application of which it was created. There can be no reason for implying in a charter, given for a valuable consideration, a power which is not only not expressed, but is in direct contradiction to its express stipulations.

From the fact, then, that a charter of incorporation has been granted, nothing can be inferred which changes the character of the institution, or transfers to the government any new power over it.   The character of civil institutions does not grow out of their incorporation, but out of the manner in which they are formed, and the objects for which they are created.   The right to change them is not founded on their being incorporated, but on their being the instruments of government, created for its purposes. The same institutions, created for the same objects, though not incorporated, would be public institutions, and, of course, be controllable by the legislature. The incorporating act neither gives nor prevents this control. Neither, in reason, can the incorporating act

*639   * change the character of a private eleemosynary institution.

We are next led to the inquiry, for whose benefit the property given to Dartmouth College was secured. The counsel for the defendant have insisted that the beneficial interest is in the people of New Hampshire. The charter, after reciting the preliminary measures which had been taken, and the application for an act of incorporation, proceeds thus: "Know ye, therefore, that we, considering the premises, and being willing to encourage the laudable and charitable design of spreading Christian knowledge among the savages of our American wilderness, and, also, that the best means of education be established, in our province of New Hampshire, for the benefit of said province, do, of our special grace," &c. Do these expressions bestow on New Hampshire any exclusive right to the property of the college, any exclusive interest in the labors of the professors? Or do they merely indicate a willingness that New Hampshire should enjoy those advantages which result to all from the establishment of a seminary of learning in the neighborhood? On this point we think it impossible to entertain a serious doubt. The words themselves, unexplained by the context, indicate that the "benefit intended for the province" is that which is derived from "establishing the best means of education therein ; " that is, from establishing in the province Dartmouth College, as constituted by the charter.   But, if these words, considered alone, could admit of doubt, that * doubt is completely removed by an inspection of the entire instrument.

640

The particular interests of New Hampshire never entered into the minds of the donors, never constituted a motive for their donation.   The propagation of the Christian religion among the savages, and the dissemination of useful knowledge among the youth of the country, were the avowed and the sole objects of their contributions.   In these, New Hampshire would participate ; but nothing particular or exclusive was intended for her.   Even the site of the college was selected, not for the sake of New Hampshire, but because it was " most subservient to the great ends in view," and because liberal donations of land were offered by the proprietors, on condition that the institution should be there established.   The real advantages from the location of the college, are, perhaps, not less considerable to those on the west than to those on the east side of Connecticut River. The clause which constitutes the incorporation, and expresses the objects for which it was made, declares those objects to be the instruction of the Indians, " and also of English youth, and any others."   So that the objects of the contributors, and the incorporating act, were the same ; the promotion of Christianity, and of education generally, not the interests of New Hampshire particularly.

From this review of the charter, it appears that
Dartmouth College is an eleemosynary institution,
incorporated for the purpose of perpetuating the application of the bounty of the donors, to the specified
objects of that bounty; that its trustees or governors
*641   * were originally named by the founder, and
            invested with the power of perpetuating
themselves; that they are not public officers, nor is
it a civil institution, participating in the administration of government; but a charity school, or a seminary of education, incorporated for the preservation
of its property, and the perpetual application of that
property to the objects of its creation.

Yet a question remains to be considered, of more
real difficulty, on which more doubt has been entertained than on all that have been discussed. The
founders of the college, at least those whose contributions were in money, have parted with the property
bestowed upon it, and their representatives have no
interest in that property. The donors of land are
equally without interest, so long as the corporation
shall exist. Could they be found, they are unaffected
by any alteration in its constitution, and probably regardless of its form, or even of its existence. The
students are fluctuating, and no individual among our
youth has a vested interest in the institution, which
can be asserted in a court of justice. Neither the
founders of the college nor the youth for whose benefit it was founded complain of the alteration made
in its charter, or think themselves injured by it. The
trustees alone complain, and the trustees have no

beneficial interest to be protected. Can this be such
a contract as the constitution intended to withdraw
from the power of state legislation? Contracts, the
parties to which have a vested beneficial interest, and
those only, it has been said, are the objects about
*642   * which the constitution is solicitous, and to
which its protection is extended.

The court has bestowed on this argument the most
deliberate consideration, and the result will be stated.
Dr. Wheelock, acting for himself, and for those who,
at his solicitation, had made contributions to his
school, applied for this charter, as the instrument
which should enable him, and them, to perpetuate
their beneficent intention. It was granted. An artificial, immortal being, was created by the crown,
capable of receiving and distributing forever, according to the will of the donors, the donations which
should be made to it. On this being, the contributions which had been collected were immediately bestowed. These gifts were made, not, indeed, to make
a profit for the donors, or their posterity, but for
something in their opinion of inestimable value; for
something which they deemed a full equivalent for the
money with which it was purchased. The consideration for which they stipulated, is the perpetual application of the fund to its object, in the mode prescribed
by themselves. Their descendants may take no interest in the preservation of this consideration. But
in this respect their descendants are not their representatives. They are represented by the corporation.
The corporation is the assignee of their rights, stands

in their place, and distributes their bounty, as they would themselves have distributed it, had they been immortal. So with respect to the students who are to derive learning from this source. The corporation is a trustee for them also. Their potential rights, which, taken distributively, * are imperceptible, amount collectively to a most important interest. These are, in the aggregate, to be exercised, asserted and protected, by the corporation. They were as completely out of the donors, at the instant of their being vested in the corporation, and as incapable of being asserted by the students, as at present.

* *643*

According to the theory of the British constitution, their parliament is omnipotent. To annul corporate rights might give a shock to public opinion, which that government has chosen to avoid; but its power is not questioned. Had parliament, immediately after the emanation of this charter, and the execution of those conveyances which followed it, annulled the instrument, so that the living donors would have witnessed the disappointment of their hopes, the perfidy of the transaction would have been universally acknowledged. Yet then, as now, the donors would have had no interest in the property; then, as now, those who might be students would have had no rights to be violated; then, as now, it might be said, that the trustees, in whom the rights of all were combined, possessed no private, individual, beneficial interest in the property confided to their protection. Yet the contract would at that time have been deemed sacred by all. What has since occurred to strip it of its inviolability? Circumstances have not changed it. In reason, in justice, and in law, it is now what it was in 1769.

This is plainly a contract to which the donors, the trustees, and the crown (to whose rights and obligations New Hampshire succeeds), were the original **644* *parties. It is a contract made on a valuable consideration. It is a contract for the security and disposition of property. It is a contract, on the faith of which real and personal estate has been conveyed to the corporation. It is then a contract within the letter of the constitution, and within its spirit also, unless the fact that the property is invested by the donors in trustees for the promotion of religion and education, for the benefit of persons who are perpetually changing, though the objects remain the same, shall create a particular exception, taking this case out of the prohibition contained in the constitution.

It is more than possible that the preservation of rights of this description was not particularly in the view of the framers of the constitution when the clause under consideration was introduced into that instrument. It is probable that interferences of more frequent recurrence, to which the temptation was stronger, and of which the mischief was more extensive, constituted the great motive for imposing this restriction on the state legislatures. But although a particular and a rare case may not, in itself, be of sufficient magnitude to induce a rule, yet it must be governed by the rule, when established, unless some plain and strong reason for excluding it can be given. It is not enough to say that this particular case was not in the mind of the convention when the article was framed, nor of the American people when it was adopted. It is necessary to go farther, and to say that, had this particular case been suggested, the language would have been so varied, as to exclude it, or it would have been made a special exception. The *645   *case being within the words of the rule, must be within its operation likewise, unless there be something in the literal construction so obviously absurd, or mischievous, or repugnant to the general spirit of the instrument, as to justify those who expound the constitution in making it an exception.

On what safe and intelligible ground can this exception stand. There is no exception in the constitution, no sentiment delivered by its contemporaneous expounders, which would justify us in making it. In the absence of all authority of this kind, is there, in the nature and reason of the case itself, that which would sustain a construction of the constitution, not warranted by its words? Are contracts of this description of a character to excite so little interest that we must exclude them from the provisions of the constitution, as being unworthy of the attention of those who framed the instrument? Or does public policy so imperiously demand their remaining exposed to legislative alteration, as to compel us, or rather permit us to say that these words, which were introduced to give stability to contracts, and which in their plain import comprehend this contract, must yet be so construed as to exclude it?

Almost all eleemosynary corporations, those which are created for the promotion of religion, of charity, or of education, are of the same character. The law of this case is the law of all. In every literary or charitable institution, unless the objects of the bounty be themselves incorporated, the whole legal interest is in trustees, and can be asserted only by them. The donors, or claimants of the bounty, if *they can appear in court at all, can appear only to complain of the trustees. In all other situations, they are identified with, and personated by, the trustees; and their rights are to be defended and maintained by them. Religion, Charity, and Education, are, in the law of England, legatees or donees, capable of receiving bequests or donations in this form. They appear in court, and claim or defend by the corporation. Are they of so little estimation in the United States that contracts for their benefit must be excluded from the protection of words which, in their natural import, include them? Or do such contracts so necessarily require new-modeling by the authority of the legislature that the ordinary rules of construction must be disregarded in order to leave them exposed to legislative alteration?

*646

All feel that these objects are not deemed unimportant in the United States. The interest which this case has excited proves that they are not. The framers of the constitution did not deem them unworthy of its care and protection. They have, though

in a different mode, manifested their respect for
science, by reserving to the government of the Union
the power " to promote the progress of science and
useful arts, by securing for limited times to authors
and inventors the exclusive right to their respective
writings and discoveries." They have so far withdrawn science, and the useful arts, from the action of
the state governments. Why, then, should they be
supposed so regardless of contracts made for the ad-
vancement of literature as to intend to exclude them
647 from provisions made for the security *of
ordinary contracts between man and man?
No reason for making this supposition is perceived.

If the insignificance of the object does not require
that we should exclude contracts respecting it from
the protection of the constitution, neither, as we conceive, is the policy of leaving them subject to legislative alteration so apparent as to require a forced
construction of that instrument in order to effect it.
These eleemosynary institutions do not fill the place,
which would otherwise be occupied by government,
but that which would otherwise remain vacant. They
are complete acquisitions to literature. They are donations to education; donations which any government must be disposed rather to encourage than to
discountenance. It requires no very critical examination of the human mind to enable us to determine
that one great inducement to these gifts is the conviction felt by the giver, that the disposition he
makes of them is immutable. It is probable that no
man ever was, and that no man ever will be, the

founder of a college, believing at the time that an act of incorporation constitutes no security for the institution; believing that it is immediately to be deemed a public institution, whose funds are to be governed and applied, not by the will of the donor, but by the will of the legislature. All such gifts are made in the pleasing, perhaps delusive hope, that the charity will flow forever in the channel which the givers have marked out for it. If every man finds in his own bosom strong evidence of the universality of this sentiment, there can be but little reason to imagine that the framers of our constitution were

*648   *strangers to it, and that, feeling the necessity and policy of giving permanence and security to contracts, of withdrawing them from the influence of legislative bodies, whose fluctuating policy, and repeated interferences, produced the most perplexing and injurious embarrassments, they still deemed it necessary to leave these contracts subject to those interferences. The motives for such an exception must be very powerful, to justify the construction which makes it.

The motives suggested at the bar grow out of the original appointment of the trustees, which is supposed to have been in a spirit hostile to the genius of our government, and the presumption that, if allowed to continue themselves, they now are, and must remain forever, what they originally were. Hence is inferred the necessity of applying to this corporation, and to other similar corporations, the correcting and improving hand of the legislature.

It has been urged repeatedly, and certainly with a degree of earnestness which attracted attention, that the trustees deriving their power from a regal source, must necessarily partake of the spirit of their origin; and that their first principles, unimproved by that re-splendent light which has been shed around them, must continue to govern the college, and to guide the students.   Before we inquire into the influence which this argument ought to have on the constitutional question, it may not be amiss to examine the fact on which it rests.   The first trustees were undoubtedly named in the charter by the crown; but at whose suggestion were they named?   By whom were they

*649   selected?   *The charter informs us.   Dr. Wheelock had represented "that, for many weighty reasons, it would be expedient that the gen-tlemen whom he had already nominated in his last will, to be trustees in America, should be of the cor-poration now proposed."   When afterwards, the trus-tees are named in the charter, can it be doubted that the persons mentioned by Dr. Wheelock in his will were appointed?   Some were probably added by the crown, with the approbation of Dr. Wheelock. Among these is the doctor himself.   If any others were appointed at the instance of the crown, they are the governor, three members of the council, and the speaker of the house of representatives of the colony of New Hampshire.   The stations filled by these persons ought to rescue them from any other imputa-tion than too great a dependence on the crown.   If, in the revolution that followed, they acted under the

influence of this sentiment, they must have ceased to
be trustees; if they took part with their countrymen,
the imputation which suspicion might excite would no
longer attach to them. The original trustees, then,
or most of them, were named by Dr. Wheelock, and
those who were added to his nomination, most probably with his approbation, were among the most eminent and respectable individuals in New Hampshire.

The only evidence which we possess of the character of Dr. Wheelock is furnished by this charter.
The judicious means employed for the accomplishment of his object, and the success which attended
his endeavors, would lead to the opinion that he
united a sound understanding to that humanity and
*650   benevolence *which suggested his under-
taking. It surely cannot be assumed that
his trustees were selected without judgment. With
as little probability can it be assumed, that, while the
light of science, and of liberal principles, pervades the
whole community these originally benighted trustees
remain in utter darkness, incapable of participating
in the general improvement; that, while the human
race is rapidly advancing, they are stationary. Reasoning *a priori*, we should believe that learned and
intelligent men, selected by its patrons for the government of a literary institution, would select learned
and intelligent men for their successors; men as well
fitted for the government of a college as those who
might be chosen by other means. Should this reasoning ever prove erroneous in a particular case, public
opinion, as has been stated at the bar, would correct

the institution. The mere possibility of the contrary
would not justify a construction of the constitution
which should exclude these contracts from the protection of a provision whose terms comprehend them.

The opinion of the court, after mature deliberation,
is, that this is a contract, the obligation of which cannot be impaired without violating the constitution of
the United States. This opinion appears to us to be
equally supported by reason, and by the former decisions of this court.

2. We next proceed to the inquiry whether its obligation has been impaired by those acts of the legislature of New Hampshire to which the special verdict
refers.

*651   *From the review of this charter, which
            has been taken, it appears that the whole
power of governing the college, of appointing and removing tutors, of fixing their salaries, of directing the
course of study to be pursued by the students, and of
filling up vacancies created in their own body, was
vested in the trustees. On the part of the crown it
was expressly stipulated that this corporation, thus
constituted, should continue forever ; and that the
number of trustees should forever consist of twelve,
and no more. By this contract the crown was bound
and could have made no violent alteration in its essential terms, without impairing its obligation.

By the revolution, the duties, as well as the powers,
of government, devolved on the people of New
Hampshire. It is admitted, that among the latter was
comprehended the transcendent power of parliament,

as well as that of the executive department. It is too clear to require the support of argument, that all contracts, and rights, respecting property, remained unchanged by the revolution. The obligations, then, which were created by the charter to Dartmouth College, were the same in the new that they had been in the old government. The power of the government was also the same. A repeal of this charter at any time prior to the adoption of the present constitution of the United States, would have been an extraordinary and unprecedented act of power, but one which could have been contested only by the restrictions upon the legislature, to be found in the constitution of the state. But the constitution of the United States has imposed this additional limitation *that the legislature of a state shall pass no act "impairing the obligation of contracts."

*652

It has been already stated that the act "to amend the charter, and enlarge and improve the corporation of Dartmouth College," increases the number of trustees to twenty-one, gives the appointment of the additional members to the executive of the state, and creates a board of overseers, to consist of twenty-five persons, of whom twenty-one are also appointed by the executive of New Hampshire, who have power to inspect and control the most important acts of the trustees.

On the effect of this law, two opinions cannot be entertained. Between acting directly, and acting through the agency of trustees and overseers, no essential difference is perceived. The whole power of governing the college is transferred from trustees appointed according to the will of the founder, expressed in the charter, to the executive of New Hampshire. The management and application of the funds of this eleemosynary institution, which are placed by the donors in the hands of trustees named in the charter, and empowered to perpetuate themselves, are placed by this act under the control of the government of the state. The will of the state is substituted for the will of the donors, in every essential operation of the college. This is not an immaterial change. The founders of the college contracted, not merely for the perpetual application of the funds which they gave, to the objects for which those funds were given; they contracted also to secure that application by the con-

*653 stitution of the corporation. * They contracted for a system which should, as far as human foresight can provide, retain forever the government of the literary institution they had formed, in the hands of persons approved by themselves. This system is totally changed. The charter of 1769 exists no longer. It is re-organized; and re-organized in such a manner as to convert a literary institution, moulded according to the will of its founders, and placed under the control of private literary men, into a machine entirely subservient to the will of government. This may be for the advantage of this college in particular, and may be for the advantage of literature in general, but it is not according to the will of the donors, and is subversive of that contract, on the faith of which their property was given.

In the view which has been taken of this interesting case, the court has confined itself to the right
possessed by the trustees, as the assignees and representatives of the donors and founders, for the benefit
of religion and literature. Yet it is not clear that the
trustees ought to be considered as destitute of such
beneficial interest in themselves as the law may respect. In addition to their being the legal owners
of the property, and to their having a freehold right
in the powers confided to them, the charter itself
countenances the idea that trustees may also be
tutors with salaries. The first president was one of
the original trustees ; and the charter provides, that
in case of vacancy in that office, " the senior professor
or tutor, being one of the trustees, shall exercise the
office of president, until the trustees shall make choice
* *654*   * of, and appoint a president." According
        to the tenor of the charter, then, the trus-
tees might, without impropriety, appoint a president
and other professors from their own body. This is a
power not entirely unconnected with an interest.
Even if the proposition of the counsel for the defendant were sustained ; if it were admitted that those
contracts only are protected by the constitution, a
beneficial interest in which is vested in the party,
who appears in court to assert that interest ; yet it is
by no means clear that the trustees of Dartmouth
College have no beneficial interests in themselves.

But the Court has deemed it unnecessary to inves-
tigate this particular point, being of opinion, on general principles, that in these private eleemosynary

institutions, the body corporate, as possessing the whole legal and equitable interest, and completely representing the donors, for the purpose of executing the trust, has rights which are protected by the constitution.

It results from this opinion, that the acts of the legislature of New Hampshire, which are stated in the special verdict found in this cause, are repugnant to the constitution of the United States; and that the judgment on this special verdict ought to have been for the plaintiffs. The judgment of the State Court must therefore be reversed.

Loughborough *v.* Blake.

NOTE.

THE main, and substantially the only, interest of the case is in the dictum thrown out by Marshall in the course of his opinion that in the Constitution the words "United States" designate the whole not any particular portion of the American empire. The exact point before him did not call for any such statement, and in the recent cases arising before the Supreme Court as to the application of the constitutional restrictions to the government of the territorial possessions gained by the Spanish war, that old dictum of *Loughborough* v. *Blake* required a great deal of explaining away on the part of the Court, and in the opinion of the Court in *Downes* v. *Bidwell*, 182 U. S., 244, at p. 262, Mr. Justice Brown said of these observations of Marshall, "So far as they apply to the territories they are not called for by the exigencies of the case." All through these Insular Cases *Loughborough* v. *Blake* was constantly and confidently cited but in truth the case contains no argument or reasoning on the topics of the Insular Cases, and written as it was with no conception of the circumstances and difficulties that later arose, has very little to do with them.

Loughborough

v.

Blake.

[5 Wheaton, 317.]

1820.

The case was argued by Mr. Jones for the plaintiff, Mr. Wirt, the Attorney-General, for the defendant.

Mr. Chief Justice MARSHALL delivered the opinion of the court: This case presents to the consideration of the court a single question. It is this: *318 * Has Congress a right to impose a direct tax on the District of Columbia?

The counsel who maintains the negative has contended, that Congress must be considered in two distinct characters. In one character as legislating for the states; in the other, as a local legislature for the district. In the latter character, it is admitted, the power of levying direct taxes may be exercised; but, it is contended, for district purposes only, in like manner as the legislature of a state may tax the people of a state for state purposes.

Without inquiring at present into the soundness of

384

this distinction, its possible influence on the application in this district of the first article of the constitution, and of several of the amendments, may not be
altogether unworthy of consideration.   It will readily
suggest itself to the gentlemen who press this argument, that those articles which, in general terms, restrain the power of Congress, may be applied to the
laws enacted by that body for the district, if it be
considered as governing the district in its character
as the national legislature, with less difficulty than if
it be considered a mere local legislature.

But we deem it unnecessary to pursue this investigation, because we think the right of Congress to tax
the district does not depend solely on the grant of
exclusive legislation.

The 8th section of the 1st article gives to Congress
the "power to lay and collect taxes, duties, imposts
and excises," for the purposes thereinafter mentioned.
This grant is general, without limitation as to place.
It consequently extends to all * places over
*319   which the government extends.   If this
could be doubted, the doubt is removed by the subsequent words which modify the grant.   These words
are, "but all duties, imposts, and excises, shall be
uniform throughout the United States."   It will not
be contended that the modification of the power extends to places to which the power itself does not
extend.   The power, then, to lay and collect duties,
imposts, and excises, may be exercised, and must be
exercised throughout the United States.   Does this
term designate the whole, or any particular portion

of the American empire? Certainly this question can admit of but one answer. It is the name given to our great republic, which is composed of states and territories. The District of Columbia, or the territory west of the Missouri, is not less within the United States than Maryland or Pennsylvania; and it is not less necessary, on the principles of our constitution, that uniformity in the imposition of imposts, duties, and excises, should be observed in the one than in the other. Since, then, the power to lay and collect taxes, which includes direct taxes, is obviously co-extensive with the power to lay and collect duties, imposts, and excises, and since the latter extends throughout the United States, it follows that the power to impose direct taxes also extends throughout the United States.

The extent of the grant being ascertained, how far is it abridged by any part of the constitution?

The 20th section of the first article declares, that "representatives and direct taxes shall be apportioned *320 among the several states which may be included *within this Union, according to their respective numbers."

The object of this regulation is, we think, to furnish a standard by which taxes are to be apportioned, not to exempt from their operation any part of our country. Had the intention been to exempt from taxation those who were not represented in Congress, that intention would have been expressed in direct terms. The power having been expressly granted, the exception would have been expressly made. But a limitation can scarcely be said to be insinuated. The words used do not mean that direct taxes shall be imposed on states only which are represented, or shall be apportioned to representatives; but that direct taxation, in its application to states, shall be apportioned to numbers. Representation is not made the foundation of taxation. If, under the enumeration of a representative for every 30,000 souls, one state had been found to contain 59,000, and another 60,000, the first would have been entitled to only one representative, and the last to two. Their taxes, however, would not have been as one to two, but as fifty-nine to sixty. This clause was obviously not intended to create any exemption from taxation, or to make taxation dependent on representation, but to furnish a standard for the apportionment of each on the states.

The 4th paragraph of the 9th section of the same article will next be considered. It is in these words: "No capitation, or other direct tax, shall be laid, unless in proportion to the census, or enumeration hereinbefore directed to be taken."

*321   * The census referred to is in that clause of the constitution which has just been considered, which makes numbers the standard by which both representatives and direct taxes shall be apportioned among the states. The actual enumeration is to be made "within three years after the first meeting of the Congress of the United States, and within every subsequent term of ten years, in such manner as they shall by law direct."

As the direct and declared object of this census is, to furnish a standard by which "representatives, and direct taxes, may be apportioned among the several states which may be included within this Union," it will be admitted that the omission to extend it to the district or the territories would not render it defective. The census referred to is admitted to be a census exhibiting the numbers of the respective states. It cannot, however, be admitted, that the argument which limits the application of the power of direct taxation to the population contained in this census is a just one. The language of the clause does not imply this restriction. It is not that "no capitation or other direct tax shall be laid, unless on those comprehended within the census hereinbefore directed to be taken," but "unless in proportion to" that census. Now, this proportion may be applied to the district or territories. If an enumeration be taken of the population in the district and territories, on the same principles on which the enumeration of the respective States is made, then the information is acquired by which a direct tax may be imposed on the

*322   district and territories, "in proportion to the *census or enumeration" which the constitution directs to be taken.

The standard, then, by which direct taxes must be laid, is applicable to this district, and will enable Congress to apportion on it its just and equal share of the burthen, with the same accuracy as on the respective states. If the tax be laid in this proportion, it is within the very words of the restriction. It is a tax in proportion to the census or enumeration referred to.

But the argument is presented in another form, in which its refutation is more difficult. It is urged against this construction, that it would produce the necessity of extending direct taxation to the district and territories, which would not only be inconvenient, but contrary to the understanding and practice of the whole government. If the power of imposing direct taxes be co-extensive with the United States, then it is contended, that the restrictive clause, if applicable to the district and territories, requires that the tax should be extended to them, since to omit them would be to violate the rule of proportion.

We think a satisfactory answer to this argument may be drawn from a fair comparative view of the different clauses of the constitution which have been recited.

That the general grant of power to lay and collect taxes is made in terms which comprehend the district and territories as well as the states, is, we think, incontrovertible. The subsequent clauses are intended to regulate the exercise of this power, not to withdraw from it any portion of the community. *The words in which those clauses are *323 expressed import this intention. In thus regulating its exercise, a rule is given in the 2d section of the first article for its application to the respective states. That rule declares how direct taxes upon the states shall be imposed. They shall be apportioned upon the several states according to their numbers.   If, then, a direct tax be laid at all, it must be laid on every state, conformably to the rule provided in the constitution.   Congress has clearly no power to exempt any state from its due share of the burden.   But this regulation is expressly confined to the states, and creates no necessity for extending the tax to the district or territories.   The words of the 9th section do not in terms require that the system of direct taxation, when resorted to, shall be extended to the territories, as the words of the 2d section require that it shall be extended to all the states.   They, therefore, may, without violence, be understood to give a rule when the territories shall be taxed, without imposing the necessity of taxing them.   It could scarcely escape the members of the convention that the expense of executing the law in a territory might exceed the amount of the tax.   But be this as it may, the doubt created by the words of the 9th section relates to the obligation to apportion a direct tax on the territories as well as the states, rather than to the power to do so.

If, then, the language of the constitution be construed to comprehend the territories and District of Columbia, as well as the states, that language confers *324 on Congress the power of taxing the district *and territories as well as the states.   If the general language of the constitution should be confined to the states, still the 16th paragraph of the 8th section gives to Congress the power of exercising "exclusive legislation in all cases whatsoever within this district."

On the extent of these terms, according to the common understanding of mankind, there can be no difference of opinion; but it is contended that they must be limited by that great principle which was asserted in our revolution—that representation is inseparable from taxation.

The difference between requiring a continent, with an immense population, to submit to be taxed by a government having no common interest with it, separated from it by a vast ocean, restrained by no principle of apportionment, and associated with it by no common feelings; and permitting the representatives of the American people, under the restrictions of our constitution, to tax a part of the society, which is either in a state of infancy advancing to manhood, looking forward to complete equality so soon as that state of manhood shall be attained, as is the case with the territories; or which has voluntarily relinquished the right of representation, and has adopted the whole body of Congress for its legitimate government, as is the case with the district, is too obvious not to present itself to the minds of all. Although in theory it might be more congenial to the spirit of our institutions to admit a representative from the district, it may be doubted whether, in fact, its interests would be rendered thereby * the *325 more secure; and certainly the constitution does not consider their want of a representative in Congress as exempting it from equal taxation.

If it were true that, according to the spirit of our constitution, the power of taxation must be limited by the right of representation, whence is derived the right to lay and collect duties, imposts and excises, within this district? If the principles of liberty, and of our constitution, forbid the raising of revenue from those who are not represented, do not these principles forbid the raising it by duties, imposts, and excises, as well as by a direct tax? If the principles of our revolution give a rule applicable to this case, we cannot have forgotten that neither the stamp act nor the duty on tea were direct taxes.

Yet it is admitted that the constitution not only allows, but enjoins the government to extend the ordinary revenue system to this district.

If it be said that the principle of uniformity, established in the constitution, secures the district from oppression in the imposition of indirect taxes, it is not less true that the principle of apportionment, also established in the constitution, secures the district from any oppressive exercise of the power to lay and collect direct taxes.

After giving this subject its serious attention, the court is unanimously of opinion that Congress possesses, under the constitution, the power to lay and collect direct taxes within the District of Columbia, in proportion to the census directed to be taken by the constitution, and that there is no error in the judgment of the Circuit Court.

Judgment affirmed.

Owings *v.* Speed *et al.*

NOTE.

THE case and the principle that it lays down seem too clear for argument or comment.

Owings

v.

Speed *et al.*

[5 Wheaton, 420.]

1820.

The cause was argued by Mr. B. Hardin for the defendants, no counsel appearing for the plaintiff.

Mr. Chief Justice MARSHALL delivered the opinion of the court : This was an ejectment brought by the plaintiff in the Circuit Court of the United States for the District of Kentucky, to recover a lot of ground lying in Bardstown. *This town *421 was laid off in 1780, on a tract of land consisting of 1,000 acres, for which, in 1785, a patent was issued by the commonwealth of Virginia to Bard and Owings. In 1788 the legislature of Virginia passed an act vesting 100 acres—part of this tract—

in trustees, to be laid off in lots, some of them to be given to settlers, and others to be sold for the benefit of the proprietors. The cause depends, mainly, on the validity of this act. It is contended to be a violation of that part of the constitution of the United States which forbids a state to pass any law impairing the obligation of contracts.

Much reason is furnished by the record for presuming the consent of the proprietors to this law; but the Circuit Court has decided the question independently of this consent, and that decision is now to be reviewed.

Before we determine on the construction of the constitution in relation to a question of this description, it is necessary to inquire whether the provisions of that instrument apply to any acts of the state legislatures which were of the date with that which it is now proposed to consider.

This act was passed in the session of 1788. Did the constitution of the United States then operate upon it?

In September, 1787, after completing the great work in which they had been engaged, the convention resolved that the constitution should be laid before the Congress of the United States, to be submitted by that body to conventions of the several states, to be convened by their respective legislatures, *422 * and expressed the opinion, that as soon as it should be ratified by the conventions of nine states, Congress should fix a day on which electors should be appointed by the states, a day on which the electors should assemble to vote for President and Vice-

President, "and the time and place for commencing proceedings under this constitution."

The conventions of nine states having adopted the constitution, Congress, in September or October, 1788, passed a resolution in conformity with the opinions expressed by the convention, and appointed the first Wednesday in March of the ensuing year as the day, and the then seat of Congress as the place, "for commencing proceedings under the constitution."

Both governments could not be understood to exist at the same time. The new government did not commence until the old government expired. It is apparent that the government did not commence on the constitution being ratified by the ninth state; for these ratifications were to be reported to Congress, whose continuing existence was recognized by the convention, and who were requested to continue to exercise their powers for the purpose of bringing the new government into operation. In fact, Congress did continue to act as a government until it dissolved on the first of November by the successive disappearance of its members. It existed potentially until the 2d of March, the day preceding that on which the members of the new Congress were directed to assemble.

The resolution of the convention might originally *423 nally * have suggested a doubt whether the government could be in operation for every purpose before the choice of a President; but this doubt has been long solved, and were it otherwise, its discussion would be useless, since it is apparent

that its operation did not commence before the first
Wednesday in March, 1789, before which time Virginia had passed the act which is alleged to violate
the constitution.

In the trial of the cause, the defendant produced a
witness to prove that the lot for which the suit was
instituted, was a part of the 100 acres vested in
trustees by the act of assembly. To this testimony
the plaintiff objected, because the witness stated
that he had sold a lot in Bardstown, with warranty,
and was in possession of another. He added, that no
suit had been brought for the said lot, and that he
was not interested in this suit. The court admitted
the witness, and to this opinion also a bill of exceptions was taken.

It is so apparent that the witness had no interest
in the suit in which he was examined, and it is so
well settled that only an interest in that suit could
affect his competency, as to make it unnecessary to
say more than that the court committed no error in
permitting his testimony to go to the jury.

There was also an exception taken to the opinion
of the court in allowing the book of the board of
trustees, in which their proceedings were recorded,
and other records belonging to the corporation, to be
given in evidence.

The book was proved by the present clerk, who
also proved the handwriting of the first clerk, and
of * the President, who were dead. The
*424   trustees were established by the legislature
for public purposes. The books of such a body are

the best evidence of their acts, and ought to be admitted whenever those acts are to be proved.   There was no error in the opinion admitting them.

There is the less necessity in this case for entering more fully into this question, because the record contains other evidence of the facts, which the testimony, to which exceptions were taken, was adduced to prove.

Judgment affirmed with costs.

Farmers' and Mechanics'
Bank of Pennsylvania
v.
Smith.

NOTE.

THIS case arose on demurrer to a plea. An action of assumpsit was brought against the defendant as indorser on a promissory note. The defendant pleaded his discharge under a Pennsylvania bankruptcy statute passed subsequent to the endorsement and also averred that the cause of action arose on a contract made in Pennsylvania, and that the plaintiffs and defendant were, at all times, citizens of that State. To that plea the plaintiff demurred and judgment was given for the defendant by the Supreme Court of Pennsylvania, affirming the validity of the Pennsylvania law. From that judgment this appeal was taken to the Supreme Court of the United States.

Marshall's decision is right since the law was subsequent to the contract, but the Court chose to rest it on the doctrine of *Sturges* v. *Crowninshield*, which, as is explained in the note to that case, *supra*, is not now law.

Farmers' and Mechanics' Bank

of Pennsylvania

v.

Smith.

[6 Wheaton, 131.]

1821.

This cause was argued by Mr. Hopkinson for the plaintiffs, and by Mr. Sergant for the defendant.

Mr. Chief Justice Marshall delivered the opinion of the court, that this case was not distinguishable from its former decisions on the same subject,[1] except by the circumstances, that the defendant in the present case was a citizen of the same state with the plaintiffs, at the time the contract was made in that state, and remained such at the time the suit was commenced in its courts. But that these facts made no difference in the cases. The constitution of the United States was made for the whole people of the Union, and is equally binding upon all the courts and all the citizens.

Judgment reversed.

---

[1] *Sturges* v. *Crowninshield*, 4 Wheat. Rep., 122; *M'Millan* v. *M'Neill*, Id. 209.

Cohens *v.* Virginia

NOTE.

THIS case came on writ of error from the Quarterly Sessions Court of the borough of Norfolk, Virginia, after appeal to the higher Virginia Court had been denied, to review the conviction of one Cohens under a Virginia statute prohibiting the sale of lottery tickets. Cohens' defense was that an act of Congress gave him the right to sell lottery tickets and overrode the Virginia law. Before the question was argued on the merits the Supreme Court considered a motion to dismiss the appeal on the ground of want of jurisdiction, and it was on that motion that Marshall's opinion was delivered.

It had already been decided by the Supreme Court in the case of *Martin* v. *Hunters' Lessee*, 1 Wheat., 304, that the Supreme Court had, under the Constitution and the Judicature Act, the power to review on appeal the determination of the highest court of any state, on a question involving the question of the construction or validity of a law of the United States or the construction of the Constitution. That decision had been delivered by Justice Story at great length, and with a force of statement and a greatness of reasoning and judicial statesmanship not unworthy of Marshall himself.

Cohens v. *Virginia* affirmed the doctrines of that case and applied them to a case where an appeal was had from a state court to the Supreme Court in a case (involving a law of the United States) where a state was a party to the action. It was argued with all the vehemence and eloquence of the Jeffersonians that the doctrines of the Martin case did not apply when a state was a party, that so cardinal a principle of state's rights must, from the very nature of the Union, be read in as a limitation on the constitutional powers of the Supreme Court, and the objection was pressed that the eleventh amendment to the Constitution expressly forbade the judicial power from taking cognizance of a suit against a state.

Marshall's opinion met and conquered every objection—with logic and convincing eloquence.   This case completed the subjugation of the state courts on federal questions and established the federal judiciary supreme.   It is hard to overestimate the importance of it.   It filled Jefferson and the state's rights party with impotent and bitter anger.   It was to them the final encroachment of the central government.   That a sovereign state should be brought before the Supreme Court was the last humiliation.

Surely *Cohens* v. *Virginia* is one of Marshall's greatest opinions. In clearness and vigor of arrangement, in splendor of cumulative argument, and in the power of phrase it ranks with any judicial effort.   Less important and far-reaching than *Marbury* v. *Madison*, *McCulloch* v. *Maryland*, and *Dartmouth College* v. *Woodward*, it is more complete and convincing, more satisfying, than any of them.

It expounds, one may say, finally and perfectly, the most important branch of the power of the federal judiciary,—emphasizing always what Marshall conceived to be the glory of the Union, the sovereign power of the central government.   There is no more wonderful passage in all his opinions than that in *Cohens* v. *Virginia* beginning: " That the United States form, for many and for most important purposes, a single nation has not yet been denied.   In war, we are one people.   In making peace, we are one people.   In all commercial regulations, we are one and the same people."

That is the keystone of the arch.

Cohens

v.

Virginia.

[6 Wheat, 264.]

1821.

For the defendants in error, on the motion to dismiss the writ of error, Mr. Barbour and Mr. Smith. Contra, Mr. D. B. Ogden and Mr. Pinkney.

Mr. Chief Justice Marshall delivered the opinion of the court :

This is a writ of error to a judgment rendered in the Court of Hustings for the borough of Norfolk, on an information for selling lottery tickets, contrary to an act of the legislature of Virginia. In the state court, the defendant claimed the protection of an act of Congress. A case was agreed between the parties, which states the act of Assembly on which the prosecution was founded, and the act of Congress on which the defendant relied, and concludes in these words : "If upon this case the court shall be of opinion that the acts of Congress before mentioned were valid, and on the true construction of those acts, the lottery tickets sold by the defendants as aforesaid, might lawfully be sold within the state of Virginia, notwithstanding the act or statute of the General Assembly of Virginia prohibiting such sale, then judgment to be entered for the defendants. And if the court should be of opinion that the statute or act of the General Assembly of the state of Virginia, prohibiting such sale, is valid, notwithstanding the said act of Congress, then judgment to be entered that the defendants are guilty, and that the commonwealth recover against them one hundred dollars and costs.

*376   * Judgment was rendered against the defendants ; and the court in which it was rendered being the highest court of the state in which the cause was cognizable, the record has been brought into this court by a writ of error.[1]

The defendant in error moves to dismiss this writ, for want of jurisdiction.

In support of this motion, three points have been made, and argued with the ability which the importance of the question merits. These points are :

1st. That a state is a defendant.

2d. That no writ of error lies from this court to a state court.

3d. The third point has been presented in different forms by the gentlemen who have argued it. The counsel who opened the cause said, that the want of jurisdiction was shown by the subject-matter of the

---

[1] The plaintiff in error prayed an appeal from the judgment of the Court of Hustings, but it was refused, on the ground that there was no higher state tribunal which could take cognizance of the case.

case.   The counsel who followed him said, that jurisdiction was not given by the judiciary act.   The
court has bestowed all its attention on the arguments
of both gentlemen, and supposes that their tendency
is to show that this court has no jurisdiction of the
case, or, in other words, has no right to review the
judgment of the state court, because neither the constitution nor any law of the United States has been
violated by that judgment.

The questions presented to the court by the two
*first points made at the bar are of great
magnitude, and may be truly said vitally to
affect the Union.   They exclude the inquiry whether
the constitution and laws of the United States have
been violated by the judgment which the plaintiffs in
error seek to review; and maintain that, admitting
such violation, it is not in the power of the government to apply a corrective.   They maintain that the
nation does not possess a department capable of restraining peaceably, and by authority of law, any
attempts which may be made, by a part, against the
legitimate powers of the whole ; and that the government is reduced to the alternative of submitting to
such attempts, or of resisting them by force.   They
maintain that the constitution of the United States
has provided no tribunal for the final construction of
itself, or of the laws or treaties of the nation ; but
that this power may be exercised in the last resort
by the courts of every state of the Union.   That the
constitution, laws, and treaties, may receive as many
constructions as there are states   and that this is not

*377

a mischief, or, if a mischief, is irremediable. These abstract propositions are to be determined; for he who demands decision without permitting inquiry, affirms that the decision he asks does not depend on inquiry.

If such be the constitution, it is the duty of the court to bow with respectful submission to its provisions. If such be not the constitution, it is equally the duty of this court to say so; and to perform that task which the American people have assigned to the judicial department.

*378   * 1st. The first question to be considered is, whether the jurisdiction of this court is excluded by the character of the parties, one of them being a state, and the other a citizen of that state?

The second section of the third article of the constitution defines the extent of the judicial power of the United States. Jurisdiction is given to the courts of the Union in two classes of cases. In the first, their jurisdiction depends on the character of the cause, whoever may be the parties. This class comprehends "all cases in law and equity arising under this constitution, the laws of the United States, and treaties made, or which shall be made, under their authority." This clause extends the jurisdiction of the court to all the cases described, without making in its terms any exception whatever, and without any regard to the condition of the party. If there be any exception, it is to be implied against the express words of the article.

In the second class, the jurisdiction depends

entirely on the character of the parties. In this are comprehended "controversies between two or more states, between a state and citizens of another state," "and between a state and foreign states, citizens or subjects." If these be the parties, it is entirely unimportant what may be the subject of controversy. Be it what it may, these parties have a constitutional right to come into the courts of the Union.

The counsel for the defendant in error have stated that the cases which arise under the constitution must grow out of those provisions which are capable *of self-execution: examples of which are to be found in the 2d section of the 4th article, and in the 10th section of the 1st article.

*379

A case which arises under a law of the United States must, we are likewise told, be a right given by some act which becomes necessary to execute the powers given in the constitution, of which the law of naturalization is mentioned as an example.

The use intended to be made of this exposition of the first part of the section, defining the extent of the judicial power, is not clearly understood. If the intention be merely to distinguish cases arising under the constitution, from those arising under a law, for the sake of precision in the application of this argument, these propositions will not be controverted. If it be to maintain that a case arising under the constitution, or a law, must be one in which a party comes into court to demand something conferred on him by the constitution or a law, we think the construction too narrow. A case in law or equity consists of

the right of the one party, as well as of the other, and
may truly be said to arise under the constitution or a
law of the United States, whenever its correct decision depends on the construction of either.   Congress seems to have intended to give its own
construction of this part of the constitution in the
25th section of the judiciary act ; and we perceive no
reason to depart from that construction.

The jurisdiction of the court, then, being extended
by the letter of the constitution to all cases arising
under it, or under the laws of the United States,
* *380* it follows that those who would withdraw
* any case of this description from that
jurisdiction, must sustain the exemption they claim
on the spirit and true meaning of the constitution,
which spirit and true meaning must be so apparent
as to overrule the words which its framers have
employed.

The counsel for the defendant in error have under-
taken to do this ; and have laid down the general
proposition, that a sovereign independent state is not
suable except by its own consent.

This general proposition will not be controverted.
But its consent is not requisite in each particular
case.   It may be given in a general law.   And if a
state has surrendered any portion of its sovereignty,
the question whether a liability to suit be a part of
this portion, depends on the instrument by which the
surrender is made.   If, upon a just construction of
that instrument, it shall appear that the state has
submitted to be sued, then it has parted with this

sovereign right of judging in every case on the justice of its own pretensions, and has entrusted that power to a tribunal in whose impartiality it confides.

The American States, as well as the American people, have believed a close and firm Union to be essential to their liberty and to their happiness. They have been taught by experience, that this Union cannot exist without a government for the whole; and they have been taught by the same experience that this government would be a mere shadow, that must disappoint all their hopes, unless invested with large portions of that sovereignty which belongs to independent states.   Under the influence of this opinion, and thus instructed by experience, * *381* * the American people, in the conventions of their respective states, adopted the present constitution.

If it could be doubted, whether from its nature, it were not supreme in all cases where it is empowered to act, that doubt would be removed by the declaration, that "this constitution, and the laws of the United States, which shall be made in pursuance thereof, and all treaties made, or which shall be made, under the authority of the United States, shall be the supreme law of the land; and the judges in every state shall be bound thereby; anything in the constitution or laws of any state to the contrary notwithstanding."

This is the authoritative language of the American people; and, if gentlemen please, of the American States.   It marks, with lines too strong to be mistaken, the characteristic distinction between the government of the Union and those of the states. The general government, though limited as to its objects, is supreme with respect to those objects. This principle is a part of the constitution ; and if there be any who deny its necessity, none can deny its authority.

To this supreme government ample powers are confided ; and if it were possible to doubt the great purposes for which they were so confided, the people of the United States have declared, that they are given " in order to form a more perfect union, establish justice, ensure domestic tranquility, provide for the common defense, promote the general welfare, and secure the blessings of liberty to themselves and their posterity."

*382   * With the ample powers confided to this supreme government, for these interesting purposes, are connected many express and important limitations on the sovereignty of the states, which are made for the same purposes. The powers of the Union, on the great subjects of war, peace, and commerce, and on many others, are in themselves limitations of the sovereignty of the states ; but in addition to these, the sovereignty of the states is surrendered in many instances where the surrender can only operate to the benefit of the people, and where, perhaps, no other power is conferred on Congress than a conservative power to maintain the principles established in the constitution. The maintenance of these principles in their purity, is certainly among the great duties of the government. One of the instruments by which this duty may be peaceably performed, is the judicial department. It is authorized to decide all cases of every description, arising under the constitution or laws of the United States. From this general grant of jurisdiction, no exception is made of those cases in which a state may be a party. When we consider the situation of the government of the Union and of a state, in relation to each other; the nature of our constitution; the subordination of the state governments to that constitution; the great purpose for which jurisdiction over all cases arising under the constitution and laws of the United States is confided to the judicial department, are we at liberty to insert in this general grant, an exception of those cases in which a state may be a *383 * party? Will the spirit of the constitution justify this attempt to control its words? We think it will not. We think a case arising under the constitution or laws of the United States, is cognizable in the courts of the Union, whoever may be the parties to that case.

Had any doubt existed with respect to the just construction of this part of the section, that doubt would have been removed by the enumeration of those cases to which the jurisdiction of the federal courts is extended, in consequence of the character of the parties. In that enumeration, we find, " controversies between two or more states, between a state and citizen of another state," " and between a state and foreign states, citizens, or subjects."

One of the express objects, then, for which the

judicial department was established, is the decision of
controversies between states, and between a state and
individuals.   The mere circumstance, that a state is a
party, gives jurisdiction to the court.   How, then, can
it be contended, that the very same instrument, in
the very same section, should be so construed as
that this same circumstance should withdraw a case
from the jurisdiction of the court, where the constitution or laws of the United States are supposed
to have been violated?   The constitution gave to
every person having a claim upon a state, a right to
submit his case to the court of the nation.   However
unimportant his claim might be, however little the
community might be interested in its decision, the
framers of our constitution thought it necessary, for

*384   the purposes of justice, to provide a tribunal
          * as superior to influence as possible, in
which that claim might be decided.   Can it be imagined, that the same persons considered a case involving the constitution of our country and the
majesty of the laws—questions in which every American citizen must be deeply interested—as withdrawn
from this tribunal, because a state is a party?

   While weighing arguments drawn from the nature
of government, and from the general spirit of an instrument, and urged for the purpose of narrowing
the construction which the words of that instrument
seem to require, it is proper to place in the opposite
scale those principles, drawn from the same sources,
which go to sustain the words in their full operation
and natural import.   One of these, which has been

pressed with great force by the counsel for the plaintiffs in error, is, that the judicial power of every well-constituted government must be co-extensive with the legislative, and must be capable of deciding every judicial question which grows out of the constitution and laws.

If any proposition may be considered as a political axiom, this, we think, may be so considered. In reasoning upon it as an abstract question, there would, probably, exist no contrariety of opinion respecting it. Every argument, proving the necessity of the department, proves also the propriety of giving this extent to it. We do not mean to say, that the jurisdiction of the courts of the Union should be construed to be co-extensive with the legislative, merely because it is fit that it should be so ; but we mean to
*385   say, that this fitness furnishes an argument
       * in construing the constitution which ought never to be overlooked, and which is most especially entitled to consideration, when we are inquiring, whether the words of the instrument which purport to establish this principle, shall be contracted for the purpose of destroying it.

The mischievous consequences of the construction contended for on the part of Virginia, are also entitled to great consideration. It would prostrate, it has been said, the government and its laws at the feet of every state in the Union. And would not this be its effect ? What power of the government could be executed by its own means, in any state disposed to resist its execution by a course of legislation ? The laws must be executed by individuals acting within the several states. If these individuals may be exposed to penalties, and if the courts of the Union cannot correct the judgments by which these penalties may be enforced, the course of the government may be, at any time, arrested by the will of one of its members. Each member will possess a veto on the will of the whole.

The answer which has been given to this argument, does not deny its truth, but insists that confidence is reposed, and may be safely reposed, in the state institutions ; and that, if they shall ever become so insane or so wicked as to seek the destruction of the government, they may accomplish their object by refusing to perform the functions assigned to them.

We readily concur with the counsel for the defendant, * in the declaration that the cases
*386   which have been put of direct legislative resistance for the purpose of opposing the acknowledged powers of the government, are extreme cases, and in the hope that they will never occur ; but we cannot help believing, that a general conviction of the total incapacity of the government to protect itself and its laws in such cases, would contribute in no inconsiderable degree to their occurrence.

Let it be admitted, that the cases which have been put are extreme and improbable, yet there are gradations of opposition to the laws, far short of those cases, which might have a baneful influence on the affairs of the nation. Different states may entertain different opinions on the true construction of the

constitutional powers of Congress. We know, that
at one time, the assumption of the debts contracted
by the several states, during the war of our revolution, was deemed unconstitutional by some of them.
We know, too, that at other times, certain taxes,
imposed by Congress, have been pronounced unconstitutional. Other laws have been questioned par-
tially, while they were supported by the great majority
of the American people. We have no assurance that
we shall be less divided than we have been. States
may legislate in conformity to their opinions, and
may enforce those opinions by penalties. It would
be hazarding too much to assert, that the judicatures
of the states will be exempt from the prejudices by
which the legislatures and people are influenced, and
will constitute perfectly impartial tribunals. In many
*387   states the judges are dependent for office
         and *for salary on the will of the legisla-
ture. The constitution of the United States furnishes no security against the universal adoption of
this principle. When we observe the importance
which that constitution attaches to the independence
of judges, we are the less inclined to suppose that it
can have intended to leave these constitutional questions to tribunals where this independence may not
exist, in all cases where a state shall prosecute an individual who claims the protection of an act of Congress. These prosecutions may take place even
without a legislative act. A person making a seizure
under an act of Congress, may be indicted as a tres-
passer, if force has been employed, and of this a jury

may judge.   How extensive may be the mischief if the first decisions in such cases should be final !

These collisions may take place in times of no extraordinary commotion.   But a constitution is framed for ages to come, and is designed to approach immortality as nearly as human institutions can approach it.   Its course cannot always be tranquil.   It is exposed to storms and tempests, and its framers must be unwise statesmen indeed, if they have not provided it, as far as its nature will permit, with the means of self-preservation from the perils it may be destined to encounter.   No government ought to be so defective in its organization as not to contain within itself the means of securing the execution of its own laws against other dangers than those which occur every day.   Courts of justice are the means most usually employed ; and it is reasonable to expect that a government should repose on its *388   * own courts, rather than on others.   There is certainly nothing in the circumstances under which our constitution was formed ; nothing in the history of the times, which would justify the opinion that the confidence reposed in the states was so implicit as to leave in them and their tribunals the power of resisting or defeating, in the form of law, the legitimate measures of the Union.   The requisitions of Congress, under the confederation, were as constitutionally obligatory as the laws enacted by the present Congress.   That they were habitually disregarded, is a fact of universal notoriety.   With a knowledge of this fact, and under its full pressure, a convention was assembled to change the system. Is it so improbable that they should confer on the judicial department the power of construing the constitution and laws of the Union in every case, in the last resort, and of preserving them from all violation from every quarter, so far as judicial decisions can preserve them, that this improbability should essentially affect the construction of the new system? We are told, and we are truly told, that the great change which is to give efficacy to the present system, is its ability to act on individuals directly, instead of acting through the instrumentality of state governments. But, ought not this ability, in reason and sound policy, to be applied directly to the protection of individuals employed in the execution of the laws, as well as to their coercion? Your laws reach the individual without the aid of any other power; why may they not protect him from punishment for performing his duty in executing them?

*389   *The counsel for Virginia endeavor to obviate the force of these arguments by saying, that the dangers they suggest, if not imaginary, are inevitable; that the constitution can make no provision against them; and that, therefore, in construing that instrument, they ought to be excluded from our consideration. This state of things, they say, cannot arise until there shall be a disposition so hostile to the present political system as to produce a determination to destroy it; and, when that determination shall be produced, its effects will not be restrained by parchment stipulations. The fate of the constitution will not then depend on judicial decisions. But, should no appeal be made to force, the states can put an end to the government by refusing to act. They have only not to elect senators, and it expires without a struggle.

It is very true that, whenever hostility to the existing system shall become universal, it will be also irresistible. The people made the constitution, and the people can unmake it. It is the creature of their own will, and lives only by their will. But this supreme and irresistible power to make or to unmake, resides only in the whole body of the people; not in any subdivision of them. The attempt of any of the parts to exercise it is usurpation, and ought to be repelled by those to whom the people have delegated their power of repelling it.

The acknowledged inability of the government, then, to sustain itself against the public will, and, by force or otherwise, to control the whole nation, is no

*390   sound argument in support of its constitutional * inability to preserve itself against a section of the nation acting in opposition to the general will.

It is true, that if all the states, or a majority of them, refuse to elect senators, the legislative powers of the Union will be suspended. But if any one state shall refuse to elect them, the Senate will not, on that account, be the less capable of performing all its functions. The argument founded on this fact would seem rather to prove the subordination of the parts to the whole, than the complete independence of any one of them. The framers of the constitution were, indeed, unable to make any provisions which should protect that instrument against a general combination of the states, or of the people, for its destruction ; and, conscious of this inability, they have not made the attempt. But they were able to provide against the operation of measures adopted in any one state, whose tendency might be to arrest the execution of the laws, and this it was the part of true wisdom to attempt. We think they have attempted it.

It has been also urged, as an additional objection to the jurisdiction of the court, that cases between a state and one of its own citizens, do not come within the general scope of the constitution ; and were obviously never intended to be made cognizable in the federal courts. The state tribunals might be suspected of partiality in cases between itself or its citizens and aliens, or the citizens of another state, but not in proceedings by a state against its own citizens. That jealousy which might exist in the first case, could not exist in the last, and therefore the judicial power is not extended to the last.

*391 * This is very true, so far as jurisdiction depends on the character of the parties ; and the argument would have great force if urged to prove that this court could not establish the demand of a citizen upon his state, but is not entitled to the same force when urged to prove that this court cannot inquire whether the constitution or laws of the United States protect a citizen from a prosecution instituted against him by a state. If jurisdiction depended entirely on the character of the parties, and was not given where the parties have not an original right to come into court, that part of the 2d section of the 3d article which extends the judicial power to all cases arising under the constitution and laws of the United States, would be mere surplusage.   It is to give jurisdiction where the character of the parties would not give it, that this very important part of the clause was inserted. It may be true, that the partiality of the state tribunals, in ordinary controversies between a state and its citizens, was not apprehended, and therefore the judicial power of the Union was not extended to such cases; but this was not the sole nor the greatest object for which this department was created.   A more important, a much more interesting object, was the preservation of the constitution and laws of the United States, so far as they can be preserved by judicial authority; and therefore the jurisdiction of the courts of the Union was expressly extended to all cases arising under that constitution and those laws.   If the constitution or

*392   laws may be violated by proceedings * instituted by a state against its own citizens, and if that violation may be such as essentially to affect the constitution and the laws, such as to arrest the progress of government in its constitutional course, why should these cases, be excepted from that provision which expressly extends the judicial power of the Union to all cases arising under the constitution and laws?

After bestowing on this subject the most attentive

consideration, the court can perceive no reason founded on the character of the parties for introducing an exception which the constitution has not made; and we think that the judicial power, as originally given, extends to all cases arising under the constitution or a law of the United States, whoever may be the parties.

It has been also contended, that this jurisdiction, if given, is original, and cannot be exercised in the appellate form.

The words of the constitution are, "in all cases affecting ambassadors, other public ministers, and consuls, and those in which a state shall be a party, the Supreme Court shall have original jurisdiction. In all the other cases before mentioned, the Supreme Court shall have appellate jurisdiction."

This distinction between original and appellate jurisdiction, excludes, we are told, in all cases, the exercise of the one where the other is given.

The constitution gives the Supreme Court original jurisdiction in certain enumerated cases, and gives it appellate jurisdiction in all others.

Among those in which jurisdiction must be exercised in the appellate *form, are cases arising under the constitution and laws of the United States. These provisions of the constitution are equally obligatory, and are to be equally respected. If a state be a party, the jurisdiction of this court is original; if the case arise under a constitution or a law, the jurisdiction is appellate. But a case to which a state is a party may arise under the

*393

constitution or a law of the United States.   What
rule is applicable to such a case?   What, then, becomes the duty of the court?   Certainly, we think,
so to construe the constitution as to give effect to
both provisions, as far as it is possible to reconcile
them, and not to permit their seeming repugnancy to
destroy each other.   We must endeavor so to construe them as to preserve the true intent and meaning of the instrument.

In one description of cases, the jurisdiction of the
court is founded entirely on the character of the
parties; and the nature of the controversy is not contemplated by the constitution.   The character of the
parties is everything, the nature of the case nothing.
In the other description of cases, the jurisdiction is
founded entirely on the character of the case, and the
parties are not contemplated by the constitution.   In
these, the nature of the case is everything, the character of the parties nothing.   When, then, the constitution declares the jurisdiction, in cases where a
state shall be a party, to be original, and in all cases
arising under the constitution or a law, to be appellate, the conclusion seems irresistible, that its
framers designed to include in the first class
*394   * those cases in which jurisdiction is given,
because a state is a party, and to include in the
second, those in which jurisdiction is given, because
the case arises under the constitution or a law.

This reasonable construction is rendered necessary
by other considerations.

That the constitution or a law of the United

States, is involved in a case, and makes a part of it, may appear in the progress of a cause in which the courts of the Union, but for that circumstance, would have no jurisdiction, and which of consequence could not originate in the Supreme Court. In such a case, the jurisdiction can be exercised only in its appellate form. To deny its exercise in this form is to deny its existence, and would be to construe a clause, dividing the power of the Supreme Court, in such a manner as in a considerable degree to defeat the power itself. All must perceive that this construction can be justified only where it is absolutely necessary. We do not think the article under consideration presents that necessity.

It is observable, that in this distributive clause, no negative words are introduced. This observation is not made for the purpose of contending that the legislature may "apportion the judicial power between the supreme and inferior courts according to its will." That would be, as was said by this court in the case of *Marbury* v. *Madison*, to render the distributive clause "mere surplusage," to make it, "form without substance." This cannot, therefore, be the true construction of the article.

*395   * But although the absence of negative words will not authorize the legislature to disregard the distribution of the power previously granted, their absence will justify a sound construction of the whole article, so as to give every part its intended effect. It is admitted, that "affirmative words are often, in their operation, negative of

other objects than those affirmed"; and that where
" a negative or exclusive sense must be given to
them, or they have no operation at all," they must
receive that negative or exclusive sense.   But where
they have full operation without it; where it would
destroy some of the most important objects for which
the power was created; then, we think, affirmative
words ought not to be construed negatively.

The constitution declares, that in cases where a
state is a party, the Supreme Court shall have
original jurisdiction ; but does not say that its appellate jurisdiction shall not be exercised in cases where,
from their nature, appellate jurisdiction is given,
whether a state be or be not a party.   It may be conceded, that where the case is of such a nature as
to admit of its originating in the Supreme Court,
it ought to originate there ; but where, from its
nature, it cannot originate in that court, these words
ought not to be so construed as to require it.   There
are many cases in which it would be found extremely
difficult, and subversive of the spirit of the constitution, to maintain the construction, that appellate
jurisdiction cannot be exercised where one of the
parties might sue or be sued in this court.

The constitution defines the jurisdiction of the
*Supreme Court, but does not define that
*396   of the inferior courts.   Can it be affirmed,
that a state might not sue the citizen of another state
in a circuit court ?   Should the Circuit Court decide
for or against its jurisdiction, should it dismiss the
suit, or give judgment against the state, might not its

It is, we think, apparent, that to give this distributive clause the interpretation contended for, to give to its affirmative words a negative operation, in every possible case, would, in some instances, defeat the obvious intention of the article.   Such an interpretation would not consist with those rules which, from time immemorial, have guided courts, in their construction of instruments brought under their consideration. It must, therefore, be discarded.   Every part of the article must be taken into view, and that construction adopted which will consist with its words, and promote its general intention.   The court may imply a negative from affirmative words, where the implication promotes, not where it defeats the intention.

If we apply this principle, the correctness of which we believe will not be controverted, to the distributive clause under consideration, the result, we think, would be this: the original jurisdiction of the Supreme Court, in cases where a state is a party, refers to those cases in which, according to the grant of power made in the preceding clause, jurisdiction might be exercised in consequence of the character of the party, and an original suit might be instituted in any of the federal courts; not to those cases in which an original suit might not be *instituted in a federal

*399   court.   Of the last description, is every case between a state and its citizens, and, perhaps, every case in which a state is enforcing its penal laws.   In such cases, therefore, the Supreme Court cannot take original jurisdiction.   In every other case, that is, in every case to which the judicial power

extends, and in which original jurisdiction is not expressly given, that judicial power shall be exercised
in the appellate, and only in the appellate form.
The original jurisdiction of this court cannot be
enlarged, but its appellate jurisdiction may be exercised in every case cognizable under the third article
of the constitution, in the federal courts, in which
original jurisdiction cannot be exercised ; and the
extent of this judicial power is to be measured, not by
giving the affirmative words of the distributive clause
a negative operation in every possible case, but by
giving their true meaning to the words which define
its extent.

The counsel for the defendant in error urge, in
opposition to this rule of construction, some *dicta* of
the court, in the case of *Marbury* v. *Madison.*

It is a maxim not to be disregarded, that general
expressions, in every opinion, are to be taken in connection with the case in which those expressions
are used. If they go beyond the case, they may
be respected, but ought not to control the judgment in
a subsequent suit when the very point is presented
for decision. The reason of this maxim is obvious.
The question actually before the court is investigated
with care and considered in its full extent. Other
principles which may serve to illustrate it, are considered *in their relation to the case decided, but
their possible bearing on all other cases
is seldom completely investigated.

*400

In the case of *Marbury* v. *Madison*, the single
question before the court, so far as that case can

be applied to this, was, whether the legislature could give this court original jurisdiction in a case in which the constitution had clearly not given it, and in which no doubt respecting the construction of the article could possibly be raised.   The court decided, and we think very properly, that the legislature could not give original jurisdiction in such a case.   But, in the reasoning of the court in support of this decision, some expressions are used which go far beyond it. The counsel for Marbury had insisted on the un- limited discretion of the legislature in the apportion- ment of the judicial power ; and it is against this argument that the reasoning of the court is directed. They say that, if such had been the intention of the article, " it would certainly have been useless to pro- ceed farther than to define the judicial power, and the tribunals in which it should be vested."   The court says, that such a construction would render the clause, dividing the jurisdiction of the court into original and appellate, totally useless ; that " affirma- tive words are often, in their operation, negative of other objects than those which are affirmed ; and, in this case (in the case of *Marbury* v. *Madison*), a negative or exclusive sense must be given to them, or they have no operation at all."   " It cannot be presumed," adds the court, " that any clause in the constitution is intended to be without *effect ; and,
401   therefore, such a construction, is inad- missible, unless the words require it."

The whole reasoning of the court proceeds upon the idea that the affirmative words of the clause giv-

ing one sort of jurisdiction, must imply a negative of
any other sort of jurisdiction, because otherwise the
words would be totally inoperative, and this reasoning is advanced in a case to which it was strictly
applicable.   If in that case original jurisdiction could
have been exercised, the clause under consideration
would have been entirely useless.   Having such
cases only in its view, the court lays down a principle
which is generally correct, in terms much broader
than the decision, and not only much broader than
the reasoning with which that decision is supported, but in some instances contradictory to its
principle.   The reasoning sustains the negative
operation of the words in that case, because otherwise the clause would have no meaning whatever,
and because such operation was necessary to give
effect to the intention of the article.   The effort now
made is, to apply the conclusion to which the court
was conducted by that reasoning in the particular
case, to one in which the words have their full operation when understood affirmatively, and in which the
negative, or exclusive sense, is to be so used as to defeat some of the great objects of the article.

To this construction the court cannot give its assent.
The general expressions in the case of *Marbury*
v. *Madison* must be understood with the limitations which are given to them in this opinion ; limita-

*402   tions *which in no degree affect the decision
in that case, or the tenor of its reasoning.

The counsel who closed the argument put several cases for the purpose of illustration, which he

supposed to arise under the constitution, and yet to be, apparently, without the jurisdiction of the court.

Were a state to lay a duty on exports, to collect the money and place it in her treasury, could the citizen who paid it, he asks, maintain a suit in this court against such state, to recover back the money?

Perhaps not. Without, however, deciding such supposed case, we may say, that it is entirely unlike that under consideration.

The citizen who has paid his money to his state, under a law that is void, is in the same situation with every other person who has paid money by mistake. The law raises an *assumpsit* to return the money, and it is upon that *assumpsit* that the action is to be maintained. To refuse to comply with this *assumpsit* may be no more a violation of the constitution than to refuse to comply with any other; and as the federal courts never had jurisdiction over contracts between a state and its citizens, they may have none over this. But let us so vary the supposed case as to give it a real resemblance to that under consideration. Suppose a citizen refuse to pay this export duty, and a suit be instituted for the purpose of compelling him to pay it. He pleads the constitution of the United States in bar of the action, notwithstanding which the court gives judgment against him. This would
*403 be a case arising under *the constitution, and would be the very case now before the court.

We are also asked, if a state should confiscate

property secured by a treaty, whether the individual could maintain an action for that property.

If the property confiscated be debts, our own experience informs us that the remedy of the creditor against his deptor remains. If it be land which is secured by a treaty, and afterwards confiscated by a state, the argument does not assume that this title, thus secured, could be extinguished by an act of confiscation. The injured party, therefore, has his remedy against the occupant of the land for that which the treaty secures to him, not against the state for money which is not secured to him.

The case of a state which pays off its own debts with paper money, no more resembles this than do those to which we have already adverted. The courts have no jurisdiction over the contract. They cannot enforce it, nor judge of its violation. Let it be that the act discharging the debt is a mere nullity, and that it is still due. Yet the federal courts have no cognizance of the case. But suppose a state to institute proceedings against an individual, which depended on the validity of an act emitting bills of credit; suppose a state to prosecute one of its citizens for refusing paper money, who should plead the constitution in bar of such prosecution. If his plea should be overruled and judgment rendered against him, his case would resemble this; and, unless the jurisdiction of this court might be exercised over it, the constitution would *be violated, and the injured party be unable to bring his case before that tribunal to which

*404

the people of the United States have assigned all such cases.

It is most true that this court will not take jurisdiction if it should not ; but it is equally true, that it must take jurisdiction if it should. The judiciary cannot, as the legislature may, avoid a measure because it approaches the confines of the constitution. We cannot pass it by because it is doubtful. With whatever doubts, with whatever difficulties, a case may be attended, we must decide it if it be brought before us. We have no more right to decline the exercise of jurisdiction which is given, than to usurp that which is not given. The one or the other would be treason to the constitution. Questions may occur which we would gladly avoid, but we cannot avoid them. All we can do, is to exercise our best judgment, and conscientiously to perform our duty. In doing this, on the present occasion, we find this tribunal invested with appellate jurisdiction in all cases arising under the constitution and laws of the United States. We find no exception to this grant, and we cannot insert one.

To escape the operation of these comprehensive words, the counsel for the defendant has mentioned instances in which the constitution might be violated without giving jurisdiction to this court. These words, therefore, however universal in their expression, must, he contends, be limited and controlled in their construction by circumstances. One of these instances is, the grant by a state of a patent of nobility. The court, he says, cannot annul this grant.

* *405*   *This may be very true; but by no
means justifies the inference drawn from it.
The article does not extend the judicial power to
every violation of the constitution which may possibly
take place, but to "a case in law or equity," in which
a right, under such law, is asserted in a court of justice. If the question cannot be brought into a court,
then there is no case in law or equity, and no jurisdiction is given by the words of the article. But if,
in any controversy depending in a court, the cause
should depend on the validity of such a law, that
would be a case arising under the constitution, to
which the judicial power of the United States would
extend. The same observation applies to the other
instances with which the counsel who opened the
cause has illustrated this argument. Although they
show that there may be violations of the constitution,
of which the courts can take no cognizance, they do
not show that an interpretation more restrictive than
the words themselves import ought to be given to
this article. They do not show that there can be "a
case in law or equity," arising under the constitution,
to which the judicial power does not extend.

We think, then, that, as the constitution originally
stood, the appellate jurisdiction of this court, in all
cases arising under the constitution, laws, or treaties of the United States, was not arrested by the
circumstance that a state was a party.

This leads to a consideration of the 11th amendment.

It is in these words: " The judicial power of the

United States shall not be construed to extend to any
*suit in law or equity commenced or prose-
*406   cuted against one of the United States, by
citizens of another state, or by citizens or subjects of
any foreign state."

It is a part of our history, that, at the adoption of
the constitution, all the states were greatly indebted;
and the apprehension that these debts might be prosecuted in the federal courts, formed a very serious
objection to that instrument.   Suits were instituted;
and the court maintained its jurisdiction.   The alarm
was general; and, to quiet the apprehensions that
were so extensively entertained, this amendment was
proposed in Congress, and adopted by the state legislatures.   That its motive was not to maintain the
sovereignty of a state from the degradation supposed
to attend a compulsory appearance before the tribunal
of the nation, may be inferred from the terms of the
amendment.   It does not comprehend controversies
between two or more states, or between a state and a
foreign state.   The jurisdiction of the court still extends to these cases; and in these a state may still be
sued.   We must ascribe the amendment, then, to
some other cause than the dignity of a state.   There
is no difficulty in finding this cause.   Those who
were inhibited from commencing a suit against a
state, or from prosecuting one which might be commenced before the adoption of the amendment, were
persons who might probably be its creditors.   There
was not much reason to fear that foreign or sister
states would be creditors to any considerable amount,

and there was reason to retain the jurisdiction of the

*407   court in those * cases, because it might be essential to the preservation of peace. The amendment, therefore, extended to suits commenced or prosecuted by individuals, but not to those brought by states.

The first impression made on the mind by this amendment is, that it was intended for those cases, and for those only, in which some demand against a state is made by an individual in the courts of the Union. If we consider the causes to which it is to be traced, we are conducted to the same conclusion. A general interest might well be felt in leaving to a state the full power of consulting its convenience in the adjustment of its debts, or of other claims upon it; but no interest could be felt in so changing the relations between the whole and its parts, as to strip the government of the means of protecting, by the instrumentality of its courts, the constitution and laws from active violation.

The words of the amendment appear to the court to justify and require this construction. The judicial power is not "to extend to any suit in law or equity commenced or prosecuted against one of the United States by citizens of another state, etc."

What is a suit ? We understand it to be the prosecution, or pursuit, of some claim, demand, or request. In law language, it is the prosecution of some demand in a court of justice. The remedy for every species of wrong is, says Judge Blackstone, "the being put in possession of that right whereof the party injured is deprived." "The instruments whereby this remedy is obtained are a diversity of suits and actions, which are defined by the * Mirror to be 'the lawful demand of one's right.' Or as Bracton and Fleta express it, in the words of Justinian, '*jus prosequendi in judicio quod alicui debetur.*'" Blackstone then proceeds to describe every species of remedy by suit; and they are all cases where the party suing claims to obtain something to which he has a right.

*408

To commence a suit is to demand something by the institution of process in a court of justice; and to prosecute the suit, is, according to the common acceptation of language, to continue that demand. By a suit commenced by an individual against a state, we should understand process sued out by that individual against the state, for the purpose of establishing some claim against it by the judgment of a court; and the prosecution of that suit is its continuance. Whatever may be the stages of its progress, the actor is still the same. Suits had been commenced in the Supreme Court against some of the states before this amendment was introduced into Congress, and others might be commenced before it should be adopted by the state legislatures, and might be depending at the time of its adoption. The object of the amendment was not only to prevent the commencement of future suits, but to arrest the prosecution of those which might be commenced when this article should form a part of the constitution. It therefore embraces both objects; and its meaning is, that the judicial power shall not be construed to extend to any suit which may be commenced, or

*409   which, if already commenced, may be *prosecuted against a state by the citizen of another state. If a suit, brought in one court, and carried by legal process to a supervising court, be a continuation of the same suit, then this suit is not commenced nor prosecuted against a state. It is clearly in its commencement the suit of a state against an individual, which suit is transferred to this court, not for the purpose of asserting any claim against the state, but for the purpose of asserting a constitutional defense against a claim made by a state.

A writ of error is defined to be a commission by which the judges of one court are authorized to examine a record upon which a judgment was given in another court, and, on such examination, to affirm or reverse the same according to law. If, says my Lord Coke, by the writ of error, the plaintiff may recover, or be restored to anything, it may be released by the name of an action. In Bacon's Abridgment, tit. Error, L., it is laid down, that "where by a writ of error, the plaintiff shall recover, or be restored to any personal thing, as debt, damage, or the like a release of all actions personal is a good plea; and when land is to be recovered or restored in a writ of error, a release of actions real is a good bar; but where by a writ of error the plaintiff shall not be restored to any personal or real thing, a release of all actions, real or personal, is no bar." And for this we have the authority of Lord Coke, both in his Commentary on

Littleton and in his Reports. A writ of error, then, is in the nature of a suit or action when it is to restore the party who obtains it to the possession of
*410   anything which is withheld from him, *not when its operation is entirely defensive.

This rule will apply to writs of error from the courts of the United States, as well as to those writs in England.

Under the judiciary act, the effect of a writ of error is simply to bring the record into court, and submit the judgment of the inferior tribunal to re-examination. It does not in any manner act upon the parties ; it acts only on the record. It removes the record into the supervising tribunal. Where, then, a state obtains a judgment against an individual, and the court, rendering such judgment, overrules a defense set up under the constitution or laws of the United States, the transfer of this record into the Supreme Court, for the sole purpose of inquiring whether the judgment violates the constitution or laws of the United States, can with no propriety, we think, be denominated a suit commenced or prosecuted against the state whose judgment is so far re-examined. Nothing is demanded from the state. No claim against it of any description is asserted or prosecuted. The party is not to be restored to the possession of anything. Essentially, it is an appeal on a single point ; and the defendant who appeals from a judgment rendered against him, is never said to commence or prosecute a suit against the plaintiff who has obtained the judgment. The writ of error is given rather than an appeal, because it is the more usual mode of removing suits at common law; and because, perhaps, it is more technically proper where a single point of law, and not the whole case, is to *be re-examined. But an appeal might be given, and might be so regulated as to effect every purpose of a writ of error. The mode of removal is form, and not substance. Whether it be by writ of error or appeal, no claim is asserted, no demand is made by the original defendant; he only asserts the constitutional right to have his defense examined by that tribunal whose province it is to construe the constitution and laws of the Union.

*411

The only part of the proceeding which is in any manner personal, is the citation. And what is the citation? It is simply notice to the opposite party that the record is transferred unto another court, where he may appear, or decline to appear, as his judgment or inclination may determine. As the party who has obtained a judgment is out of court, and may, therefore, not know that his cause is removed, common justice requires that notice of the fact should be given him. But this notice is not a suit, nor has it the effect of process. If the party does not choose to appear, he cannot be brought into court, nor is his failure to appear considered as a default. Judgment cannot be given against him for his non-appearance, but the judgment is to be re-examined, and reversed or affirmed, in like manner as if the party had appeared and argued his cause.

The point of view in which the writ of error, with

its citation, has been considered uniformly in the
courts of the Union, has been well illustrated by a
reference to the course of this court in suits instituted
by the United States.   The universally received opin-
*412   ion is, that no suit can be commenced *or
             prosecuted against the United States ; that
the judiciary act does not authorize such suits.   Yet
writs of error, accompanied with citations, have uniformly issued for the removal of judgments in favor
of the United States into a superior court, where they
have, like those in favor of an individual, been re-examined, and affirmed or reversed.   It has never been
suggested, that such writ of error was a suit against
the United States, and, therefore, not within the
jurisdiction of the appellate court.

It is, then, the opinion of the court, that the defendant who removes a judgment rendered against him
by a state court into this court, for the purpose of
re-examining the question, whether that judgment be
in violation of the constitution or laws of the United
States, does not commence or prosecute a suit against
the state, whatever may be its opinion where the
effect of the writ may be to restore the party to the
possession of a thing which he demands.

But should we in this be mistaken, the error does
not affect the case now before the court.   If this writ
of error be a suit in the sense of the 11th amendment, it is not a suit commenced or prosecuted " by
a citizen of another state, or by a citizen or subject of
any foreign state."   It is not, then, within the amendment, but is governed entirely by the constitution as

originally framed, and we have already seen, that in
its origin, the judicial power was extended to all
cases arising under the constitution or laws of
the United States, without respect to parties.

* *413*   * 2d. The second objection to the jurisdiction of the court is, that its appellate power
cannot be exercised, in any case, over the judgment
of a state court.

This objection is sustained chiefly by arguments
drawn from the supposed total separation of the judiciary of a state from that of the Union, and their
entire independence of each other. The argument
considers the federal judiciary as completely foreign
to that of a state; and as being no more connected
with it, in any respect whatever, than the court of a
foreign state. If this hypothesis be just, the argument founded on it is equally so; but if the hypothesis be not supported by the constitution, the
argument fails with it.

This hypothesis is not founded on any words in
the constitution, which might seem to countenance it,
but on the unreasonableness of giving a contrary construction to words which seem to require it; and on
the incompatibility of the application of the appellate
jurisdiction to the judgments of state courts, with
that constitutional relation which subsists between
the government of the Union and the governments
of those states which compose it.

Let this unreasonableness, this total incompatibility, be examined.

That the United States form, for many, and for

most important purposes, a single nation, has not yet been denied. In war, we are one people. In making peace, we are one people. In all commercial regulations, we are one and the same people. In * many other respects, the American people

* *414*

are one ; and the government which is alone capable of controlling and managing their interests in all these respects, is the government of the Union. It is their government, and in that character they have no other. America has chosen to be, in many respects, and to many purposes, a nation ; and for all these purposes, her government is complete ; to all these objects, it is competent. The people have declared, that in the exercise of all powers given for these objects it is supreme. It can, then, in effecting these objects, legitimately control all individuals or governments within the American territory. The constitution and laws of a state, so far as they are repugnant to the constitution and laws of the United States, are absolutely void. These states are constituent parts of the United States. They are members of one great empire—for some purposes sovereign, for some purposes subordinate.

In a government so constituted, is it unreasonable that the judicial power should be competent to give efficacy to the constitutional laws of the legislature? That department can decide on the validity of the constitution or law of a state, if it be repugnant to the constitution or to a law of the United States. Is it unreasonable that it should also be empowered to decide on the judgment of a state tribunal enforcing

such unconstitutional law ?   Is it so very unreasonable as to furnish a justification for controlling the
words of the constitution ?

We think it is not.   We think that in a government * acknowledgedly supreme, with re-
* 415   spect to objects of vital interest to the
nation, there is nothing inconsistent with sound reason, nothing incompatible with the nature of government, in making all its departments supreme, so far
as respects those objects, and so far as is necessary
to their attainment.   The exercise of the appellate
power over those judgments of the state tribunals
which may contravene the constitution or laws of the
United States, is, we believe, essential to the attainment of those objects.

The propriety of entrusting the construction of the
constitution, and laws made in pursuance thereof, to
the judiciary of the Union, has not, we believe, as
yet, been drawn into question.   It seems to be a
corollary from this political axiom, that the federal
courts should either possess exclusive jurisdiction in
such cases, or a power to revise the judgment rendered in them, by the state tribunals.   If the federal
and state courts have concurrent jurisdiction in all
cases arising under the constitution, laws, and treaties
of the United States; and if a case of this description
brought in a state court cannot be removed before
judgment, nor revised after judgment, then the construction of the constitution, laws, and treaties of the
United States, is not confided particularly to their
judicial department, but is confided equally to that

department and to the state courts, however they may be constituted. "Thirteen independent courts," says a very celebrated statesman (and we have now more than twenty such courts), "of final jurisdiction over the same causes, arising upon the same laws, is a hydra in government, from * which nothing but contradiction and confusion can proceed."

416

Dismissing the unpleasant suggestion, that any motives which may not be fairly avowed, or which ought not to exist, can ever influence a state or its courts, the necessity of uniformity, as well as correctness in expounding the constitution and laws of the United States, would itself suggest the propriety of vesting in some single tribunal the power of deciding, in the last resort, all cases in which they are involved.

We are not restrained, then, by the political relations between the general and state governments, from construing the words of the constitution, defining the judicial power, in their true sense. We are not bound to construe them more restrictively than they naturally import.

They give to the Supreme Court appellate jurisdiction in all cases arising under the constitution, laws, and treaties of the United States. The words are broad enough to comprehend all cases of this description, in whatever court they may be decided. In expounding them, we may be permitted to take into view those considerations to which courts have always allowed great weight in the exposition of laws.

The framers of the constitution would naturally examine the state of things existing at the time ; and

their work sufficiently attests that they did so. All
acknowledge that they were convened for the purpose
of strengthening the confederation by enlarging the
powers of the government, and by giving efficacy

*417   * to those which it before possessed, but
              could not exercise. They inform us them-
selves, in the instrument they presented to the American public, that one of its objects was to form a more
perfect union. Under such circumstances, we certainly should not expect to find, in that instrument, a
diminution of the powers of the actual government.

Previous to the adoption of the confederation,
Congress established courts which received appeals
in prize causes decided in the courts of the respective
states. This power of the government, to establish
tribunals for these appeals, was thought consistent
with, and was founded on, its political relations with
the states. These courts did exercise appellate jurisdiction over those cases decided in the state courts,
to which the judicial power of the federal government
extended.

The confederation gave to Congress the power
"of establishing courts for receiving and determining
finally appeals in all cases of captures."

This power was uniformly construed to authorize
these courts to receive appeals from the sentences of
state courts, and to affirm or reverse them. State
tribunals are not mentioned; but this clause in
the confederation necessarily comprises them. Yet
the relation between the general and state governments was much weaker, much more lax, under the

confederation than under the present constitution; and
the states being much more completely sovereign, their
institutions were much more independent.

The convention which framed the constitution, on
*turning their attention to the judicial
418 power, found it limited to a few objects, but
exercised, with respect to some of those objects, in
its appellate form, over the judgments of the state
courts.   They extend it, among other objects, to all
cases arising under the constitution, laws, and treaties
of the United States; and in a subsequent clause declare, that in such cases, the Supreme Court shall
exercise appellate jurisdiction.   Nothing seems to be
given which would justify the withdrawal of a judgment rendered in a state court, on the constitution,
laws, or treaties of the United States, from this
appellate jurisdiction.

Great weight has always been attached, and very
rightly attached, to contemporaneous exposition.   No
question, it is believed, has arisen to which this principle applies more unequivocally than to that now
under consideration.

The opinion of the *Federalist* has always been considered as of great authority.   It is a complete commentary on our constitution; and is appealed to by
all parties in the questions to which that instrument
has given birth.   Its intrinsic merit entitles it to this
high rank; and the part two of its authors performed
in framing the constitution, put it very much in their
power to explain the views with which it was framed.
These essays having been published while the con-

stitution was before the nation for adoption or rejection, and having been written in answer to objections
founded entirely on the extent of its powers, and on
its diminution of state sovereignty, are entitled to the
more consideration where they * frankly
* 419
avow that the power objected to is given,
and defend it.

In discussing the extent of the judicial power, the
Federalist says : " Here another question occurs :
what relation would subsist between the national and
state courts in these instances of concurrent jurisdiction ?   I answer, that an appeal would certainly lie
from the latter to the Supreme Court of the United
States.   The constitution in direct terms gives an
appellate jurisdiction to the Supreme Court in all the
enumerated cases of federal cognizance in which it is
not to have an original one, without a single expression to confine its operation to the inferior federal
courts.   The objects of appeal, not the tribunals from
which it is to be made, are alone contemplated.   From
this circumstance, and from the reason of the thing,
it ought to be construed to extend to the state tribunals.   Either this must be the case, or the local
courts must be excluded from a concurrent jurisdiction in matters of national concern, else the judicial
authority of the Union may be eluded at the pleasure
of every plaintiff or prosecutor.   Neither of these
consequences ought, without evident necessity, to be
involved ; the latter would be entirely inadmissible,
as it would defeat some of the most important and
avowed purposes of the proposed government, and

would essentially embarrass its measures. Nor do I
perceive any foundation for such a supposition.
Agreeably to the remark already made, the national
and state systems are to be regarded as one whole.
The courts of the latter will of course be natural
* 420   auxiliaries to the execution * of the laws of
the Union, and an appeal from them will as
naturally lie to that tribunal which is destined to unite
and assimilate the principles of natural justice, and
the rules of national decision. The evident aim of
the plan of the national convention is, that all the
causes of the specified classes shall, for weighty
public reasons, receive their original or final determination in the courts of the Union. To confine, therefore, the general expressions which give appellate
jurisdiction to the Supreme Court, to appeals from
the subordinate federal courts, instead of allowing
their extension to the state courts, would be to
abridge the latitude of the terms, in subversion of the
intent, contrary to every sound rule of interpretation."

A contemporaneous exposition of the constitution,
certainly of not less authority than that which has
been just cited, is the judiciary act itself. We know
that in the Congress which passed that act were many
eminent members of the convention which formed
the constitution. Not a single individual, so far as
is known, supposed that part of the act which gives
the Supreme Court appellate jurisdictiom over the
judgments of the state courts in the cases therein
specified, to be unauthorized by the constitution.

While on this part of the argument, it may be also

material to observe that the uniform decisions of this court on the point now under consideration, have been assented to, with a single exception, by the courts of every state in the Union whose judgments have been

*421

revised. It has been the unwelcome *duty of this tribunal to reverse the judgments of many state courts in cases in which the strongest state feelings were engaged. Judges, whose talent and character would grace any bench, to whom a disposition to submit to jurisdiction that is usurped, or to surrender their legitimate powers, will certainly not be imputed, have yielded without hesitation to the authority by which their judgments were reversed, while they, perhaps, disapproved the judgment of reversal.

This concurrence of statesmen, of legislators, and of judges, in the same construction of the constitution, may justly inspire some confidence in that construction.

In opposition to it, the counsel who made this point has presented in a great variety of forms, the idea already noticed, that the federal and state courts must, of necessity, and from the nature of the constitution, be in all things totally distinct and independent of each other. If this court can correct the errors of the courts of Virginia, he says it makes them courts of the United States, or becomes itself a part of the judiciary of Virginia.

But, it has been already shown that neither of these consequences necessarily follows. The American people may certainly give to a national tribunal a supervising power over those judgments of the state courts, which may conflict with the constitution, laws, or treaties of the United States, without converting them into federal courts, or converting the national into a state tribunal. The one court * still derives its authority from the state, the other still derives its authority from the nation.

* *422*

If it shall be established, he says, that this court has appellate jurisdiction over the state courts in all cases enumerated in the 3d article of the constitution, a complete consolidation of the states, so far as respects judicial power, is produced.

But, certainly, the mind of the gentleman who urged this argument is too accurate not to perceive that he has carried it too far ; that the premises by no means justify the conclusion. " A complete consolidation of the states, so far as respects the judicial power," would authorize the legislature to confer on the federal courts appellate jurisdiction from the state courts in all cases whatsoever. The distinction between such a power, and that of giving appellate jurisdiction in a few specified cases in the decision of which the nation takes an interest, is too obvious not to be perceived by all.

This opinion has been already drawn out to too great a length to admit of entering into a particular consideration of the various forms in which the counsel who made this point has, with much ingenuity, presented his argument to the court. The argument in all its forms is essentially the same. It is founded, not on the words of the constitution, but on its spirit,

a spirit extracted, not from the words of the instrument, but from his view of the nature of our Union,
and of the great fundamental principles on which the
fabric stands.

To this argument, in all its forms, the same answer
may be given.   Let the nature and objects
* 423   of * our Union be considered; let the great
fundamental principles, on which the fabric stands,
be examined; and we think the result must be, that
there is nothing so extravagantly absurd in giving to
the court of the nation the power of revising the decisions of local tribunals on questions which affect the
nation, as to require that words which import this
power should be restricted by a forced construction.
The question, then, must depend on the words themselves; and on their construction we shall be the more
readily excused for not adding to the observations
already made, because the subject was fully discussed
and exhausted in the case of *Martin* v. *Hunter.*

3d. We come now to the third objection, which,
though differently stated by the counsel, is substantially the same.   One gentleman has said that the
judiciary act does not give jurisdiction in the case.

The cause was argued in the state court, on a case
agreed by the parties, which states the prosecution
under a law for selling lottery tickets, which is set
forth, and further states the act of Congress by which
the city of Washington was authorized to establish
the lottery.   It then states that the lottery was regularly established by virtue of the act, and concludes
with referring to the court the questions, whether the

act of Congress be valid? whether on its just construction, it constitutes a bar to the prosecution? and,
whether the act of Assembly, on which the prosecution is founded, be not itself invalid? These questions were decided against the operation of the act of
Congress, and in favor of the operation of the act
of the state.

* *424*   * If the 25th section of the judiciary act be
inspected, it will at once be perceived that it
comprehends expressly the case under consideration.

But it is not upon the letter of the act that the
gentleman who stated this point in this form, founds
his argument. Both gentlemen concur substantially
in their views of this part of the case. They deny
that the act of Congress, on which the plaintiff in
error relies, is a law of the United States; or, if a law
of the United States, is within the second clause of
the sixth article.

In the enumeration of the powers of Congress,
which is made in the 8th section of the first article,
we find that of exercising exclusive legislation over
such district as shall become the seat of government.
This power, like all others which are specified, is conferred on Congress as the legislature of the Union;
for, strip them of that character, and they would not
possess it. In no other character can it be exercised.
In legislating for the district, they necessarily preserve the character of the legislature of the Union;
for, it is in that character alone that the constitution
confers on them this power of exclusive legislation.
This proposition need not be enforced.

The 2d clause of the 6th article declares, that "this constitution, and the laws of the United States, which shall be made in pursuance thereof, shall be the supreme law of the land."

The clause which gives exclusive jurisdiction is, unquestionably, a part of the constitution, and, as such, binds all the United States. Those who contend that acts of Congress, made in pursuance of *this power, do not, like acts made in pursuance of other powers, bind the nation, ought to show some safe and clear rule which shall support this construction, and prove that an act of Congress, clothed in all the forms which attend other legislative acts, and passed in virtue of a power conferred on, and exercised by Congress, as the legislature of the Union, is not a law of the United States, and does not bind them.

*425

One of the gentlemen sought to illustrate his proposition that Congress, when legislating for the district, assumed a distinct character, and was reduced to a mere local legislature, whose laws could possess no obligation out of the ten miles square, by a reference to the complex character of this court. It is, they say, a court of common law and a court of equity. Its character, when sitting as a court of common law, is as distinct from its character when sitting as a court of equity, as if the powers belonging to those departments were vested in different tribunals. Though united in the same tribunal, they are never confounded with each other.

Without inquiring how far the union of different

characters in one court may be applicable, in principle, to the union in Congress of the power of exclusive legislation in some places, and of limited legislation in others, it may be observed, that the forms of proceedings in a court of law are so totally unlike the forms of proceedings in a court of equity, that a mere inspection of the record gives decisive information of the character in which the court sits, and consequently of the extent of its powers.

* 426   But * if the forms of proceeding were precisely the same, and the court the same, the distinction would disappear.

Since Congress legislates, in the same forms, and in the same character, in virtue of powers of equal obligation, conferred in the same character, in virtue of powers of equal obligation, conferred in the same instrument, when exercising its exclusive powers of legislation, as well as when exercising those which are limited, we must inquire whether there be anything in the nature of this exclusive legislation which necessarily confines the operation of the laws made in virtue of this power to the place with a view to which they are made.

Connected with the power to legislate within this district, is a similar power in forts, arsenals, dockyards, &c.   Congress has a right to punish murder in a fort, or other place within its exclusive jurisdiction ; but no general right to punish murder committed within any of the states.   In the act for the punishment of crimes against the United States, murder committed within a fort, or any other place or

district of country, under the sole and exclusive jurisdiction of the United States, is punished with death.
Thus Congress legislates in the same act, under its
exclusive and its limited powers.

The act proceeds to direct, that the body of the
criminal, after execution, may be delivered to a surgeon for dissection, and punishes any person who
shall rescue such body during its conveyance from
the place of execution to the surgeon to whom it is to
be delivered.

*427
* Let those actual provisions of the law,
or any other provisions which can be made
on the subject, be considered with a view to the character in which Congress acts when exercising its
powers of exclusive legislation.

If Congress is to be considered merely as a local
legislature, invested, as to this object with powers
limited to the fort, or other place, in which the murder may be committed, if its general powers cannot
come in aid of these local powers, how can the offense
be tried in any other court than that of the place in
which it has been committed? How can the offender
be conveyed to, or tried in, any other place? How
can he be executed elsewhere? How can his body
be conveyed through a country under the jurisdiction of another sovereign, and the individual
punished, who, within that jurisdiction, shall rescue
the body?

Were any one state of the Union to pass a law for
trying a criminal in a court not created by itself, in
a place not within its jurisdiction, and direct the

sentence to be executed without its territory, we should all perceive and acknowledge its incompetency to such a course of legislation. If Congress be not equally incompetent, it is because that body unites the powers of local legislation with those which are to operate through the Union, and may use the last in aid of the first; or because the power of exercising exclusive legislation draws after it, as an incident, the power of making that legislation effectual, and the in-
*428   cidental power may be exercised * through-
out the Union, because the principal power is given to that body as the legislature of the Union.

So, in the same act, a person who, having knowledge of the commission of murder, or other felony, on the high seas, or within any fort, arsenal, dockyard, magazine, or other place, or district of country within the sole and exclusive jurisdiction of the United States, shall conceal the same, &c., he shall be adjudged guilty of misprision of felony, and shall be adjudged to be imprisoned, &c.

It is clear, that Congress cannot punish felonies generally; and, of consequence, cannot punish misprision of felony. It is equally clear, that a state legislature—the state of Maryland, for example—cannot punish those who, in another state, conceal a felony committed in Maryland. How, then, is it that Congress, legislating exclusively for a fort, punishes those who, out of that fort, conceal a felony committed within it?

The solution, and the only solution of the difficulty

is, that the power vested in Congress, as the legislature of the United States, to legislate exclusively
within any place ceded by a state, carries with it, as
an incident, the right to make that power effectual.
If a felon escape out of the state in which the act has
been committed, the government cannot pursue him
into another state, and apprehend him there, but must
demand him from the executive power of that other
state.   If Congress were to be considered merely as
the local legislature for the fort or other place in
which the offense might be committed, then this principle would apply to them as to other local
*429   * legislatures, and the felon who should es-
cape out of the fort, or other place, in which the
felony may have been committed, could not be apprehended by the marshal, but must be demanded from
the executive of the state.   But we know that the
principle does not apply ; and the reason is, that
Congress is not a local legislature, but exercises this
particular power, like all its other powers, in its high
character, as the legislature of the Union.   The
American people thought it a necessary power, and
they conferred it for their own benefit.   Being so
conferred, it carries with it all those incidental powers
which are necessary to its complete and effectual
execution.

Whether any particular law be designed to operate
without the district or not, depends on the words of
that law.   If it be designed so to operate, then the
question, whether the power so exercised be incidental to the power of exclusive legislation, and be

warranted by the constitution, requires a consideration of that instrument.   In such cases the constitution and the law must be compared and construed.
This is the exercise of jurisdiction.   It is the only
exercise of it which is allowed in such a case.   For
the act of Congress directs, that " no other error shall
be assigned or regarded as a ground of reversal, in any
such case as aforesaid, than such as appears on the
face of the record, and immediately respects the be-
forementioned questions of validity or construction
of the said constitution, treaties," &c.

The whole merits of this case, then, consist in the
construction of the constitution and the act of Congress.   * The jurisdiction of the court, if
* 430
acknowledged, goes no further.   This we
are required to do without the exercise of jurisdiction.

The counsel for the state of Virginia have, in support of this motion, urged many arguments of great
weight against the application of the act of Congress
to such a case as this ; but those arguments go to
the construction of the constitution, or of the law,
or of both ; and seem, therefore, rather calculated to
sustain their cause upon its merits, than to prove a
failure of jurisdiction in the court.

After having bestowed upon this question the most
deliberate consideration of which we are capable,
the court is unanimously of opinion, that the objections to its jurisdiction are not sustained, and that
the motion ought to be overruled.

Motion denied.

NOTE.—When this case came on to be argued on the merits the following opinion (reported in 6 Wheaton 440) was given :

The opinion of the court was delivered by *Mr. Chief Justice Marshall :*

This case was stated in the opinion given on the motion for dismissing the writ of error for want of jurisdiction in the court. It now comes on to be decided on the question whether the Borough Court of Norfolk, in over-ruling the defense set up under * the act of Congress, has misconstrued that act. It is in these words :

* *441*

" The said corporation shall have full power to authorize the drawing of lotteries for effecting any important improvement in the city, which the ordinary funds or revenue thereof will not accomplish. Provided, that the sum to be raised in each year shall not exceed the amount of $10,000. And provided, also, that the object for which the money is intended to be raised shall be first submitted to the President of the United States, and shall be approved of by him."

Two questions arise on this act:

1st. Does it purport to authorize the corporation to force the sale of these lottery tickets in states where such sales may be prohibited by law? If it does,

2d. Is the law constitutional?

If the first question be answered in the affirmative, it will become necessary to consider the second. If it should be answered in the negative, it will be unnecessary, and consequently improper, to pursue any inquiries, which would then be merely speculative, respecting the power of Congress in the case.

In inquiring into the extent of the power granted to the corporation of Washington, we must first examine the words of the grant. We find in them no expression which looks beyond the limits of the city. The powers granted are all of them local in their nature, and all of them such as would, in the common course of things, if not necessarily, be exercised * within the city. The subject on which Congress was employed when framing this act was a local subject ; it was not the establishment of a lottery, but the formation of a separate body for the management of the internal affairs of the city, for its internal government, for its police. Congress must have considered itself as delegating to this corporate body powers for these objects, and for these objects solely. In delegating these powers, therefore, it seems reasonable to suppose that the mind of the legislature was directed to the city alone, to the action of the being they were creating within the city, and not to any extraterritorial operations. In describing the powers of such a being, no words of limitation need be used. They are limited by the subject. But, if it be intended to give its acts a binding efficacy beyond the natural limits of its power, and within the jurisdiction of a distinct power, we should expect to find, in the language of the incorporating act, some words indicating such intention.

* *442*

Without such words, we cannot suppose that Congress designed to give to the acts of the corporation any other effect, beyond its limits, than attends every act having the sanction of local law, when anything depends upon it which is to be transacted elsewhere.

If this would be the reasonable construction of corporate powers generally, it is more especially proper in a case where an attempt is made so to exercise those powers as to control and limit the penal laws of a state. This is an operation which was not, * we think, in the contemplation of the legislature, while incorporating the city of Washington.

* *443*

To interfere with the penal laws of a state, where they are not leveled against the legitimate powers of the Union, but have for their sole object, the internal government of the country, is a very serious measure, which Congress cannot be supposed to adopt lightly, or inconsiderately. The motives for it must be serious and weighty. It would be taken deliberately, and the intention would be clearly and unequivocally expressed.

An act, such as that under consideration, ought not, we think, to be so construed as to imply this intention, unless its provisions were such as to render the construction inevitable.

We do not think it essential to the corporate power in question, that it should be exercised out of the city. Could the lottery be drawn in any state of the Union? Does the corporate power to authorize the drawing of a lottery imply a power to authorize its being drawn without the jurisdiction of a corporation, in a place where it may be prohibited by law? This, we think, would scarcely be asserted. And what clear legal distinction can be taken between a power to draw a lottery in a place where it is prohibited by law and a power to establish an office for the sale of tickets in a place where it is prohibited by law? It may be urged, that the place where the lottery is drawn is of no importance to the corporation, and therefore the act need not be so construed as to give power over the place, but that the right to sell tickets throughout the United * States is of importance, and therefore ought to be implied.

* *444*

That the power to sell tickets in every part of the United States might facilitate their sale, is not to be denied ; but it does not follow that Congress designed, for the purpose of giving this increased facility, to overrule the penal laws of the several states. In the city of Washington, the great metropolis of the nation, visited by individuals from every part of the Union, tickets may be freely sold to all who are willing to purchase. Can it be affirmed that this is so limited a market that the incorporating act must be extended beyond its words, and made to conflict with the internal police of the states, unless it be construed to give a more extensive market?

It has been said that the states cannot make it unlawful to buy that which Congress has made it lawful to sell.

This proposition is not denied ; and, therefore, the validity of a law punishing a citizen of Virginia for purchasing a ticket in the city of Washington,

might well be drawn into question.   Such a law would be a direct attempt
to counteract and defeat a measure authorized by the United States.   But
a law to punish the sale of lottery tickets in Virginia, is of a different character.   Before we can impeach its validity, we must inquire whether Congress
intended to empower this corporation to do any act within a state which the
laws of that state might prohibit.

* 445   * In addition to the very important circumstance, that the act
contains no words indicating such intention, and that this extensive construction is not essential to the execution of the corporate power,
the court cannot resist the conviction, that the intention ascribed to this
act, had it existed, would have been executed by very different means from
those which have been employed.

Had Congress intended to establish a lottery for those improvements in
the city which are deemed national, the lottery itself would have become the
subject of legislative consideration.   It would be organized by law, and
agents for its execution would be appointed by the President, or in such other
manner as the law might direct.   If such agents were to act out of the district,
there would be, probably, some provision made for such a state of things, and
in making such provisions Congress would examine its power to make them.
The whole subject would be under the control of the government, or of
persons appointed by the government.

But in this case no lottery is established by law, no control is exercised by
the government over any which may be established.   The lottery emanates
from a corporate power.   The corporation may authorize, or not authorize it,
and may select the purposes to which the proceeds are to be applied.   This
corporation is a being intended for local objects only.   All its capacities are
limited to the city.   This, as well as every other law it is capable of making,
is a by-law, and, from its nature, is only co-extensive with the city.   It is not
* 446   probable that such * an agent would be employed in the execution of a lottery established by Congress ; but when it acts, not
as the agent for carrying into effect a lottery established by Congress, but
in its own corporate capacity, from its own corporate powers, it is reasonable
to suppose that its acts were intended to partake of the nature of that capacity
and of those powers ; and, like all its other acts, be merely local in its nature.

The proceeds of these lotteries are to come in aid of the revenues of the
city.   These revenues are raised by laws whose operation is entirely local,
and for objects which are also local ; for no person will suppose, that the
President's house, the Capitol, the Navy Yard, or other public institution,
was to be benefited by these lotteries, or was to form a charge on the city
revenue.   Coming in aid of the city revenue, they are of the same character
with it ; the mere creature of a corporate power.

The circumstances, that the lottery cannot be drawn without the permission of the President, and that this resource is to be used only for important improvements, have been relied on as giving to this corporate power

a more extensive operation than is given to those with which it is associated. We do not think so.

The President has no agency in the lottery. It does not originate with him, nor is the improvement to which its profits are to be applied to be selected by him. Congress has not enlarged the corporate power by restricting its exercise to cases of which the President might approve.

* *447*   * We very readily admit, that the act establishing the seat of government, and the act appointing commissioners to superintend the public buildings, are laws of universal obligation. We admit, too, that the laws of any state to defeat the loan authorized by Congress, would have been void, as would have been any attempt to arrest the progress of the canal, or of any other measure which Congress may adopt. These, and all other laws relative to the district, have the authority which may be claimed by other acts of the national legislature ; but their extent is to be determined by those rules of construction which are applicable to all laws. The act incorporating the city of Washington is, unquestionably, of universal obligation ; but the extent of the corporate powers conferred by that act, is to be determined by those considerations which belong to the case.

Whether we consider the general character of a law incorporating a city, the objects for which such law is usually made, or the words in which this particular power is conferred, we arrive at the same result. The corporation was merely empowered to authorize the drawing of lotteries ; and the mind of Congress was not directed to any provision for the sale of the tickets beyond the limits of the corporation. That subject does not seem to have been taken into view. It is the unanimous opinion of the court, that the law cannot be construed to embrace it.

Judgment affirmed.

END OF VOLUME I